WORKING OUT DESIRE

Gender, Culture, and Politics in the Middle East

miriam cooke, Simona Sharoni, and Suad Joseph, *Series Editors*

1. Women exercising at Kartal ISMEK, from knees below, May 17, 2012.

WORKING OUT
DESIRE

Women, Sport, and Self-Making
in Istanbul

Sertaç Sehlikoglu

Syracuse University Press

All photographs by Sertaç Sehlikoglu.

Copyright © 2021 by Syracuse University Press
Syracuse, New York 13244-5290

First Edition 2021
21 22 23 24 25 26   6 5 4 3 2 1

∞ The paper used in this publication meets the minimum requirements
of the American National Standard for Information Sciences—Permanence
of Paper for Printed Library Materials, ANSI Z39.48-1992.

For a listing of books published and distributed by Syracuse University Press,
visit https://press.syr.edu.

ISBN: 978-0-8156-3693-9 (hardcover)
      978-0-8156-3695-3 (paperback)
      978-0-8156-5505-3 (e-book)

Library of Congress Cataloging-in-Publication Data
Names: Sehlikoglu, Sertaç, author.
Title: Working out desire : women, sport, and self-making in Istanbul /
    Sertaç Sehlikoglu.
Description: First edition. | Syracuse, New York : Syracuse University Press, [2021] |
    Series: Gender, culture, and politics in the Middle East | Includes bibliographical
    references and index. | Summary: "In "Working Out Desire," Sehlikoglu presents
    the ways in which women's changing habits, leisure, and self-formation in the Muslim
    world and the Middle East are connected to their agentive capacities to shift and
    transform their conditions and socio-cultural capabilities"— Provided by publisher.
Identifiers: LCCN 2020012640 (print) | LCCN 2020012641 (ebook) | ISBN
    9780815636939 (hardback ; alk. paper) | ISBN 9780815636953 (paperback ; alk.
    paper) | ISBN 9780815655053 (ebook)
Subjects: LCSH: Women—Turkey—Identity. | Self-perception in women—Turkey.
    | Exercise for women—Social aspects—Turkey. | Women—Turkey—Social
    conditions. | Sports—Sociological aspects.
Classification: LCC HQ1726.7 .S44 2021 (print) | LCC HQ1726.7 (ebook) |
    DDC 305.409561—dc23
LC record available at https://lccn.loc.gov/2020012640
LC ebook record available at https://lccn.loc.gov/2020012641

Manufactured in the United States of America

I dedicate this book to my father, Tahir Sehlikoğlu, whom I lost unexpectedly while writing this book. He was a national athlete, so I grew up surrounded by sportspeople.

*I also dedicate it to
Istanbulite women, whose desires have become my fascination.*

Contents

Illustrations

Figures

Table

Acknowledgments

The journey of writing this book has not been an individual, isolated one but the result of constant conversations, engagements, confrontations, and support.

I am endlessly grateful to my interlocutors, without whom this book could never have been written. Some are now friends—the exceptional Meziyet and Elif Ayşe as well as Nurhayat, Zuhal, Yadigar, Filiz, Sare, Sema, Hatice Teyze, Fatma Abla—and there is a long list of women who remain anonymous here. I also thank those who participated in my research not as gym members per se but as owners, trainers, role models, and others: Spor AŞ, Selim Terzi, Ebru Şallı, Saba Tümer, Özlem Yeprem, B-Fit, Feridun Kunak, the crew of *Doktorum*, Serap Bay Becerik, Zahide Yetiş, and especially Dr. Aytuğ Kolankaya and his sympathy for anthropological research.

Henrietta L. Moore has been a valuable mentor who not only advised and supervised me as I worked on my PhD but cared for, understood, stimulated, and elevated my work and me to levels I could not have anticipated. Her support has extended beyond the limits of academia. In November 2011, I underwent two operations on my lungs at a hospital in Istanbul: the first in the emergency room and the second one under a failed anesthetic in full awareness and thus unbearably painful and terribly traumatic. Henrietta, knowing how writing is never a singular path and not separated from life, offered her active support, which helped me to endure the distressing period after the trauma, to get back on my feet, and to make a faster recovery from the haunting memories of that experience.

I offer special thanks to a few people. Deniz Kandiyoti has been an anchor to my academic journey and to this work. Esra Özyürek has provided her intellectual mentorship and invaluable support. Rüstem Ertuğ Altınay, Giulia Liberatore, Alice Wilson, and Fiona Wright constantly reminded me of the value of friendship and peer support. Our interactions and the insights from their critical, inspiring, and creative minds have been among the most precious gifts I received in the process of writing.

I wrote different parts of this book as a visiting scholar at different institutions: Bilgi University, Koç University, and London School of Economics' European Institute. I am forever indebted to my colleagues at these institutions, who provided invaluable hospitality and whose feedback has contributed to this work and friendship has allowed me to return home with sweet memories: Itır Erhart, Aslı Tunç, Esra Ercan Bilgiç, Halil Nalçaoğlu, Aylin Dalsalgüler, Zeynep Merve Uygun, Başak Can, Osman Şahin, Mustafa Avcı, Banu Çankaya, and Erdem Yörük.

The great majority of this book was rewritten, edited, and reedited during a research fellowship at Pembroke College, University of Cambridge, that was generously provided by the Abdullah Al-Mubarak Al-Sabah Foundation. I thank Sheikh Mubarak A.M. Al Sabah and Sir Roger Tomkys for making this fellowship possible. During my time at Pembroke College, I have received incredible support from the fellows (Iza Hussin, Mina Gorji, Waseem Yaqoob, my neighbor Hannah Mumby, Anil Madhavapeddy, Nicky Kindersley, and Sanne Cottaar, to name a few) and the staff (especially Ladan Rastan, Nadjim Nemiri, Savino Cafagna, Nina Rhodes, Carlos, Danny, Jeanette Ferguson, Natalie Kent, Joanna Lubanska, and Matthew Mellor). The master of Pembroke College during my tenure there, Chris Smith, and his hard work to make the college an inclusive space had a tremendous impact on my academic life (and emotional well-being) in an institution like Cambridge, which was established through systematic exclusion. I thank him dearly.

I would not have been able to write this book without the generous comments and suggestions of scholars at the two graduate programs I have completed: during my PhD work in the Division of Social Anthropology at the University of Cambridge, Sian Lazar, Leo Howe, Nikolai Ssorin-Chaikov, Liana Chua, James Laidlaw, Harri Englund, and Susan Bayly; and during my MA work in the Department of Anthropology at the University of Toronto, Shiho Satsuka, Andrea Muehlebach, Amira Mittermaier, Janice Boddy, Valentina Napolitano, Alissa Trotz, and Michael Lambek.

Earlier chapters of this book were presented at a number of institutions, including the London School of Economics and Political Science, Oxford University, University of St. Andrews, University of Cambridge, Bilgi University, Yıldız Technical University, Centre for Cultural Studies, Cambridge Muslim College, Newnham College, Qatar University, University of Nottingham, and Northeastern University.

Sometimes luck needs to be credited, along with the hard work. I was lucky enough to cross paths with and to discuss parts of my work and receive invaluable comments from various scholars. I thank Homa Hoodfar, Gül Özyeğin, Afsaneh Najmabadi, Niko Besnier, Robert (Bob) Hefner, Khaled Fahmy, Samuli Schielke, Jessica Winegar, Lara Deeb, Mahfoud Amara, Rosi Braidotti, Suad Joseph, Berna Turam, Valentina Moghadam, Selin Akyüz, Atif Imtiaz, and Richard Irvin.

I took the most difficult steps toward condensing the core arguments of this book through helpful interactions with friends. I thank Aslı Zengin, Dılar Dirik, Jasmijn Rana, Magda Craciun, Sima Aprahamian, Seçil Dağtaş, Ryan Davey, Hildegard Diemberger, Andrew Sanchez, Laurie Denyer-Willis, Clara Devlieger, Chloe Nahul-Claudel, Andrea Grant, Maryon Macdonald, Lauren Wilcox, Jeremy Walton, Rebecca Skreslet Hernandez, Matthew McGuire, Claudia Liebelt, Sebastian John, Ceren İlikan, Felix Stein, Nikolay Mintchev, Yasemine Moataz, Jessica Johnson, Anna Grigoryeva, Yu Qui, Tom Neumark, Ross Porter, Maximillian Spiegel, John McManus, Çağrı İdiman, Sabiha Alluche, Erol Sağlam, Elisabetta Costa, Samaya Farooq, Alice von Bieberstein, Eona Bell, Marlene Schäfers, Marilena Frisone, Eirini Avramapoulu, Feyza Akınerdem, Gülay Türkmen-Derviş, Mezna

Qato, and Sümeyye Ulu. One of the Pembroke fellows, Allegra Fryxell, whom I met as I completed this book, has offered generous help and read almost half of the book and helped me improve it.

There are people who influence you without perhaps knowing it, people for whom a mere listing in the references seems inadequate because their writing has been such a huge influence on your thinking: I would like to acknowledge publicly the intellectual debt I owe to Nazan Üstündağ, Lois McNay, Lisa Rofel, and Katherine Ewing.

The fieldwork and writing of this book have benefitted from generous financial support, including a fieldwork grant from the University of Cambridge William-Wyse Fieldwork Fund, a British Institute at Ankara Study Grant, and a British Institute of Middle Eastern Studies PhD Scholarship.

It is not only the academic and emotional support or intellectual stimulation that makes a book but also the joyful "leisure moments" one has along the way. For me, those moments often involve coffee. In Turkish, there is a saying that "one cup of coffee is cherished for forty years." As a coffee lover, I am compelled to thank two special friends whose Turkish coffees (along with warm friendship and intellectual support) helped me to type several parts of this book: Esra Ercan Bilgiç and Merve R. Kayıkçı.

I thank my family: my father, Tahir Sehlikoğlu, who was a sportsman and a national athlete; my sister, Sevtap Bihter Sehlikoğlu; my beautiful, cheerful nieces, Nazra and Meyra; especially my mother, Sema Sehlikoğlu, who is an exercising Istanbulite woman, not an interlocutor for this project but an inspiration for me; as well as dear Zeynep Yıldız, Ekin Bodur, and Ayşe Su Polat, who have supported me as if they were family.

Finally, my beloved partner, Fahri Karakaş, who championed the true sense of the word *partner*. He walked with me over the rocky path of everything else that was happening while the book was progressing, through the moments of joy and tears, often one close behind the other.

Prologue

I am in Fatih, often known as the "religious" or "Islamic" district of Istanbul. I left Hamza Yerlikaya Sports Center and am moving toward Unkapanı from Topkapı on Fevzipaşa Road to conduct an interview later. It is May 2012, and combined with the concrete and the crowd, the heat is getting on everyone's nerves. The bus I am in is stuck in traffic, and since I am going to need my temper later in the day, getting off and taking a slow walk seems like a wise choice. I am a fully equipped ethnographer, with my iPad, voice recorder, notepad, and camera, all purchased with the grants for which I would publicly give thanks in my book to be published. My load is heavy; my curiosity is at its peak.

I leave the bus where it is stuck in traffic and start to walk toward Unkapanı without hassle. I take some random photos, peeking into the shops. After a short while, my looking at the shops and their display windows gains a quasi-academic dimension. I discover a connection between the diversity of the women I have been meeting, working out alongside, and sitting down with for almost a year and the diverse desires and aspirations framed by those display windows. The bridal gowns flash from the display windows, the mannequins positioned to exhibit the glow of the dresses: they raise their arms to reveal the embroidery stitched on the bodice or step one leg onto a high platform to exhibit skirt patterns—all making the mannequins look more brazen. The women who are shopping, in contrast, do not show a shred of brazenness. If anything, they blend in; some of them even look timid.

2. Divergent desires on display: a store display window in Fatih, Istanbul, May 4, 2012.

The display windows reflect the heterogeneity of the Fatih crowd, its various members moving toward their collective and individual desires. Take, for instance, the display window shown in figure 2, where there are two mannequins wearing different costumes, reflecting two contrasting identities. A turquoise engagement costume with long sleeves and a head scarf loaded with beads and patterns is displayed side by side with a strapless wedding gown. The latter is no less weighed down with patterns, no less aglow than its veiled counterpart; the mannequin raises her arms, amplifying the alluring look of the low-cut dress in a strange way. Both mannequins pose with pride, the glittering dresses almost promising to provide a lifetime of sparkle to whoever wears them.

Here in a district often referred to as "traditional" or "Islamic" or both, I come face to face with one of the most vibrant shopping hubs of the city in all its burlesque glory. The radiant display windows are designed not to mimic the customers but to appeal to their desiring selves.

And if the display windows are formed to appeal to their customers' desires, then capturing those desires would be exciting.

The gyms I have been attending are not different from those display windows. In those windows before my eyes, diverse social and political subjectivities are on display, the two mannequins serving as synecdoches of divergent but somehow connecting desires and embodying how individuals interact with multiple tastes and how the perspectives associated with those tastes are interleaved with one another in everyday life.

This book is a product of my scholarly enchantment with what I call "women's desiring subjectivities" in the way these subjectivities enable a pastiche of social belongings and bear unforeseen, unexpected formations.

Working Out Desire

Introduction

A Eulogy to Sporty Aunties

"How Can a Grown-Up Woman Not Be Ashamed to Jump Like a Bouncing Ball?!"

In an episode of what was once one of the most popular Turkish TV series, *Bizimkiler* (Our Folks/Those of Us),[1] the German wife, Ulrike/Ulviye,[2] is exercising in the morning and coercing her overweight Turkish husband, Davut; her clumsy son, Halis; and her husband's even clumsier nephew, Galip, to exercise with her at home. Halis seeks compliments for his ability to follow Ulrike's instructions, which Davut and Galip fail to accomplish properly. As I watch this twenty-year-old episode, I try to remember the responses of the audience back then. What were we thinking when we saw this scene on TV in the 1990s? I vaguely remember that it was amusing to see the big bodies of the male Turkish relatives poorly imitating Ulrike's

---

1. *Bizimkiler* was a popular TV series that ran every week for thirteen years from 1989 to 2002 on the national channel TRT. It told the stories of residents living in different apartments in the same modern, middle-class building. Its primary subject was Istanbul in the 1990s, and it focused on modern values with all their contradictions and contestations. One of the families living in the building is a Turkish German family; the Turkish father decides to return to Turkey after spending long years in Germany with his German wife, Ulrike (Ulviye), and their only son.

2. The German wife's original name was "Ulrike," although she was called by her Turkish(ized) name "Ulviye."

I

movements. We were also probably admiring the German discipline embodied in Ulrike, a slim woman in her late forties. Yet I am not quite sure how exactly the public reacted to a woman in her late forties exercising.

The answer to my question is luckily provided in a few minutes, pouring from the mouth of Ulrike's grumpy neighbor Sabri Bey: "How can a grown-up woman not be ashamed to jump like a bouncing ball?!"[3] The sort of movements physical exercise entail have long been associated with immaturity and preadolescence. Paradoxically, exercising (i.e., running, jumping) female bodies would also be sexually arousing after puberty and thus needed to be reduced and controlled after that point. My middle-aged interlocutors are very familiar with both perspectives.

A Eulogy to Sporty Aunties

The formation of sport as a gendered *object of desire* in Turkey dates back to 1930, when it began to be marked as a tool for and signifier of transformation by the republicanist Turkish state. Highly influenced by widespread eugenics discourses of the time (Alemdaroğlu 2005), the republican ideology aimed to mold the unfit Eastern bodies of Turks into new healthy, Western, and civilized bodies through a series of initiatives, often targeted specifically at women.

Yet even after Turkey's decades-long investment in biopolitics, exercise, gymnastics, sports, and women's and girls' physical education, the idea of exercising female bodies remained somewhat incongruent if not outrageous or repugnant in the minds of the nonelite majority. Girls famously used notes from doctors to opt out of compulsory physical education classes in high schools, and gymnastics performances of the annual Youth and Sport Fest celebrations have always been a matter of public anxiety when mixed-sex groups of youths are seen parading in shorts.

---

3. See this episode of *Bizimkiler* at http://youtu.be/U1pjnqBB7Xc?t=21m38s.

However, by the time I started my research in 2008 the middle-aged Istanbulite women who went walking in the parks had already become city legends known as *sporcu teyzeler* (sporty aunties). Although the outdoor gyms replacing playgrounds were strange to the majority of Istanbul's inhabitants and the municipal governments have built the outdoor gyms to attract the youth, the middle-aged women (often wearing long robes and large head scarves) acted more quickly to occupy the equipment—which eventually marked the outdoor gyms as spaces for the aunties rather than the youth.

Working Out Desire

Women exercising in public spaces—ordinary, middle-aged "sporty aunties" from lower-middle-class or rural backgrounds or both—present a stark contrast to the republican ideals promulgated to increase women's participation in sports. Whereas the republican ideal promoted Western-garbed, serious, disciplined, and elite bodies, the sporty aunties are often rural looking, joyful, Eastern, and covered. Whereas the former emphasized the fit, young, and able, sporty aunties are fervent, chubby, and not so able. Women-only gyms are also far from mimicking the Western fitness trends. When you walk into a women-only gym in Istanbul—unlike a gym in, say, the United States, the United Kingdom, or Canada—you don't walk into a space full of determined, skinny, muscular, flexible bodies. Instead, you witness a slower pace and relaxed atmosphere that dominates the space. The women are often in comfortable outfits, with their sweatpants, T-shirts, and cotton scarves used as gym towels, creating an almost homely feel.

This book looks closely at what Turkish women often call *spor meraki*, "interest or curiosity in sport," as an object of desire shared by a broad and diverse group of Istanbulite women. *Spor meraki* is not like "exercise trend" or "exercise craze" in the Western sense as used in English. Neither is it descriptive, not unlike how men refer to their exercise as "doing sports," "lifting weights," "having a match," "running." As women do with many other objects of desire, in the case of exercise they often undersell their yearnings and aspirations, presenting the latter as simple interests or innocuous curiosities. To appreciate the distinctiveness of Istanbulite women's *spor merakı*, I follow women's own words and use their language as a gateway to their imaginations.

This book is not an ethnographic account of women exercising across Istanbul. Rather, it is an ethnographic account of the formation of desiring subjectivities, the human capacity to desire that is not only informed and shaped by sociohistorical constraints but also marked in its agentive aptitude.

Desiring subjectivity is rooted in aspirations, in fantasy, and in anticipation within and beyond the realms of sex and sexuality. Tracing a form of subjectivity with such extensive operations is possible by focusing on a single *object* of desire, through which women manifest their desiring subjectivities.

Spor merakı connects a diverse body of women to one another as a collective object of desire. What does this connection tell us about the formations of an object of desire? This book studies the connections among women according to a three-angle approach: through (gendered) self, through space (Istanbul), and through perspectives of time (neoliberal times).

In a context like Turkey, where any womanly entertainment is perceived as trifling and even foolish, it is unsurprising that young and educated Istanbulites see middle- to lower-class women's *spor merakı* as a trivial matter. After all, the vocabulary on women's leisure is often used for pejorative references. For example, the terms *kadınlar hamamı* (women's hamam or bath) and *kadınlar matinesi* (women-only stage performance) are phrases used to refer to any setting or moment that stops being serious and becomes frivolous. If someone says, "You have turned here into a *kadınlar hamamı*," that means you need to get back to serious business and stop displaying a flippant attitude.

It is almost as if jumping middle-aged female bodies in public inflict frivolousness on an otherwise serious act, sport. The dominant perspective tends to mark these women's bodies as familial (i.e., as aunties) yet also equally inappropriate and irritating, to the extent that this perspective has turned exercising women into a subject of public mockery. Even the oxymoronic moniker given to this particular group of *spor merakı* devotees—*sporcu teyzeler,* "sporty aunties"—is an expression of contempt. Like the phrases *flying chickens* and *running turtles,* the nickname *sporcu teyzeler* highlights the inappropriateness of sports for *teyze*—a category of women branded as local, non-Western, familial, traditional, and domestic. Caricatures, jokes, and Photoshopped memes have circulated on social media and the internet, some arguing that these aunties should not be engaging in sports. The consensus suggested by these ridiculing memes is that these women are pursuing something beyond their reach.[4]

The normative impulse embedded in public mockery pops up in various ways, articulated by people of various socioeconomic and ideological backgrounds. Women themselves are quite aware of the contrast that turns their bodies into subjects of ridicule.[5] They are also aware of the phrase used to refer to them, *sporty aunties,* yet they do not seem to care about becoming a matter of public mockery. The way they ignore this public mockery is a small reflection of their agentive processes of self-formation, just as they are aware of the nationalist, secularist, and Islamist discourses that limit their physicality.

4. During the London Summer Olympics in 2012, Zaytung, a satirical news channel similar to the Onion in the United States, published a mock interview with sports authorities discussing how Turkey's failure to win medals in certain categories might be related to Turkish youth having lost their enthusiasm for sports after seeing sporty aunties working out at the outdoor gyms. "We installed these outdoor gyms in the parks in the hopes that they might enable poor teenagers to exercise and engage in sports. Instead, they have attracted women over the age of fifty. Pardon me for saying this, but it's as though the entire neighborhood has descended upon the parks in the hopes of reducing their bum fat! Any young people still interested in fitness must wait in line to get on the equipment. We have now introduced legislation prohibiting anyone over twenty-five from using the outdoor gyms" ("The Ministry of Sports" 2012).

5. One YouTube video titled *Uçan türbanlı* (The Flying Headscarved), of a stout woman in a long robe using swinging equipment in a standing position to strengthen core muscles was video-recorded from behind by two young people walking their dog, which signifies a class gap, the pet owners being upper class (at http://www.youtube.com/watch?v=-5TH2kD6Fdw).

In this context, reducing Istanbulite women in their pursuit of *spor merakı* to mindless followers of a neoliberal trend would be careless. Istanbulite women's desiring subjectivities have a nonlinear and intermittent relationship with structures, rules, systems, and the linguistic and discursive limits of life, which are often hidden in social crevices that easily escape analytical scrutiny under the tools offered by traditional ethnography, from the study of language to observation.

Thus, this book develops a polyvalent analysis of how women use *spor merakı* to sprout and form a desiring subjecthood over time. *Spor merakı* takes women out of the domestic zone physically, emotionally, and imaginatively.

Exercising Istanbulite women help us to think about how different rationales and norms for desire operate differently on different bodies. In the context of Turkey, gender norms are configured differently for male and female desire. Whereas male desire is to be fed, female desire is to be disciplined. Whereas male desire is seen as the essence of manhood, female desire is seen as perverse and selfish. Because of these distinctions, women often form and articulate their desire in indirect and subtle ways. Women's connections to their desires thus need to be detected and carefully excavated. Women will not discuss their desires unless they feel completely free of the possibility of disapproval. Female desire thus shies away from judgment. It giggles and flourishes in private enjoyment and comfort.

Istanbulite women's transformative pursuits are purposefully non-threatening, understated, and veiled—which is one of the reasons why they have heretofore not received the ethnographic attention they deserve. A second reason why this practice of embodiment is often dismissed in academic literature concerns the scholarly mind. Despite decades-long discussions of leisure in leisure studies, non-elite women's leisure has not emerged as a serious area of research in anthropology or become perceived as an arena of emancipation in Middle Eastern studies.[6] Why?

6. Important exceptions would be Asef Bayat (2007) and Laleh Khalili (2016), who have studied leisure in the areas of emancipation. Also please see chapter 2 for the discussion of other scholarly work that focuses on leisure in the Middle East.

Perhaps it is because leisure has long been understood as being about class and privilege. Yet we need to rethink these categories of analysis when considering a large number of *ordinary* women, most of whom are housewives and married to working-class men. Leisure is also about time, and time is regulated by gender (see chapters 7, 8, and 9). Through leisure, Istanbulite women not only navigate through the time regimes imposed on them but also actively recalibrate their own temporalities.

An Anthropology of Desire

Desire exists beyond the moment it is felt, experienced, or even yearned for. Desire is formed through a series of social and historical makings. In recent years, anthropology has developed the concept of desire to denote new lifestyles, new ways of being, new consumption patterns, and new ways of engaging with a world enhanced by neoliberalism— all of which were formerly labeled "modernity." This book is built on the anthropological literature that is interested in the fluidity, multiplicity, and temporality of subjecthood (Ortner 2005; Luhrmann 2006; Moore 2007). Its ethnographic account is of the daily lives of exercising Istanbulite women who have developed multiple subject positionings, self-stylizations, and self-imaginations through a dynamic relationship between desire and the social.

Anthropology can learn more about the human subject by exploring how individuals think about themselves in relation to the world. With this aim, instead of trying to disentangle multiple, ambiguous macroconcepts such as "modernity," "capitalism," and "neoliberalism," I approach the social through the ways women experience and encounter the world. I look closer at the ways women experience spatial and temporal regimes imposed on them through neoliberalism or kinship dynamics and how they navigate these macro-operations and find the cracks where they can form new selves.

Using desire as an anthropological concept formulated within the discipline nonetheless requires a careful approach. In the Western (androgenic) philosophical tradition, desire is often depicted as the opposite of reason. Several scholars, perhaps reflecting a masculine (almost an alpha male) sense of rivalry, have even felt the need to place desire within some sort of a competitive comparison: reason ought to win over desire, autonomous desiring subjectivity should be idealized and assigned to men and not to women. In G. W. F. Hegel's infamous comparison, men and not women have the right to desire and an untainted ethical life ([1807] 2010, 399). The constant problematic need to create contrasting binaries leaves little room for nuanced analysis (see chapter 2).

As often happens in response to such binary accounts, the scholars of gender studies have developed a more nuanced formulation of desire, connecting it to the complex operations of power mechanisms and their significance to the formation of desire and desiring subjectivity. Feminist psychoanalyst Jessica Benjamin states, for example, "The question of woman's desire actually runs parallel to the question of power" (1986, 78). In the anthropological and gender studies literature, desire is often linked to the realms of sex and sexuality. The problem of a woman's desire in particular is portrayed primarily through her object status, centralizing the androgenic position or male gaze and assuming its centrality in women's self-makings, too.

Desire, however, is also related to the human capacity to crave new possibilities and the ability to dream and fantasize, which are not only aspects of subjectivity but also deeply rooted in human agency (see chapter 2). These agentive capacities of desiring subjectivity enable women to transform the meanings and categories that limit their bodies physically, temporally, and spatially. These agentive capacities, as will be explored in the following chapters, are unthreatening. They are often divergent, concealed, and left unenunciated—which is also why such agentive capacities often escape the ethnographic gaze and have not become objects of anthropological inquiry. They can, however, be detected through a longitudinal research by comparing women's transformative power across time.

Not Sport but *Spor Meraki* as an Object of Anthropological Inquiry

In women's everyday language, the sort of involvement at stake is not "exercise" or "fitness" or "training" or "jogging," but *sport*. Any form of exercise—heavy or light, performed at home, in the park, on the streets, or at the gym—is called "doing sport," in Turkish *spor yapmak*. If they go to the gym or even take a half-hour walk in the morning in the park, women say that they are "going to sport" *spora gitmek*. They—or their children—share their exercise photos on social media and receive comments about what a *sporcu*, "sportsperson" or "sporty person," they are, and that term is also usually found in the photo caption.[7]

Building on Pierre Bourdieu, contemporary scholarship on the sociology or anthropology of sports often uses various forms of sports as a venue to observe and analyze how habitus forms "body capital" by making and remaking both the bodies and souls of individuals. In this literature, sport not only disciplines the body but also reinforces existing gendered, classed, and ethnic hierarchies (Sfeir 1985; Messner 1990; Joseph Maguire 1993; Duncan 1994; Defrance 1995; Hargreaves 2000; Horne 2000; Bolin and Granskog 2003b; Yarar 2005; Markula and Pringle 2006; Farooq 2010; Besnier and Brownell 2012; Raab 2012; Sehlikoglu 2013a; Hoodfar 2015). The most immediate scholarly interest in the studies of exercising gendered bodies is also physical embodiment and its effect on women's social and interpersonal relations (Jacob 2011; Paradis 2012). However, Istanbulite women's *spor merakı* is less often about bodily physicality. *Spor merakı* is more concerned with women's self-imaginations, with what women imagine themselves doing, and with how those aspirations are formed and collectively articulated toward triggering the creation of a new market. It is in this context that *spor merakı* has gained currency among women in the formation of desiring selves. How women are able to manifest their gendered subjectivities in everyday life and strive for the change they desire is a more fundamental question to explore.

7. Depending on the context, *sporcu* can be translated as "sportsman," "sportswoman," or "sporty person." There is no gender distinction, nor is there a separate term for "sporty" in Turkish.

From the Object of Desire to the Desiring Subject

Istanbulite women's *spor merakı* presents a perfect object of desire and thus sheds light on the constitutions, operations, and limits of desiring subjectivity and its agentive capacity. The agentive capacity of women is visible in their ability (1) to create a seismic hiatus in the consistency of social structures and norms, of gender and sexuality, and of economic, familial, and even religious conditions affecting their lives; (2) to remake the pace and materiality of the city via their flesh; and, most importantly, (3) to manifest more desiring selves.

The way *spor merakı* circulates indicates new ways of imagining selfhood and womanhood and reflects a craving for change and even advancement. Women's particular interest at stake in *spor merakı* is not merely an interest in sport, as the term suggests, but an interest in changing and establishing a new self that is separate from conventional feminine duties as well as an investment in doing something for *oneself* rather than for other family members (children, partners, parents, in-laws) or social networks (neighbors, other relatives, classmates).

I use the phrase *desiring subjectivity* and *desiring subject* for two reasons. First, the term *desiring subject* refers to the individual who desires, longs, aspires, wills, and dreams. I call all of these various forms of volition, combined with an element of fantasy and anticipation, "desire." Second, the term *desiring subject* suggests that desire is informed by social makings and is also a human capacity. In this vein, the way desire connects to the processes of self-making and subjectification deserves attention.

Women aspire not only to have a body that looks slimmer and "healthier" but also to *feel* slimmer and healthier, and so they are quickly pleased with any little progress. The immediate effects of exercise include being more energetic and having better posture. In turn, having better posture makes women *look* and *feel* more confident.

As Lara Deeb explains in developing Lisa Rofel's analysis, "Gender is a basic component of discourses about being modern, 'one of the central modalities through which modernity is imagined and desired'" (2006, 29, quoting Rofel 1999, 19). This approach is built in part on the conceptualization of Lacanian desire vis-à-vis the imaginary toward a unified and coherent self, placing the self and its image in relation to the orders of the symbolic and the real. Psychoanalytical theory enables us to situate the subject's imagination as part of a desiring process while recognizing the unrealizable fantasies as energizing forces directed toward the "desired" (Kramer 2003; Belghiti 2013). These debates are inevitably linked to imagining the self as a modern being, which is very similar to what Deeb refers to as "enchanted modern" subjectivities. Modernity—as a social imaginary shared among women and other subjects—provides desirable and fashionable narratives of liberation, equality, and development; it also propagates discourses of achieving "ideal" conditions of health, society, morality, gender, progress, and advancement.

Turkish women have long been enchanted by "global waves" and promises of being modern, cosmopolitan, and progressive. Turkey—Istanbul in particular—has recently witnessed a shift in its culture of health and sports, where global trends and practices, such as gym culture, are taking hold and transforming understandings of exercise, self, and social relations. Istanbulite women do not merely absorb global trends and concepts. As I examine throughout the book, they actively engage with them and shape them through an alternative imagination and cosmopolitanism, through *spor merakı*, and through women-only gyms. In so doing, they create new possibilities of authentic and plural forms of self-fashioning. This book contributes to a growing body of ethnographic literature on how women around the world are becoming involved in exercise (Spielvogel 2003; Andrews, Sudwell, and Sparkes 2005; J. S. Maguire 2007) as a means of remaking their own cosmopolitan selves in distinctive ways that borrow from but also transform Western globalizing forms.

An analysis of how women remake their desiring selves requires a concept of the self that is endowed with reflexivity, fluidity, and agency as it performs actions to manage multiple, shared, or fragmented subject positionings. As a result, the boundaries of the self expand, producing a participating and relational self. Indeed, interviews with women reflect a more fluid connectivity. Women feel they are bound to others, actively involved in anticipating others' needs and sharing their interests and passions, and see themselves as extensions of each other. Therefore, the process of forming desiring selfhood is a dynamic one. Desiring subjectivity is interwoven in a pattern of relationships and women's "fluid connectivity" within social boundaries.

Subjectivity and Istanbulite Women

The name "Istanbulites" does not signify merely that my interlocutors live in Istanbul. Neither does "desiring Istanbulite women" assume a homogeneous cluster. The city represents a physical reality and a psychophysical field as a behavioral environment (Pile 1996). Geographical imaginations are in fact multiple, and they map subjectivity (Pile 2008).

On the contrary, in a study that focuses on fluid and vibrant desiring subjectivities, use of the name "Istanbulite" captures, among other things, the dynamic aspirations of remaking and refashioning seemingly contradictory desires that contribute to the processes of self-formation. "Istanbulite" refers to the physical conditions that surround my interlocutors and through which *spor merakı* is molded.

The Istanbulite Muslim women devotees of *spor merakı* are more diverse than is immediately apparent, differing in age and class as well as along urban–rural, political, religious (at both levels of religiosity and sect), and ethnic lines (Anatolian, eastern European, Kurdish, and other). Although all of my interlocutors were born to Muslim families, a few are atheists.

The sort of diversity I have encountered does not fit into the easy categories we often assume in thinking about non-Western women. There are those like Sibel and Seval who are educated young professionals and devout Kemalists (Turkish nationalist secularists) who do not pray five times a day or wear a head scarf and who enjoy occasional drinking but do fast during Ramadan and read the Qur'an (which requires knowledge of the Arabic script) after funerals. For instance, Gülay, an Alevi (Alawite) woman, fasts for twelve days during Muharram but avoids alcohol during Ramadan as well.[8] Serra is offended when people judge her by her "European" appearance (blue eyes, long blond hair, tight jeans), assume she is a secularist, and fail to recognize her religiosity. She never drinks alcohol and prays five times a day.

We do not have the proper vocabulary for such a complex matrix of Muslimhoods either. In fact, the participants of my research reflect the true fabric of Turkish Muslimhoods—Türkiye Müslümanlığı—something notoriously understudied. Turkish Muslimhoods often combine visiting shrines with candle lighting (a Christian practice) and drinking rakı (an aniseed-flavored alcoholic drink) with attending *bayram namazı* (prayers on the morning of religious festivals). Turkish Muslimhoods cannot be studied solely by relying on religious texts or *fetvas* (or fatwas, jurists' opinions on Islamic law) but also by realizing that religious texts and rules are not the central part of these Muslim self-makings. With that said, though, Turkish Muslimhoods are not the focus of this book, although it has been written with an awareness that these Muslimhoods must be taken into consideration with great care and not forced into vulgar binaries. Another concern here has to do with the conceptual categories that scholars and nonscholars alike tend to think through, as elaborated in detail in chapter 2. The binaries that limit our conceptual mappings are the reason why simple and ordinary but forceful forms of self-making can be difficult to recognize, capture, and articulate.

This book focuses its ethnographic binoculars on women's desiring subjectivity as one of the understudied aspects of selfhood that might also be one of the factors that make Turkish Muslimhoods possible and acceptable. If scholars continue to ignore the elements of desire, pleasure, and imagination, they fail to capture moments when pleasure supersedes the meaning in marking Turkish Muslimhoods—for

8. Although Alawites in Turkey are diverse in their belief systems and religious practices, they traditionally often do not observe Ramadan.

instance, moments in which the (Arabic) Qur'an is not read, translated, and discussed but recited for the joy of hearing it, just as music is enjoyable to one's ears.

In this book, the name "Istanbulite" is more than a simple reference to one's city of residence, as elaborated in chapter 4. Istanbul stimulates certain urges in its residents against the feelings of being trapped, contained, and limited, on the one hand, and expands the contours or physical limits of desire by providing new opportunities, on the other. Through this dualistic operation, Istanbul demarcates the shared subjectivities of its residents and thus of the participants in this research.

When it comes to *spor merakı*, "Istanbulite" captures not only the diversity but also the vibrant, spirited, and overstimulated aspects of the everyday lives of women residents of the city. Of course, their status as residents of the same city is one of the main shared aspects of the diverse women you will encounter in this book. As a significant body of scholarship has established, categories related to class, religion, political affiliation, and ethnicity matter. They shape the possibility of individual identities and complicate their subjectivities. Beyond considering the deeply structural nature of taste and distinction produced by these divisions (Bourdieu 1984), following Istanbulite women closely enables us to see the processes through which a shared object of desire is formed through parallel admirations, aspirations, dislikes, and concerns. In this vein, figuring out what makes exercise desirable and a concern central to women, despite the social differences between them, becomes the key to understanding such processes.

Landscapes of Exercise

When I first began my research on exercise among Istanbulite women in 2008, there was an exponential increase in the number of women-only gyms: between 2005 and 2008, the number had risen sevenfold, and by 2012 twentyfold. The (unofficial) number of women involved in exercise at the gyms and in public parks was around 1.5 million by 2012. The leader of this gym market in Istanbul is Spor AŞ (Sports Inc.), an Istanbul Metropolitan Municipality–owned company responsible for providing sports facilities to "make the residents of the city healthier." B-Fit, which followed behind the Spor AŞ gyms, was founded by a secular feminist entrepreneur, Bedriye Hülya. The motto of B-Fit is "*for* women *by* women."

The exercise trend became so widespread among women that even women's charities and training centers, established to provide skills for women such as accounting, computing, traditional and modern handicrafts, now offer step, aerobics, and Pilates sessions for a couple of hours a week in their often poorly air-conditioned rooms. In short, the new Istanbulite public-exercise landscape brought about a fundamental turnaround in women's engagement in fitness activities.

Methodology

This study draws on long-term ethnographic fieldwork in 2008 and 2011–12. The first period of ethnographic research was conducted in 2008 with the support of Women Living under Muslim Laws[9] and involved twenty-three women who attended Cemal Kamacı Sports Center, a municipal public gym with women-only hours, and Okyanusfly, a women-only private leisure center with a gym, swimming pool, spa, and sauna for middle- to upper-class clientele. In 2008, the various municipal governments in Istanbul[10] started installing outdoor gyms in city parks to meet the demand of middle-aged Istanbulite women, *sporcu teyzeler*, "sporty aunties," walking in the parks. Cemal Kamacı is located on the European side of Istanbul, in Okmeydanı, whereas Okyanusfly is on the Asian side in Ümraniye. Both were squatter districts (*gecekondu*) in the 1980s but are now considered to be middle-class districts (Erder 1999; Yonucu 2008) that are part of central Istanbul. Although the gym trainers at Cemal Kamacı told me that they have customers from various socioeconomic

9. Women Living under Muslim Laws is an international solidarity network that provides information, support, and a collective space for women whose lives are shaped, conditioned, or governed by laws and customs said to derive from Islam.

10. Istanbul is composed of forty-one local municipal governments, all connected to the Istanbul Metropolitan Municipality.

backgrounds, a significant proportion of them are middle class. Aslı, one of the trainers there, mentioned that "wealthy" women prefer to take sessions privately at their homes or in the center.[11]

I conducted interviews with ninety-eight people in total, seventy-eight of whom are Istanbulite women from upper-, middle-, and lower-class backgrounds and between eighteen and sixty-eight years old.[12] Of those ninety-eight people, I interviewed twenty-one in 2008 (eighteen customers, two trainers, and one manager) and the remaining seventy-seven in the second and more extensive period of ethnographic fieldwork in 2011–12. Out of those seventy-seven people, forty-seven were women attending the gyms, and thirteen were women exercising in parks. The remaining seventeen included trainers, gym managers, and gym owners, people who run magazines for women, exercise celebrities, and daytime health-themed TV program hosts and producers. I held three focus-group meetings and thirty-seven follow-up interviews.

In 2011 and 2012, I visited Hamza Yerlikaya Sports Center, a municipal-owned sports center in suburban Istanbul; Istanbul Metropolitan Municipality Lifelong Learning Center (ISMEK); and two private gyms: Yeşilvadi (Green Valley) of Ümraniye, which was targeting a VIP clientele (according to its own description), and B-Fit of Bulgurlu, both offering women-only hours. I also visited Okyanusfly Leisure Center in Ümraniye.

Hamza Yerlikaya and Yeşilvadi are located at opposite ends of Istanbul: the former on the European side, and the latter on the Asian

11. Having personal trainers was not common up to 2008 in Turkey, so it was a signifier of wealth.

12. None of my interlocutors was living below the poverty line. The class differences are not as sharp in Turkey as they are, for instance, in the United Kingdom. I define class as based on income, occupation, and lifestyle: the lower class consists of blue-collar workers and their wives; the middle class includes small-business owners; the white-collar class includes doctors and engineers and their wives; and the upper class comprises the employers of the white-collar workers and their wives. For an extensive study on the formation of class in Turkey, see Keyder 1987.

side. The former, by virtue of its location, serves lower- to middle-class customers, whereas the latter is the "trendiest" gym among the rising Islamic bourgeoisie of Turkey. The Hamza Yerlikaya Sports Center is a sports-and-leisure center located in the Istanbul suburb of Sultançiftliği in Sultangazi district. Now with a quarter of a million inhabitants, Sultançiftliği was only four decades ago a village on the outskirts of Istanbul. Many of them first- and second-generation migrants, residents of Sultançiftliği come from different parts of Turkey and the Balkans—mostly rural areas—and therefore reflect the ethnic diversity of Istanbul. Hamza Yerlikaya is one of thirty-five sports centers established and run by Spor AŞ, a company owned by the Istanbul Metropolitan Municipality and responsible for providing sports facilities for the city's residents. I attended one of the "free sessions" there that target (and reach) low-income residents. The 10-lira ($3)[13] fee for a two-and-a-half-month membership covers the cost of the membership card and a digital card that regulates attendance and ensures that members observe the maximum attendance of two visits a week. There were usually around forty to sixty women at any time in the heavily mirrored fitness room during these "free sessions," working out or queuing in front of the treadmills, which could be used for no longer than fifteen minutes per person due to overcapacity.

The Yeşilvadi gym, in contrast, is located in the high-security, gated residential community Yeşilvadi Sitesi, which is populated by the new rising Islamic bourgeoisie (see chapter 4). This gym was initially intended for the exclusive use of the community's residents, but it was later taken over by Spor AŞ, which designed it for what the company describes as "VIP" customers. The gym is considered the new, "trendy" spot for upper-class women who wish to exercise in a homosocial space and practice a new classed leisure. The annual membership fee is considerably less (1,350 liras or $450) than the membership fee for the upper-class mixed gyms in other parts of the city but

13. The fees and the conversion rate are from the period I conducted my research.

is several times higher than the regular membership fees of the other Spor AŞ gyms in the city. Members can train on equipment with a view of the pool or watch their choice of TV channel on the screens embedded on each elliptical trainer, exercise bike, and treadmill. What CCTV monitors see in the daycare is aired on the screens placed near the swimming pool and in the fitness room, allowing women to monitor their children—a service several women appreciate. The Yeşilvadi facilities offer fitness programs such as Pilates, spinning, step aerobics, and yoga and include a sauna, steam room, and spa. Members can also receive a massage from the therapist.

In addition to Hamza Yerlikaya and Yeşilvadi, I also visited four other centers: Okyanusfly and the Bulgurlu branch of B-Fit are private women-only gyms, whereas Cemal Kamacı and Kartal ISMEK are not-for-profit gyms. B-Fit is a national gym franchise modeled after Curves in North America, specializing in women's fitness and equipped with training machines that develop "feminine" muscles and ensure weight loss. I interviewed two women at B-Fit Bulgurlu as well as the manager of this branch, Özlem Yeprem. Özlem is not just a manager; she is also a minor celebrity, especially in Islamic circles, as a former fashion model like her husband, Reha Yeprem. Both chose a religious life in the late 1990s, when an Islamic revival was taking place in Turkey (Gülalp 2001; Saktanber 2002; Altınay 2013b). At Kartal ISMEK, one of my interlocutors, Filiz, was a trainer for step, aerobics, and Pilates classes. The classes were free and took place in the branch's poorly ventilated basement. The participants did not have to bring their own equipment, though, because small dumbbells, exercise balls, bands, and matts were provided by the municipal government. Filiz not only participated in my research as an interlocutor but also kindly hosted me in her classes, allowed me to video-record her sessions, and even arranged her class so that trainees who wear a head scarf outside the classroom would not be captured during the shooting.

Several months before I started my second fieldwork project, I arranged a visit for March 2011 and sent out emails to people I thought might help me, such as former interlocutors and owners and managers of gyms I knew from my work in 2008. Curiously, none of my former contacts seemed able to help me. I found that the "field" had changed rapidly. The number of gyms as well as gym members had increased, and the managers of older gyms had been replaced because the gyms that had once been popular were now "out" just four years later. Then I met Meziyet,[14] a woman who is very active on social media, with about two thousand followers on Twitter and more than four thousand followers on Instagram. She responded to one of the desperate emails I had started sending out not only to former interlocutors but also to anyone who might be remotely interested in my study.

Meziyet is a young independent soul whose intellectual curiosity and thirst for new discoveries meant that my research was very appealing to her. She is a blessing for any ethnographer. The networks she introduced me to were upper class and would not otherwise be immediately accessible to me or to any outsider. With her introduction, I met people crucial to my study, such as the manager of the upper-class Yeşilvadi gym and the owners of *Âlâ* magazine. I also went to the places she frequented with her friends, such as hamams and spas in upmarket hotels and ostentatious gallery openings for the new Islamic arts.

However, none of these "introductions," in my opinion, were as valuable as her willingness to invite me into her life and into her emotions, frustrations, yearnings, and dreams. She invited me to her home, into her life, and even into the lives of her friends. Her willingness to provide me with access to individuals and networks was very little compared to her ability to make herself vulnerable to a stranger.

I spent about four months in 2011 at Meziyet's triplex villa in Yeşilvadi. I lived with Meziyet, her three energetic and energizing children, and her two maids of eastern European origin—*yardımcılar*

---

14. Among the women I interviewed, aside from the media celebrities, the only person I did not assign a pseudonym to was Meziyet, upon her approval and owing to her public profile. All other names are pseudonyms.

(helpers), as they are called in Turkey—a mother and daughter who were also living in Meziyet's house. During my time in her villa, I received invitations to join both leisure and religious activities that were exclusive to the upper-class women in Meziyet's small network. These activities included some weekly religious meetings, *sohbet*s, exclusively targeted at women living in the villa-type houses of Yeşilvadi.

Because the focus of my research is to capture desire and enjoyment, it was crucial to create friendly relations with the people I met, interviewed, and worked out with. I consciously avoided formal and distant tones to encourage comfortable conversations about *womanly* matters. This approach meant, however, that I never interviewed women I had not befriended.

Creating the atmosphere for a smooth and relaxed conversation was not always easy. Awkwardness arose when my interlocutors felt pressured to speak "smart" with me, especially if they perceived an educated woman living and studying abroad when they looked at me. I needed to strip away those markers and remain attuned to women's everyday language—which would sometimes vary from one neighborhood to another.[15]

In cases where my interlocutors were more than a few years older than I, switching to their "language" would not work. Owing to the age hierarchy between women in Turkey, it was impossible for me to strike impromptu casual conversations with older peers. At those times, I would search for shared backgrounds, as I did with Feray Teyze (age forty-seven),[16] who had moved to Istanbul from Kayseri,

---

15. The differences among the everyday languages I needed to switch to and from in order to create a friendly environment were sometimes so stark that shifting from one style to another became very confusing for me. In the end, ethnography for me has been "an intense, intersubjective engagement" (Clifford 1983, 119).

16. The attribute *teyze* refers to a maternal aunt in Turkish and is also a warm way of addressing an elderly woman. As women of this age and I became close to each other, I dropped the more formal title *hanım* (lady or Mrs.) and called them *teyze*—except in the case of the few who might find the latter form of address *laubali* (too cavalier).

the city where my mother was born and raised,[17] or would approach women through their daughters, as in the cases of Sabriye Teyze (forty-eight), Belgin Teyze (fifty), and Hilâl Teyze (fifty-seven).

During my time in Istanbul, the women who participated in my study and I shared hundreds of hours together. In ethnographic research, this method is called "participant observation," a term I find apathetic. We not only exercised and worked out together but also spent leisurely time together and shared multiple tastes: we drank many, many cups of tea and Turkish coffee, talked, watched TV, smoked *nargile* (shisha or waterpipe), ate breakfast, went to *ev oturması* (tea parties—literally "home sitting"), read magazines, and followed each other on social media (which we still do). Toward the end of my time in Istanbul, we went to hamams, beauty parlors, massage therapies, trendy and not-so-trendy coffee shops, restaurants, *nargile* cafes, and basketball games (with free tickets provided by the municipal government to increase the number of female spectators).

Toward the end of my fieldwork, in order to delve deeper into relevant issues and emergent themes, I organized three focus groups with small numbers of women (four or five) who shared common characteristics, such as socioeconomic status or age, to speak more about three main themes: ageing, pregnancy, and religion. These three themes seemed to be appearing with great frequency during my fieldwork, but there was no consensus around them. Group conversations in a relaxed and conversational atmosphere helped to bring out the women's underlying stories, opinions, attitudes, and feelings, such as their fascinations, frustrations, and, of course, contradictions and disagreements. The focus-group interviews served as a way to gain insight into the intersubjective aspects of women's interests and enabled me more than once to perceive how certain interests were circulated.

---

17. In my conversation with Feray Teyze, we also discovered that she and my mother were in fact from the same village, Kayseri, which led to another discovery—that my grandfather was her husband's primary-school teacher.

An important theme of desiring subjectivity is how women interact with the environments that surround them and with other social actors in their lives, including families, significant others, friends, role models, favorite TV personalities and actresses, as well as the social classes they may aspire to join. I looked closely at how my interlocutors perceived these individuals and social groups in order to explore the factors that triggered these women's fascination with exercise. In this pursuit, in addition to my primary interlocutors, I also interviewed third parties whom my interlocuters mentioned frequently during my fieldwork as figures who had exerted a significant influence on the women's interest in exercise. I interviewed Fatma Bayram, a female preacher, and a prominent figure among the rising Islamic bourgeoisie in Istanbul; Ebru Şallı, former fashion model and Pilates guru who has been teaching Pilates on TV for years; Saba Tümer, a daytime TV program host known for her "ideal Turkish femininity," as one of my interlocutors put it—a well-polished, perhaps advanced version of the "girl next door" with her curves, cheerful laughter, and bleached hair; Dr. Feridun Kunak, an orthopedic surgeon who hosts a popular daytime health program; and Dr. Aytuğ Kolankaya, a gynecologist who also hosts a popular daytime health program.

On Proximity and Fieldwork

As a woman who was born and raised in Istanbul, who has socialized with people from diverse neighborhoods in the same city, diverse classes, and diverse religious (as well as nonreligious) affiliations, and who was born into an "ordinary," secular, lower-middle-class family but who invested in becoming familiar with different religious circles in the city, I had multiple levels of proximity to the field and to the women I met. The proximities I am talking about both leave limited space for objectification and strengthen the ethnography, as discussed earlier. Positivists have previously critiqued proximity to the field as weakening the researcher's objectivity (see, e.g., Chavez 2008). Objectivity, however, as anthropologists have now realized, was only a claim made in early anthropology to gain recognition of the field as a legitimate branch of social sciences.

In the late 1800s and early 1900s, anthropologists were occupied with the methods of natural sciences, such as cataloging, categorizing, and keeping a distance so that they could get this new field accepted as a discipline in institutions. That was also the period of cultural evolutionism, armchair anthropology, and several other approaches that we now have left behind. Claiming objectivity gained anthropology the recognition it was looking for, but it also became an obstacle. The anthropologist or the ethnographer always carries his or her own biases to the field. The scholars who pretend otherwise are either not aware of their own biases and signification in the field or are trying to find ways to deny their own affect. For instance, a white male scholar who assumes that his informants are not tailoring their answers to him in the aftermath of a colonial experience and who writes accordingly does not have to account for the ethnographic shortcomings—or the politics—of his work when he claims objectivity. In other words, *claiming* objectivity makes the anthropologist immune to his or her own flaws.

Questioning proximity as an issue in ethnographic fieldwork is deeply connected to this fetishism of objectivity and to the determined denial that it is always lacking. In response, a number of ethnographers and anthropologists have chosen to nourish their anthropological gaze by developing a personal touch with the field to penetrate the illusion of objectivity.

I had a personal and particularly close relationship with the subject I was researching, which enabled me to have a more vigorous rapport with the field and my interlocutors. In my experience, proximity and building rapport are much more complicated than the classical insider/outsider question. I admit that I had multiple advantages in reaching the women I studied, such as an insider's awareness of the multiple behavioral codes of different classes (lower, middle, upper) and lifestyles (religious, secularist, neither); awareness of languages and dialects in relation to level of education; knowledge of the different regions and cultures of Turkey; and more. These advantages enabled me to be aware of what to say, when to say what, whom to talk to, when to talk to them, and how to address them. Nevertheless, what enabled my research beyond these advantages was the level of mutual trust I managed to establish with all of the different participants in my study, from trainers to administrators, from the female gym members with whom I spoke almost every day to the women who let me talk to them more intimately. Especially in the case of the upper-class, educated Islamic women I met during my fieldwork, who are (like many upper-class, educated individuals in many other contexts) more skeptical than lower- and middle-class women, it was their willingness to include me in their private lives that made the fieldwork possible. They not only opened their homes to me and shared their lives with me but also trusted me as a person, as a friend, and as a researcher.

In order to approach our research subjects with more than mere intellectual curiosity and to avoid positivist tendencies in the social sciences, we anthropologists need to develop either *inherited* or *invested relationality*. I define *inherited relationality* as the structural advantages an ethnographer might have that enable her to make the field more accessible for herself, such as knowing the language of the people she talks to. This relation is easily referred to as being an "insider," yet in fact it is more complicated than simply being born in the same region as the research subjects, as it was in my case. I view *invested relationality*, in contrast, as independent from whether one was born into a particular region or social environment, and I define it as seeing the world through the eyes of one's interlocutors and sharing their joys and sorrows. Invested relationality makes one feel obliged to carry the interlocutors' relationship with the world into theory in as strong and well-tailored a form as possible.

Mapping the Formation of Desiring Subjectivity across the Book

One of the challenges of studying subject making is related to the fact that it is a multilayered, multifaceted, dynamic, and fluid process. Writing about the formation of desiring selves also bears similar challenges. Accordingly, the book provides cross-references in one chapter to the ethnographic moments described in previous or later chapters. The reader may also want to read two different chapters side by side (e.g., chapters 3 and 6) to trace the connections between different types of relationalities and intersubjectivities.

To organize the fluidity of the self-making processes under analysis, however, I followed the broader dimensions through which desiring selves are formed—space, self, and time—and accordingly divided the book into three parts.

The first part, "Self," is composed of three chapters. Chapter 1, "Forming an Object of Desire," delves into the imaginative aspects of sport through a historical analysis of how sport was used as a tool for transformation in republican Turkey and how from the beginning of the history of sport in the Republic of Turkey women's involvement in sports has challenged existing norms about women's public sexuality. Chapter 2, "Desiring Istanbulite Women," starts with a discussion of Muslim women as desiring subjects as a feminist inquiry. It formulates the conceptual foundations of the desiring subjectivity. Moving beyond recent critiques of ethical self-fashioning, this chapter unpacks the notion of "desiring subjectivity" and its grounding in relational forms of Turkish female agency. Chapter 3, "Mediating Desires," follows women's *spor merakı* and connects their desires to role models, TV personalities, Pilates gurus, and other *mediating figures* in order to map out the interactive process of desire formation. The interactive aspect, as becomes apparent throughout the chapter, concerns how these mediating figures invest in their own selfhood to meet the expectations of potential followers and to become role models.

The second part, "Space," looks at the spatial dimensions of Istanbulite women's self-making practices at two levels. Chapter 4, "Leisurely Istanbul," approaches Istanbulite women as individuals who are living in the affective milieu of a metropolitan city and who are suffused with longing and dreams. It looks closer at the interactions among women's desires, their exercising flesh, and the city's materiality. In the second layer of my spatial analysis, I move on to the issue of segregation. Women constantly control the erotics of their public bodies, their attire, and their body movements at different levels in the public sphere. That constant control, however, is challenged when they attempt to exercise, as their breasts and legs start jiggling. Chapter 5,

"Men-Free Exercise," locates women's concern to avoid the foreign male gaze when they exercise at the center of queer theory. It analyzes this concern as part of the Islamicate culture of *mahremiyet* (intimacy, privacy) that operates as an institution of intimacy that provides a metacultural intelligibility for heteronormativity. Chapter 6, "Homosociality and the Female Gaze," is written against the liberationist accounts of women-only spaces, which suggest that any women's space freed from men can immediately indicate emancipation. By focusing on the normative capacity of the female gaze and the intersubjectivity among women in the gym changing rooms, this chapter instead brings out the complex dynamics between self-making, homosociality, and changing and shifting norms.

Istanbulite women's engagement in *spor merakı* and the relative autonomy they experience through exercise may appear to be about reclaiming space for desiring selfhoods through exercise. However, women's *spor merakı* involves shifting and trespassing the cognitive limits in which these selfhoods are embedded. Thus, women's process of desiring self-making is more complicated than simply opening up new spaces because it involves opening new temporalities as well. Therefore, the third part, "Time," explores subjectification and temporality. By examining the self-making processes constituted through perspectives of time, it also engages with the anthropological concern with human agency and the significance of agency in hindering or catalyzing social change. Chapter 7, "Embodied Rhythms and Self-Time," analyzes how the changes in daily routines and rhythms reflect women's desire to form a new selfhood by using exercise as an "altchronic practice," a practice that alters former temporalities and forms new, idiosyncratic ones. Chapter 8, "Gendered Temporalities," further investigates exercise as an altchronic practice, not something that simply has alternate rhythm but rather something that breaks and sometimes reverses the gendered life cycles imposed on women. This chapter is derived from a series of interviews and focus-group meetings about women's pregnant and postpartum bodies. The last chapter, "*Emanet* Corporalities," deals with the Islamic notion of *emanet*, which is often translated as "trust" and refers to the body's temporality. By looking closely at the ways in which women define this concept, the chapter suggests that Istanbulite women shift from the understanding of it as guarding certain body parts in order to avoid committing sins to an Islamic understanding of it as caring for one's body. In this shift in understanding, I argue, my interlocutors also change the ways in which the body is thought of in relation to a larger cosmology (i.e., the afterlife).

Self

1

Forming an Object of Desire

One of the first things I noticed in Istanbul during fieldwork was how sports was discussed, especially by the trainers and gym owners, as a matter of improving the self and body and becoming civilized. Often the term used to signify this sense of advancement was *spor bilinci,* literally "sport consciousness." In one such conversation, the assistant director of Hamza Yerlikaya, Serkan Bey, said, "Women come here just to lose weight, but we give them sport consciousness."[1] This sentence was the verbatim repetition of what the director of Cemal Kamacı said to me three years earlier. Considering his background as a graduate of sports management from one of the highest-ranking universities in that discipline (Marmara University), Serkan Bey had enough academic background to know that doing fitness, Pilates, or step aerobics is not categorized as "sport" but as "exercise." In his account, however, sport consciousness would be gained through body discipline acquired via any form of physical exercise—not just through professional sports. The trainers Fatma, Öykü, Sema, Nehir, and Sinem—all graduates of physical education—told me many times that women develop "sport consciousness" when they start attending a gym.

The idea of consciousness continued to echo during my journey through Istanbulite landscapes of exercise. For forty-seven-year-old Feray Teyze, who came to Istanbul from a rural town in Kayseri and

---

1. Field notes, July 23, 2011.

married a car mechanic, "sport consciousness" was one of the phrases she used to explain how she established a habit of regular exercise. "In time, I gained sport consciousness. Now it's part of my life."[2] Thirty-two-year-old Seda, an upper-class woman who had been swimming and skiing since she was a little girl, also proudly articulated her and her children's involvement in exercise as a matter of consciousness. Seda told me how she sent her son to capoeira (Brazilian martial arts) lessons, although her son's primary-school teacher did not approve. The teacher insisted that capoeira is not suitable for boys and suggested basketball instead. According to Seda, this comment proved that the teacher, although an educator, "lacks sport consciousness": "I once told his [her elder son's] teacher that he does capoeira, and she tells me that it involves violence, and I should rather send him to basketball. Why should I send such a flexible boy to basketball? Nonsense! He is talented at this, and it involves defense but no violence. Capoeira is based on gymnastics, if anything. Her comment comes from complete lack of sport consciousness."[3]

Seda considered herself more conscious than the forty-year-old trainer of her gym, too, she explained to me. The trainer, who occasionally appears on TV and is a small-scale celebrity, suggested that capoeira is not for girls, whereas Seda recommended it to her neighbor's daughter.

This ethos of sport consciousness is a matter of knowledge, attitude, and performance for those who claim to have it. Women who can run faster or have better endurance do not rate their performance only in terms of physical prowess. They feel superior in terms of "sport consciousness" as well. In fact, it is almost as if exercise elevates women, providing them with a higher status akin to higher education. It was also often the case, as became apparent in my conversations with Esma, a lower-middle-class woman of forty-two, that a sense of sport consciousness goes hand-in-hand with a sense of greater

2. Interview, Jan. 10, 2012.
3. Interview, Dec. 1, 2011.

education, of being educated; my interviewees would tell me how we were *bilgili* (knowledgeable), unlike others: "Women here are ignorant; they are not knowledgeable [*bilgili değiller*]. But you live abroad [*dış ülke*]. You understand what I mean. You see this. I don't talk to many women here, but I am a soft-hearted person: I help them when they do something wrong."[4]

From this perspective, the forms of knowledge gained in higher education and physical education are comparable. Both make one more cultivated, knowledgeable, and aware of the world. The moments I have shared here include glimpses of the ways in which sport is constructed as a *desired asset*, a source of status and a reflection of improvement that resonates with the modernizing impulses that initially framed sport promotion in the early years of the Turkish republican project (Yarar 2005).

Spor Merakı to Exercise New Selves

Sport is a curious word in English and in French, from which Turkish initially borrowed it. Aside from referring to athletic activities requiring physical endurance and prowess, *sport* also denotes leisurely or playful activity that is not expected to produce any benefit aside from personal or communal satisfaction as well as an act of mockery, a jest, or ostentatious dress. In this broad sense, *sport* is untranslatable into Turkish; its original polyvalence in English and French refers to a concept or set of practices that did not exist previously in Turkish culture. The idea of doing sport for no immediate benefit was introduced to the Middle East in the late 1800s when the first European and American sports clubs opened across the Ottoman Empire (Sehlikoglu 2017).[5] Thus, without an historically equivalent concept, the word *sport* is used in Turkey to refer exclusively to athletic activities.

---

4. Field notes, Jan. 12, 2012.

5. For a more thorough discussion of the colonial transition from "military training" to "sports" during the 1800s, please refer to Di-Capua 2006 and Sehlikoglu 2017.

Moreover, like the final *t* in the word, the additional French connotations did not survive the word's transfer into Turkish. Once imported firmly into the fabric of Turkish social life, sport began to acquire new cultural meanings and practices.

The historical background laid out in this chapter explains how sport and exercise emerged as one of the first activities women contemplate when they want to make a change in their lives. Importantly, not all forms of physical activity are referred to as *sport*—certainly not domestic activities that require heavy physical exertion. Although cleaning a carpet may require squatting, scrubbing, and weight lifting, in no way is it considered a "sport." This distinction in women's own understanding of sport lies not in the physical strength or endurance necessary for the activity but in the symbolic references that surround it.

Women I interviewed often reflected on the masculinist public discourse that mocks women for no longer doing housework in the traditional way, such as washing the laundry by hand. "If women did in fact continue doing their traditional duties," Kadir, the husband of one of my interlocutors explained mockingly, "then they would have had no need to exercise." Several of the women I met at the gyms shared similar opinions: "Of course, I should have been doing housework [at the moment]. Perhaps I would lose more weight if I did more housework instead of exercise," Sabiha mentioned mere days before Kadir made his facetious remark.

The reason why women referred to many of their activities as sport is deeply related to particular ways of imagining, perceiving, and performing exercise as a cultivating and civilizing ritual. As a consequence, the notion of "sport consciousness" is deeply related to the ways in which sport has been presented to the Turkish public through a series of historical moments, including the Turkish republican project. Women's attitudes toward exercise is related to broader public attitudes about sport; together with the historical and cultural connotations of sport, these attitudes influence and reflect women's aspirations and desires (Sehlikoglu 2014). Modernity in particular was one of the components of the early republican project that constantly highlighted concepts such as "knowledge," "awareness," and "rationality" and reconciled them with tradition (Akşit 2005; Özyürek 2006; Altınay 2013a). Early republican (1923–50) investment in sport took root in the minds of the public by the mid–twentieth century, branding sport as a civilizing, modern, classed, and therefore desirable act. This historical intervention played a significant role in shaping contemporary sport consciousness in Turkey.

Turkey and Sports: Civilizing a Nation

Western sports began to emerge in the Middle East in the mid-1800s, when under the aegis of European colonial institutions such as embassies and schools several Western sport clubs were established for men in major regional cities, such as Cairo, Alexandria, Istanbul, and Beirut (Fişek 1985; Yurdadön 2004; Di-Capua 2006). These clubs offered sports such as cricket, hockey, rugby, soccer, tennis, and basketball. The emergence of Western sports and sport clubs served a variety of purposes; in addition to providing exercise, sports fortified the colonialist aspirations and aimed to civilize the public, targeting youth in particular from the late 1800s to early 1900s in the Middle East and elsewhere in the colonial world (Besnier and Brownell 2012). These sports were significantly different from "traditional" Middle Eastern sports—namely, archery, racing, wrestling, horseback riding, and swimming—all of which were part of official military training for men (Fişek 1980; Yurdadön 2004; Di-Capua 2006), with the goal to promote "honour, bravery, and male group spirit" (Di-Capua 2006, 440) as part of the civilizing mission.

By the early 1900s, nationalist movements began to emerge across the Middle East, resulting in a transformation in perceptions and approaches to sport. During the interwar period, these nationalist desires replaced European sport clubs with local alternatives. Whereas colonialism used sport as a tool to *civilize*, early twentieth-century nationalist movements used it to create and transform a healthy "nation." According to Yoav Di-Capua, sport was part of the rising nationalist ideology that "promoted the European idea that a physically and mentally healthy individual is a precondition for the well-being of a robust nation, for the nation itself was the sum of these healthy individuals" (2006, 440). What remained unchanged was the perception of sport as a tool to control and transform the public, especially the minds and bodies of the youth.

The nationalization of sport clubs and sports started in Turkey during the late Ottoman period. After the establishment of the Republic of Turkey in 1923, the new country endured a series of social transformations until 1950, retrospectively deemed the "Republican Project," which aimed to create a modern, nationalist, secular, and Western Turkey. Sport was an important part of this transformation. The founder and first president of the Turkish Republic, Mustafa Kemal Atatürk, combined both colonial and nationalist perspectives in his approach to sport as a tool for nation building. Ayça Alemdaroğlu (2005) argues that Atatürk was influenced by the early twentieth-century eugenics discourse popular in this period as well as by the mind–body dichotomy of Enlightenment philosophy. Indeed, reflecting the body culture of nationalist ideologies of the time, Atatürk claimed that sport "concerns the improvement and development of the race" and "is also a matter of civilization" (quoted in Tuzcuoğulları, Tuzcuoğulları, and Tuzcuoğulları 2001, 55).[6] According to Atatürk, the bodies of Turkish people "remained in the East while their thoughts inclined towards the West" (quoted in Tuzcuoğulları, Tuzcuoğulları, and Tuzcuoğulları 2001, 57). In this binary, East and West had different physicalities: a fit, strong, muscular, erect posture was associated with the West, modernity, progression, and enlightenment, whereas a loose, chubby, large, and weak posture was associated with the East, tradition, the past, and darkness. Cemal Nadir's cartoon entitled *History of the Last Fifteen Years: Before and After* from 1938 visually encapsulates this dichotomy. The left depicts "before," and the right depicts "now" or "after": in the latter, the citizens are in Western clothing, slimmer, younger, and

6. From Atatürk's speech at the opening ceremony of the Alliance of Exercise Association of Turkey in 1938.

taller—not to mention fairer in color. In Atatürk's dualist formulation of nationalism, modernity, and fitness (in a social Darwinist sense), the Turks' supposedly Eastern bodies had to be molded—quite literally—into better shape, thereby enabling the formation of a new civilization.

As a consequence of this formulation, early republican intellectuals presented sporting culture to the public as an inherently Turkish characteristic (Kepecioğlu 1946; Yıldız 1979, 2002; İşcan 1988; Güven 1999). Formerly sporty characteristics such as bravery, physical strength, endurance, heroism, and military strength were now described using a new nationalist rhetoric. In this new rhetoric, sport-associated characteristics were inherently Turkish: *millî* (national) characteristics of Turks that had been forgotten during the Ottoman period. This viewpoint comes from the nationalist myth that suggests that all pre-Islamic and pre-Ottoman Turkic tribes were once a homogeneous nation; the early republican project thus promised to give this stable heritage "back" to the Turkish nation.[7]

National Pride in Women's Sporting Bodies

Women's participation in sports played an even more crucial role in the definition of the nation. The transformation of the nation was understood to parallel the physical transformation of its women (Sirman 2005). Focusing on the discursive and cultural productions of the nation-state, Nükhet Sirman notes: "Women were made part of the nation through the control of their bodies and, through cultural elaborations of femininity, the definition and control of the cultural boundaries of the nation" (2005, 149).[8] The symbols of a new Turkey

7. In this discourse, the pre-Anatolian and pre-Islamic Turkic tribal groups were imagined to be strong sportsmen because of their adaptation to the harsh geographic conditions in which they lived.

8. Sirman's argument is in line with the debate Nira Yuval-Davis and Floya Anthias (1989) started on women's role in the nation-state and the ways in which nation-states treat women as second-class citizens while simultaneously locating them at the center of nationalist projects.

and the new Turkish nation were crystallized in the definitions and displays of the "New Turkish Woman." Hence, popular journals of the 1930s "almost exclusively illustrate only women's bodies" (Baydar 2002, 238) when discussing the importance of sports and exercise, just as male novelists of the time pictured the "ideal Turkish woman" as someone who exercises and loves sports (among other things) for her health and her beauty (Baydar 2002, 238).

The transformation of women's rural-looking, veiled, "unhealthy," and therefore uncivilized bodies into disciplined, liberated, eugeni-cized, and therefore civilized bodies (Alemdaroğlu 2005) was per-ceived not only as an indicator of the country's westernization and modernization but also as a means of creating and defining the ideal "New Turkish Woman" (Kandiyoti 1989; Göle 1996). As in Nadir's caricature of the (fantasized) transition of Turkey over fifteen years, the new ideal woman was supposed to be unveiled, fit, and dressed in Western clothes—as well as somehow taller and blond. The veiled woman on the left represents "before," and the woman on the right represents "after."

In line with the contemporary eugenics theory, reproducing the nation was "an honor and privilege, if not a duty" (Kevles 1995, 184) for any woman who had the capacity to give birth. In order to ensure the desired physical transformation and to revive the Turkish charac-teristics embedded in the genes of Turkish citizens, sport was presented to the public as a patriotic duty (Üçok 1985; Arıpınar, Atabeyoğlu, and Cebecioğlu 2000; Tuzcuoğulları, Tuzcuoğulları, and Tuzcuoğulları 2001; Atalay 2007b) and as an act of *devotion* to the country. This link between sport and patriotism was inevitably enhanced when for-mer military commanders emerged as managers of the first republican sports clubs (Yurdadön 2004; Alemdaroğlu 2005).

First Sportswomen of the Republic: Elite and Engineered

The republican investment in sport to increase the fitness of the Turk-ish nation in physical as well as social Darwinist terms resulted in the introduction of a national program in 1926, the Çapa Teachers' School for Girls, to train professional female instructors in physical education and to encourage women to become involved in diverse branches of sports (Lüküslü and Dinçşahin 2013). Atatürk personally committed to the project—for instance, by asking managers of sports clubs who were former military men to encourage female relatives to become involved in sports at amateur and professional levels (Tuzcuoğulları, Tuzcuoğulları, and Tuzcuoğulları 2001; Yıldız 2002). Women whose close male relatives, especially husbands and fathers, were members of these sport clubs were the first to start playing Western sports (Yıldız 2002; Di-Capua 2004; Atalay 2007a; Koca and Hacısoftaoğlu 2009).

The first sportswomen were those who had familial relationships with former military officers and leaders of the new republic. They were encouraged to participate in sports at Atatürk's personal behest because, it was argued, developing disciplined bodies would strengthen the Turkish nation. The first generation of sportswomen were also those who could afford club membership fees. Such factors (being related to someone with a high military rank and being able to afford membership fees) reflected these women's elite status. They were meant to be not only role models for the wider public but also symbolic carriers and representatives of republican ideals and were widely known as the "daughters of the Republic" (Z. Arat 1998; Durakbasa and Ilyasoglu 2001; Altan-Olcay 2009; Altınay 2013a). Most of them assumed other professions in the following years. Suat Aşeni and Halet Çambel, for instance, were the first Turkish women to compete in fencing in the Olympic Games, representing the Turkish Republic in Berlin in 1936. Halet Çambel was born in Berlin, and her family was able to afford private fencing classes. Çambel later became the first and one of the best-known professors of archaeology in Turkey (Arıpınar, Atabeyoğlu, and Cebecioğlu 2000). Another leading sportswoman, Sabiha Rıfat, became the first female volleyball player in 1929 and was one of very few female members of a national men's sport club, Fenerbahçe. Rıfat was an educated woman from an elite family and part of the construction team for Anıtkabir, Atatürk's mausoleum, as Turkey's first female engineer. This particular history laid the foundations of an imagined narrative in the minds of the public that located women's involvement in sport as an upper-class act.

Women's participation in sports was regarded as an opportunity to prove and showcase the physical transformation of the Turkish nation. Turkish reform was therefore embodied in and represented by the bodies of Turkish elite sportswomen. The presentation of Turkish female bodies to a global (i.e., Western) audience was important for the republican project to confirm its success in the eyes of the idealized other; international games consequently provided the perfect platform for performance. Scholars on the subject often give the following quotation from a resource on Turkish women's involvement in the Olympic Games: "The Turkish Republic, which proceeds on the pathway of modernization with giant steps, should have shown the world that the Turkish woman now is no longer under the black veil [*çarşaf*] or behind the wooden curtain[9] [*kafes*]" (quoted in Arıpınar, Atabeyoğlu, and Cebecioğlu 2000, 7).[10]

Women's participation in sports was perceived as a means of representing and demonstrating to the Western gaze that the Turkish nation was succeeding in modernizing itself (Yarar 2005; Talimciler 2006; Atalay 2007a, 2007b). In her article on the emotive aspects of Turkey's negotiations to become part of the European Union, Meltem Ahıska suggests the term *Occidentalism* "to conceptualize how the West figures in the temporal/spatial imagining of modern Turkish national identity." She argues that "in theorizing the construction and representation of Turkish modernity, we can neither unproblematically herald the Western model nor dismiss the fantasy of 'the West'" that informs the hegemonic national imaginary" (2003, 353). In Ahıska's analysis, Turkey's republican reforms were not aimed simply at addressing contemporary political and social problems in Turkey but also at presenting Turkey to Europe. In other words, the reforms

9. A wooden curtain or cage was used when gender segregation was practiced. It ensured that women would not be seen by men, but women could watch the men in such places as mosques, palaces, and certain houses.

10. "Çağdaşlık yolunda dev adımlarla ilerleyen Türkiye Cumhuriyeti, Türk kadınının da artık çarşaf altından ve kafes arkasından çıkmış olduğunu dünyaya göstermeliydi."

were "part of a performance geared for the gaze of the West" (2003, 355). Similarly, elite sportswomen of the early republican era were presented to a "Western" gaze, a presentation that reflected the ways in which Turkey had developed a hegemonic yet inferior relationship with the West under the ideology of Occidentalism.

Sporting as a Heroic Masculine Act

Daughters of the republic were heroic figures who sacrificed their lives and their needs in the making of a new (and heavily wounded) country (Kandiyoti 1988; Y. Arat 1998; İnel and Inel 2002; J. White 2003; Kadıoğlu 2010). Early republican sportswomen were among those figures who used sport, a masculine act, to represent their nation on the international stage. Yet the representations of these early sportswomen as heroic paradoxically further widened the gender gap in sport. The sportswomen of this period were presented as heroes who *sacrificed* their femininity and *bravely* took up masculine qualities by playing sports for the sake of the nation. This was different from sport in post–World War II Europe and North America, wherein women were recalled to their feminine duties, and gender binaries reemerged in sexual identity and child-rearing practices. These elite Turkish women were looked upon as heroic figures, and the tales about their successes continue to inform republican history books, narrating how they sacrificed their femininity (but not necessarily their feminine duties) by participating in international-level sports competitions.

The republican ideology highlighted the bravery of elite women in order to promote them as role models. In doing so, it simultaneously deepened the gender binaries regarding sports and qualities of sports that paradoxically contributed to the public's rejection of women's involvement in sports after the early republican years (1930–50)— despite the compulsory physical education classes in schools and the emphasis on sportswomen in state and media propaganda. From 1930 to 1950, when Turkish sportswomen received several medals in the international arena, the overall number of Turkish women involved in sport remained quite limited (Amman 2005). Women's involvement in both sport and physical exercise was not supported by an important majority of the population, despite the curious reality that the Turkish state financially and structurally invested in women's exercise during this period (Sfeir 1985; Baydar 2002; Kay 2006; Benn, Pfister, and Jawad 2010). Obtaining a fake medical excuse in order to avoid compulsory physical education classes at public schools was common in Turkey even into the 1980s (Fasting et al. 1997). This lack of interest in sport (if not actual resistance to it) was, I believe, related to the tension created between sportswomen's exalted status and a desire to retain women's strong connection to the ideals of motherhood, family, and domesticity (according to republican ideals). Moreover, this tension was compounded by the ways in which norms of femininity were challenged by sports.

Women's Sport and Female Normativity: Gender Trouble

As is apparent in the history of women's sport in twentieth-century Turkey, women's athletic bodies are troubling because they trespass into a masculine zone of physicality, strength, and activity, thus challenging traditional definitions of femininity. Sport, as a type of physical involvement, is considered masculine. However, exercise is also related to the ways in which a moving female body is considered seductive. Therefore, exercise troubles heteroerotic boundaries in the Islamicate Turkish context. This aspect subsequently emerged as a main reference point of the *fetva*s (fatwas) that aimed to regulate women's sporting bodies. Before we can understand the *fetva*s, we must understand women's sexuality in the context of everyday harassment of women in relation to their participation in sport.

In 1978, the Women's Volleyball National Championship took place in the Adapazarı indoor facility. In a fully booked facility with a seating capacity of three thousand, the entire audience was composed of men: as these male spectators watched women jump and run around the volleyball court in exercise shorts, many of them used slingshots to throw metal objects at the players' legs in a form of sexual harassment. This gendered spectatorship and intervention was not an isolated incident; in fact, high school girls were still being harassed by male peers during compulsory physical education classes in 1980 (Hoşer 2000). In the Turkish context, women's moving bodies were imagined as hypersexual and therefore were under constant threat of sexual harassment and physical abuse.

Similar problems arose during the annual Remembrance of Atatürk Youth and Sports Fest (Atatürk'ü Anma Gençlik ve Spor Bayramı) celebrated annually on May 19 with parades and gymnastics displays by high school students. In the early republican period, performances by teenage girls were highly significant for the state elite as symbolic of the Turkish nation's transformation. Whereas fit female bodies represented physical civilization and Europeanization, their tight outfits reflected secularization. Yet Havva Abla remembered this event as solely about how the girls tried to find excuses not to attend the festival or rehearsals: "Boys were always trying to see our legs, and we would try to find corners to hide from them," she said. She then added with a wicked smile in her face, "But they could never do a thing to me."[11] She said this with pride, as if her strength of character kept the boys at bay. I later on learned that her father was a teacher at her school. Melek and Halime, two neighbors, conversely remembered Youth and Sport Fests with horror. "I used to hate them," said Melek, a gentle, pious woman who never stated any strong feeling about almost anything during several months of conversations: "Our physical education teacher would force us to attend them. I used to hate the classes, and the boys were harassing us afterward, but she refused to listen to me and my concerns."

In a way, these girls' everyday agenda was not about transforming a nation or looking "more European" or even secular when it came to the Youth and Sport Fests but about avoiding harassment by their schoolmates or simply about hiding their bodies.

In addition, several myths that prevented women and girls from exercising remained prevalent until the 1980s. These myths often indicated that by becoming involved in sports, women would mar

11. Field notes, Feb. 18, 2012.

their womanhood by either *becoming* masculine or losing their virginity (Sfeir 1985; De Knop et al. 1996). The women older than fifty whom I met during my fieldwork were able to confirm the circulation of such myths.

Düriye Teyze, fifty-eight, could recall former practices and attitudes about women's exercise in Turkey. She revealed some of the myths very clearly during a conversation in the Hamza Yerlikaya Sports Center changing room, and as we talked, the conversation also fleshed out the ways in which in her mind sport symbolizes a better, more educated self, a symbolism deeply connected with the notion of "sport consciousness" discussed earlier:

> DÜRIYE: Was there any sport back then [Eskiden spor mu vardı]?
>
> SERTAÇ: Why not? There has always been sport at schools.
>
> DÜRIYE: [Raising her eyebrows] No, no. That was for boys, not for us.
>
> SERTAÇ: Why not?
>
> DÜRIYE: Nobody did it, why would you? [She paused, fixed her shoelace, and then continued.] Even if we wanted to, our mothers and fathers would not let us anyway.
>
> SERTAÇ: But then how about in later years? There has always been something for women, hasn't there?
>
> DÜRIYE: We used to think that if we do sport, we would become like a man. Like those on TV [i.e., female body builders].[12]

Asiye Abla (forty-nine) interrupted our conversation and said, "Our elders used to tell us that we would lose our girlhood." Losing one's girlhood meant losing one's virginity, a common fear of damaging the hymen through jumping or excessive physical activity. When Asiye Abla mentioned losing their girlhood, *kızlık*, Zarife Teyze (sixty-three) commented, "Cehalet işte [ignorance]." Düriye and Asiye, like other women older than forty-five whom I talked to at gyms, referred to this past as their "ignorant" age. The national

12. Field notes, Jan. 22, 2012.

discourse of sport was internalized as a way to claim superiority over those who did not exercise and thus to position oneself as an elite relative to everyone else. Sport is still considered an upper-class activity, hence the pride these two women feel for leaving those times behind, for changing, improving, and becoming more urban and civilized. This sport pride is also about a process of intellectual growth within womanhood: that is, the knowledge that they will not lose their virginity through sport. The changing perceptions of womanhood, as I elaborate further in the next section, have been in continuous contestation in Islamic circles with respect to the rules and regulations about women's sporting bodies.

Islamic Perceptions of Women's Sporting Bodies: A Question of Physicality and Sexuality

As republican ideology sought to transform Turkish women by glorifying women's participation in the masculine realm of sport, Islamist intellectuals, preachers (*vaizler*), imams, and *hocalar* (religious teachers) emphasized the "protection" of women (by not allowing women to exercise in the presence of men) and the preservation of women's traditional roles in the household. According to this traditionalist Islamic perspective, the transformation of Turkish women during the early republican era represented a process of degeneration and distancing from their traditional roles. The word *fitne* (or *fitnah*, secession and chaos) thus came to embody the process of women's emancipation from domestic life, unveiling, and entry into the public sphere (Kandiyoti 1988; Saktanber 2002). In this conservative discourse, sport was one of the modern "inventions" causing chaos in Turkish society as it took women outside of normative boundaries.[13]

---

13. Although political opposites of one another, both Islamic traditionalist and Kemalist (Turkish secular nationalist) views "work by objectifying women's bodies and subjecting them to patriarchal systems of representation, thereby negating and distorting women's own experience of their corporeality and subjectivity" (Mahmood 2005, 158). Therefore, following Saba Mahmood's definition, I find it relevant to refer to both ideologies as patriarchal.

Despite the former prohibitions, Turkish women's contemporary interest in exercise and sport in the Muslim world pressured the Islamic authorities to soften their *fetva*s in Turkey. Hayrettin Karaman is one of the most cited and referenced scholars in *fıkıh* (or *fiqh*, Islamic jurisprudence) in Turkey, the author of fifteen books and hundreds of articles and essays on *fetva*s. He regularly contributes to a daily Islamic newspaper, *Yeni Şafak*, and makes all of his writings available on his personal website. In a limited number of articles, he discusses sport as an extension of daily life and fun (Karaman 2000, 2003, 2005).[14] Karaman writes, "The sport activities that do not harm humans at an individual and social level, that do not contain cruelty or torture, that are not made part of game of chance or gambling, that do interrupt time management, those that do not violate modesty and morality were supported and even performed by our Prophet himself (peace be upon him)" (2003, 245). Among those four warnings, Karaman cites the fourth one as important to both men and women, stressing modesty for both equally. In relation to the third warning, time management, Karaman reminds women not to neglect their child-bearing and domestic duties. Although he tries to draw attention to gender equality (segregation for both sexes), he also repeats exactly the same tension between womanhood and exercise raised in the early republican period with his emphasis on motherhood and household duties. This tension continues to haunt state discourse around women and sport in contemporary Turkey.

Karaman's immediate focus on the gender issues (rather than on fanaticism) when discussing sports is no different from the focus in the rest of the Muslim world.[15] The fatwas regarding sports that circulate

14. In the "Entertainment" section of his book *Günlük hayatımızda helaller ve haramlar* (Permitted and Forbidden Acts in Our Everyday Lives), Karaman designates entertainment as a human "need" (2000, 177).

15. An exception is Mustafa İslamoğlu, who repetitively warns his followers against football (soccer) fanaticism (İslamoğlu 1999, 2000, 2003, 2005) because he considers it an "addiction" (İslamoğlu 2003) and "social drug" (İslamoğlu 1999).

across the Muslim world from Malaysia to Cairo to North America also overwhelmingly center on gender and modesty issues.

Women's involvement either by participating in or by watching sports exacerbates an already-existing ambivalence toward sports in Islamic attitudes, often leading to heated debates in Islamic circles about women in sports, thus shaping the sporting experience of women as gendered subjects. Almost all of the *fetva*s concerning physical exercise begin with the importance of sports for health and encourage individuals to be physically active, with minor warnings about violence, fanaticism, and hooliganism, similar to Karaman's account. The most conservative interpretations may warn adherents of Islam against wasting time in sports.[16]

When it comes to women's involvement in sports, however, the fatwas engage stricter and more regulative language. Almost all of the suggested regulations and rules about women's involvement in sports are related to gender segregation and, more importantly, to bodily exposure. They commonly specify several rules that must be followed. Men and women must be segregated because mixed environments may open channels for seduction, temptation, and corruption. *Fetva*s reject any physical exercise that stirs sexual urges or encourages moral perversion, such as women dancing and being watched by the public. These acts are coded as sexual (i.e., sexually appealing) and *fitne/fitnah*.

The requirements to be met for a Muslim woman to practice sport relate at all scales to her duty to cover the *awrah* (Arabic transliteration),

16. This interpretation is in line with the fatwas elsewhere. For instance, IslamQA, one of the most visited Islamic fatwa websites, which provides in twelve languages (Russian, Arabic, Turkish, Uyghur, Chinese, Japanese, Urdu, Indonesian, Hindi, English, French, and Spanish) the fatwas declared by Sheikh Mohammad Salih al-Munajjid, discusses sports as a form of leisure and therefore subject to time-management issues within Islam. According to Sheikh al-Munajjid, "If [an activity] distracts you from something that is obligatory, then it becomes forbidden [*haram*], and if it becomes a person's way of life so that it takes up most of his time, then it is a waste of time, and in this case at the very least it is disgraced [*mekruh/makrooh*]" (al-Munajjid 2003).

or *avret* in Turkish: the parts of the body one is supposed to cover, according to Islamic rules. For men, the *avret/awrah* is the area from navel to knee, whether in a mixed or men-only sphere. For women, however, the *avret/awrah* is the area from navel to knee only in the presence of women. In the presence of (foreign) men, the *avret/awrah* is all of a woman's body except hands, feet, and face.

Contemporary Islamic debates are evidently highly influenced by the anxiety over the loosening of values, as is more visible in the case of Saudi Arabia; this anxiety haunts Karaman's fatwa as well. Indeed, an overemphasis on control, especially on control of women as bodies to be protected and preserved, is a reflection of this anxiety. Women's involvement in sports is regulated in terms of modesty, which summons up Islamic accounts of female sexuality as being "dangerously active, rather than intrinsically passive" (Lewis and Mills 2003, 15; also argued in Mernissi 1975 and Ong 1990). Therefore, when women's sporting bodies are a matter of fatwas, they are discussed in terms of regulation, control, and segregation.

Although pious Muslim sportswomen do not undervalue bodily regulative accounts of Islam, they do not necessarily internalize or centralize the normative perception shared in the *fetva*s. What is even more interesting is the extent of the debate: the *fetva*s on women's sports I have discussed are taken more seriously by the non-Muslim world at both the academic (Antoun 1968) and nonacademic levels (Abu Zahra 1970; for a critique of media, see Samie and Sehlikoglu 2014).

Conclusion

References to early republican ideals in contemporary Turkey usually reflect an aspiration for knowledge of sports, which is associated with an idea of an enhanced knowledge of the self and specifically the self in relation to the world. Women's imagination of their selves as sporting bodies, which extends to referring to regular fast walks as "sport," reflects an aspiration for this knowledge and for a better self. In this context of permanent state investment in women's sports as a signifier of social transformation, a collective affective memory was built around the notion of sport. Sport came to signify the desire for change toward a "civilized," improved, and better self and nation. It is in this context that *spor merakı* took on historical nuances, becoming an object of desire, a signifier of change, self-improvement, and advancement.

Contemporary debates about women's sporting, exercising, and moving bodies encapsulate a particular perception about my interlocutors that has become part of their everyday subjectifications. Discourses surrounding Muslim women's sporting bodies should be regarded as diverse and dynamic as the sociocultural or geopolitical contexts with which women are in conversation. This chapter highlights the importance of accounting for these global discourses and unpacking women's subjectivities. In fact, women's position within these discourses is in line with current theories of subjectivity, which define it as a process composed of cultural and historical aspects (Ortner 2005; Luhrmann 2006), just as desire is defined as an historically and socially mediated phenomenon (Rofel 2007). Women's desiring selves are also about how they see themselves through the lenses of others and how they navigate by means of those lenses.

Women's exercise is connected to the broader discussions about sport in the Muslim world. The collection of national, Islamic, and Western perspectives suggests that Muslim women's involvement in sport is not a coherent universal entity but shaped by a diverse set of culturally embedded, socially constructed, and locally produced discourses. Each of the levels—national and international, Islamic and Western perceptions and debates—defines and idealizes particular criteria about Muslim women's exercising bodies. Istanbulite women attending women-only gyms are equally subjects of the early republican project in Turkey, of Islamic debates and constraining accounts of *fetva*s, and of caricatured "Western" accounts obsessed with how Muslim women are deprived of sport.

The way my interlocutors imagine themselves as *sporcu*[17] has been informed by the history of women in sports in Turkey and sports'

---

17. *Sporcu* is a gender-neutral term in Turkish meaning "sportsperson" or "sportperson."

defined role in forming a civilized, enhanced, and elite self. For my interlocutors—Turkish Muslim Istanbulite women who do not have a desire to become professional athletes but are part of the women's *spor merakı* in the city—"sports" embodies the change in the nation. The early republic's investment in sport from 1923 to 1950 built up a collective emotional memory in modern Turkey. As a result, sport became and continues to be a reflection of the desire for change—the desire for a civilized, improved, and "better" self.

"Sport consciousness" neatly fits this paradigm of transformation. The way both trainers and exercising women invoke the notion of "sport consciousness" is related to widespread perceptions of sport as a tool for change. According to this perspective, any form of physical exercise that is able to transform bodies is enough to raise a certain kind of cognitive awareness and an enhanced knowledge about life, about the world, and about the self. The words that women choose to describe their experiences of sport, therefore, are related to broader public attitudes toward sport and its connotations. In sum, these debates both influence and reflect women's aspirations and desires, which is why I trace the ways in which my interlocutors' sporting bodies are imagined, represented, appropriated, estranged, or idealized.

However, sport also lies at the crossroads of contrasting assumptions and discursive practices about women's physicality, femininity, and womanhood in different ideological, geographical, political, and historical spheres, as explored in this chapter. Interestingly, conservative fatwas and the Western media agree on many points; both fail to understand Muslim women's sporting bodies beyond the binary terms of modesty and sexuality. While Islamic fatwas relentlessly remind us that women's sporting bodies raise anxieties about the violation of public modesty codes, Western media similarly obsesses over the veil, which, as I argue elsewhere, is a reflection of colonial eroticized fantasies of the Orient (Samie and Sehlikoglu 2014). Although both accounts focus on public sexuality and modesty when discussing Muslim women's exercising bodies, both also paradoxically end up neglecting the everyday concerns of the women themselves, who exist at the border where women's moving bodies trouble or transgress boundaries of sexuality and modesty in public. My research in Turkey reveals a more complex—and colorful—picture of how as women exercise, they navigate modesty culture and sexuality norms that regulate their public identities.

2

Desiring Istanbulite Women

My favorite spots at the gyms were where the most vibrant conversations took place. At Hamza Yerlikaya, that spot was at the far end of the room across from the changing-room entrance, where five lower-body machines were located, the third and fourth ones facing each other at a ninety-degree angle. Women arrived there after they jogged on the treadmill and worked out their upper body. At my favorite corner, they caught their breath while sitting and working out their lower body and so chatted about all sorts of things. It was one of the best spots to strike up a conversation.

One cold, hazy, late-March day in Istanbul, the free women-only session at Hamza Yerlikaya was very crowded because it was a school day. In the fitness room, two middle-aged women were using the lower-body machines at that corner. One of the two was wearing a bonnet, the type that head-scarf-wearing women wear under their scarves to keep them neatly in place. The other one was wearing her hair in a ponytail. The one with the bonnet was explaining how to use the leg machines when Hazine Abla,[1] Züleyha, and Nida approached the corner. They spread their mats on the floor just next to the lower-body machines, hoping to join the chat while doing floor exercises. Hazine Abla and Züleyha agreed to follow Nida while she led the training. They started exercising, but the conversation on how to use

1. *Abla*, meaning "elder sister," is an honorific deictic term of address for a younger woman who is older than yourself.

52

the lower-body machines ended as soon as the other three joined. Now we all were speaking about Züleyha's newly shaved head. "I wanted to have stronger hair," she explained. The woman with the bonnet agreed. She shaved each of her three sons' heads when they were little, and they all had very thick hair now. "Would that work on adults too?" the pony-tailed woman asked. Nida replied with a big smile, "She [Züleyha] has put on nourishing ointments; of course it will work." Nida was always protective of Züleyha, I remember thinking. Nida probably did not want Züleyha to lose her motivation. Meanwhile, Hazine Abla was bored and stood up to walk to the CD player. "What sort of ointment do you use?" the pony-tailed woman asked as Hazine Abla was changing the music. Züleyha's face lit up: "I use something with *acıbadem yağı* [apricot seed oil], but be careful, don't use *badem yağı* [almond oil]." Her sentence was interrupted by the new loud music Hazine Abla had just put on. Everybody in the large room seemed to be happy with the music intervention. We all turned our heads to the CD player and watched Hazine Abla approaching, half-walking and half-dancing. She interrupted the floor training Nida was leading, just as she had interrupted the chat and taken over the whole fitness room with the loud music. Hazine Abla, in her late forties, charmed seven women into joining her belly dance, and at least eight others clapped their hands to the rhythm of the music.

After about fifteen minutes of belly dancing, the group grew tired, and we all slowly moved to the changing room, chatting, with Hazine Abla's voice louder than the rest. She was trying to organize a *çay keyfi* (tea indulgence) event, and the indulgence part seemed to refer to what would be served with the tea. Hazine Abla reminded the women to bring low-fat, low-carb, home-made snacks and *mezes* (appetizers). She told those who were hesitating to join the feast that they "had lost enough [weight/calories]. Let's indulge ourselves!"[2]

This chapter traces the elements of desiring subjectivity. To be clear, my use of the term *desiring subjectivity* does not simply harness

---

2. Field notes, Mar. 27, 2012.

desire to the subject. Rather, it uses this particular aspect of human subjectivity—desire—to expand the conceptual limits of studies in the social sciences, especially those in gendered area studies concerning a group of people, Middle Eastern women, whose subjectivity has long been reduced to a limited number of tropes. Nor is my use of this term meant to set the foundations of yet another binary. By drawing our attention to the complexities of self-formation as articulated through desire, I hope to inspire the use of other colors beyond the usual black-and-white conceptual pallet (see page 72 for discussion).

The Linguistic Ambiguity of Agentive Desires

Hilâl Teyze (Aunt Hilâl) is a fifty-seven-year-old *ev hanımı* (house-wife)[3] who came to Istanbul after her marriage into an Anatolian upper-middle-class family. The way Hilâl Teyze spoke about exercise was not much different from the way other women her age spoke about it: she wanted to find that one ever-elusive perfect solution to her health problems and regretted not taking up exercise when she was younger. Although self-discipline has never been a core feature of women's *spor merakı*, in Hilâl Teyze's case her ability to afford multiple alternatives seemed to have resulted in an inability to stick to a consistent schedule. Unlike women from lower economic classes, she could try out many different options, each for a short period. Despite this inconsistency, like many other women I talked to, Hilâl Teyze linked her *spor merakı* to a range of self-fashioning and self-making activities. With a carefully concealed pride, she went down her list— anti-aging creams, face-lift exercises, visits to renowned nutrition-ists, samplings of all the gyms in the area, exercise equipment, and a "to learn" sublist that included swimming, skiing, and driving. The amount of money women spend on such tools of self-fashioning var-ies with income level; whereas Hilâl Teyze would purchase high-end

---

3. I use the English translation "housewife" throughout the book for the women who call themselves *ev hanımı*.

brands such as Dior, a woman from a lower-income household might opt to mix olive oil with bay leaf or yogurt with cucumber as a cream. Eleven of the women I talked to received free nutrition advice either at state hospitals or through their budget gyms.

Hilâl Teyze frequented up-market exercise venues in Bağdat Caddesi, an upper-class residential neighborhood on the Anatolian side of Istanbul, whereas other women stuck to municipally owned centers available to them within walking distance.

During our conversation, Hilâl Teyze took me upstairs to show me her exercise equipment with much excitement. I tried to ask questions, but she was too distracted by her excitement in sharing her exercise goodies with me, some of which were not yet unpacked. "Do you know how to use this?" she asked me, interrupting my question to show me some kind of exercise band. "You need to pull this end," she explained, not waiting for my response. I let her excitement hijack our conversation. She showed me her dumbbells, her new sneakers, her sport suits, her resistance bands, her sauna suit, even her knee braces, most of which were gifts. As I joined in her enthusiasm, she became more stimulated, then suddenly blurted out, "Exercise takes me away from everything else."

At this point in my fieldwork, I had become aware that women would not typically talk to strangers about their pleasures because they instinctively felt that doing so might make them sound selfish. In Turkey, desires, ambitions, and cravings for satisfaction are perceived as being related to sexual desire. The way gender norms work on desire is visible within child-rearing practices. From early childhood, desire is constructed in contrasting ways for males and females. It is seen as central to the gendered subjectivity of men and boys. Because it is imagined to be the core component of manhood, from an early age appealing objects such as food and toys and activities such as cycling and driving are ideally provided to boys so as to preclude disappointment. It is assumed that appetites left unsated in a boy will lead to a loss of desire altogether, thus threatening the desiring male self. To ensure that the boy's masculinity—in other words, his male self—is kept intact, his ability to desire must be maintained and never disturbed or discouraged. A boy who has lost his desires would be deemed at risk of becoming passive.

The frequent daily referencing of male desire and its prioritization in social life contrasts sharply with the omission of female desire in everyday references. Any form of autonomous desire in a female subject is traditionally seen and treated as either selfish or immoral. Both of these qualities contrast to the qualities of the ideal woman, the mother, who should be both selfless and virtuous—that is, without desire. Turkish novels, films, and other media regularly depict desiring, wishful, and capable women as chaos bringers and *fettan kadınlar*—enticing femme fatales and witchy women (Kandiyoti 1997; Seber 2013; Aslan Ayar 2014; Yumlu 2014; İnceoğlu 2015; Işık and Eşitti 2015).[4]

Because normative expectations hold that women should have relational, devout, and most often exclusively maternal desires, women's desire easily escapes from language and is left unexpressed. Having internalized such normative discourses, women are cautious about the activities that would result in their being labeled selfish. More crucially, normative discourses shape one's self-perceptions. Thus, there are times women avoid certain activities that would make them *feel* selfish.

Normative attitudes toward female desire result in a complex process through which women manifest a desiring self that is unthreatening, docile, and relational. It is essential for women that in following their desires, they also maintain their relational value as selfless mothers.

Because of these normative constraints on women's desiring selves, when Hilâl Teyze said, "Exercise takes me away from everything else,"

---

4. Deniz Kandiyoti (1997) links this distinction between types of women to the larger Middle Eastern feminist debate and the ways in which women's sexuality is perceived as *fitne* (bringer of chaos). Although she has focused on sexuality and sexual desire, a parallel argument can be developed for desire in a larger sense, as I attempt to formulate here.

I needed to press her further so as to connect with her world of desire. We were in the third hour of our meeting, and she and I had already become friends. I had interviewed her daughter several weeks earlier. "What do you mean by *everything else*? What is the *else*?" I asked her. She first provided a cavalier answer. "Everything else," she repeated, waving her hand around her head. After a moment's thought, she shrugged and said, "Oyalanıyorum [I keep myself busy]." The term *oyalanmak*, "to keep oneself busy," is ordinarily used to refer to activities that pass the time and stave off boredom.[5] It is used especially for and by people who once had a busy life, are addicted to work, but are no longer burdened by their former workload—for instance, military men who used to work long hours under strict discipline but who have retired early and are left with the need to fill the time. Hilâl Teyze's choice of words was not accidental and hinted at a time when she was occupied with her young children and household chores. Far from the retired military man freed from his workload, Hilâl Teyze still took care of her grandchildren, a duty that required trips to different parts of the big city. The sort of dishes she cooked at home for her husband were traditional, all thus requiring hard work, such as rolling out dough and wrapping things in grape leaves, so much more difficult than my daily stir-fries. All such dishes were present when I visited her, not prepared especially for me but simply as part of her everyday menu. Despite her depiction of exercise as an act of *oyalanmak*, everything I knew about her suggested that her involvement in exercise was more than a simple matter of passing time. So I pushed her a bit. "But you are busy. You are always working—the housework, taking care of your grandchildren," to which she replied, "Kendimi *kendimle* oyalıyorum [I keep myself busy with *myself*]," with a clear emphasis on the *self*.

5. The concept of boredom is also bound up with desire (Svendsen 2005) and time (Musharbash 2007). Yasmine Musharbash writes that "boredom comes into being in the nexus of old and new regimes" (2007, 315), yet she also calls for a closer look at sociocultural and historical understandings of each particular context.

Hilâl Teyze's choice of words allowed her to avoid directly telling me that she wanted to spend time just for herself. She instead moderated her language and framed her practice of autonomy within more acceptable terms of reference—that is, acceptable in the eyes of her family, in particular her husband. Telling me that she was merely keeping herself busy was a way to camouflage her very real individualistic desires. As she told me about her adventures in exercise, she monitored my responses to gauge whether I shared her enthusiasm or if I was surprised by or disapproved of her sense of adventure and enjoyment in exercise.

Hilâl Teyze's story of *spor merakı* and her strategic use of hedges about it were shaped by her contentious relationship with her husband, who found his wife's *spor merakı* unnecessary. Her habit of using the word *oyalanmak* helped her to smooth the way for her cause. Because she knew that she would eventually go against her husband's wishes anyway, such mitigating language allowed her to make her requests sound less objectionable.

When she showed me her skiing photos, she was visibly proud of having become accomplished in such a difficult-looking sport. It took more than a year to get herself into a center with ski lessons, she told me, the waiting list was so long. This seemingly ordinary challenge is worth taking a closer look at because Hilâl Teyze needed to establish her case for skiing vis-à-vis gender norms about desire so that she wouldn't be perceived as wanting to ski out of selfish desire. The most useful way to enable this complex process of manifesting her desiring self was to bring her husband and his selfishness into the conversation. In the midst of expressing her pride of self, Hilâl Teyze slipped in a slightly bitter indignation. "He always goes to skiing with his friends," she told me in a thin, peevish voice. I was a fish on a hook. "What do you do when he goes?" I asked, giving her a chance to make her point. "He used to tell me to stay home, but I would go anyway. Then I would be imprisoned in the hotel with snow everywhere. I didn't know how to ski. In the end, I learned how."

In a context where women's selfhood is valued relative to familial relations, Hilâl Teyze articulated her story in a way that would not jeopardize her existing ties but would nevertheless draw attention to her negligent husband. By describing her husband as someone who ignored his wife to go skiing, her own desire to learn to ski was shielded from accusations of selfishness. On the surface, it may appear from within a Lacanian reading through the concept of *manqué* that Hilâl Teyze's husband acted as her *other*, signifying what she lacked (Lacan 1981, 1988; Glynos and Stavrakakis 2008). I believe that this assumption is too easy, however, in that it ignores the Turkish context of the gendered formation of acceptable desire. Normative linguistic limitations require women to use multiple hedging strategies when articulating their desires. While Hilâl Teyze was most certainly expressing her frustration with her husband, she was also drawing attention to his selfishness. If he was seen to be the kind of man who easily abandons his wife to go skiing, then her own skiing adventure, linked together with his in this way, could not be seen as self-centered. Hilâl Teyze ended the story of her skiing escapade with a scene where her husband walked into the ski instructor's office to find a photo of his wife hanging on the wall. She told me how she was caught in the photo with a cheeky grin on her face. Her next project, she explained, was to learn to drive—also an aspiration that flew in the face of her husband's will.

Most of the women I spoke with were like Hilâl Teyze in the sense that it was difficult for them simply to tell another person straightforwardly that they *want* to do what they do. It was hard for them to say that they enjoy exercise for no other reason than the immediate pleasure it brings or that they long to do something that is not for someone else—for their child, friend, or family. Despite their difficulty in expressing selfish pleasures and desires, they occasionally said something along the lines of "What the hell, everyone lives for themselves in this world." Hatice Abla, one of my interlocutors, said this to comfort another gym member whose mother-in-law found her daughter-in-law's exercise regime to be an unnecessary waste of precious time—time that the mother-in-law felt could be better spent on domestic and familial duties. For many women, it was difficult to explain even to themselves, let alone to another person, that they exercised simply for the pleasure of spending self-time, freed from all the duties imposed upon them. Few women I spoke with were able to formulate their pleasure or desires in this way. Tuba, an articulate university graduate and housewife in her midthirties with two children at home, was one of the few who could do so. "Sport," she declared, "is in the same category as a manicure, paying a visit to a beauty salon, or getting my hair done. It is something I do just for myself." Tuba enumerated other beauty regimens to highlight the modest cost of exercise at her local municipal gym.

For a young housewife like Nida, who married into a working-class family, *spor merakı* can easily become part of a larger project of investment in a more secure future. Nida and I became friends very quickly during the early weeks of my time at the budget gym she frequented. She preferred to arrange our first interview session at a location away from the hectic setting of her home, where she was subject to her three children's needs and her in-laws' surveillance. She said we should pick a place other than her home or the gym so we could "spoil ourselves." We decided to meet in one of the modern-looking but inexpensive franchised patisseries of Istanbul in the suburban area of Sultangazi. During our conversation, she told me many times how she did everything for herself, *kendim için*. A tragic incident had led her to decide to "take care of herself." "I realized that I should be stronger, more confident," she recalled. She began implementing a series of changes in her life, including training for a proper degree, first finishing middle school and then high school, then getting a diploma in accounting in case she needed a job in the future. She mentioned her *bilgi açlığı*, her hunger for knowledge, multiple times during the interview. As she switched from the topic of exercise to education, she was also letting me know that she considered exercise to be part of a larger project of the self, something that triggers new knowledge of the self. Her *spor merakı*, she said, was what kept her going, giving her strength that was "hem maddi hem manevi [both physical and spiritual]." Class differences cast aside, what is common here is that women see and use their *spor merakı* as part of a self-project available even to those less ambitious than Hilâl Teyze or Nida.

Doing something for oneself simply for individual enjoyment rather than for the good of the children, husband, or family and doing it unapologetically and impenitently do not come naturally in this context. Even when Turkish women do not find it too outlandish to want to enjoy something just for and by themselves, they often find it unfitting to speak of their desire for it.

Women also tailored their "excuses"—that is, their reasons— for why they exercise to different audiences—neighbors, husbands, in-laws, and other relatives. Even in my field notes I find that the same individual provided different accounts for why she "does sport." Many spoke of relieving a backache, losing weight or having smaller hips, becoming healthier or more beautiful. They then went on to speak about the fun they had, referring to the inexplicable joy exercise brought them. If they wanted to sound smarter, they mentioned the hormones the body secretes during exercise. At least half-a-dozen times, I overheard women telling their husbands on the phone, "I came here to become more beautiful for you," then contradicting themselves by telling the gym trainer a few minutes later, "I only exercise because I am now more sport conscious." Use of such woolly and health-related language was common among many of the women I talked to and came in especially handy when they needed to negotiate their new habits with their husbands or relatives. I realized that it would be too elitist to dismiss women's strategies as futile. As I explore in the following pages and as the longitudinal research reveals, they carry a transformative capacity.

These sometimes overlapping and often confusing and conflicting accounts draw our attention to the shifts in the language they used to talk about exercising. Grounding her conceptualization of gender and agency in a Lacanian understanding of desire as a never-fulfilled lack that "always exceeds or slips away in language," Lois McNay asserts that "it is possible to express demands in speech, but it is impossible to express all that underlies this demand. Desire then is constituted in this residue or gap, between the articulated demand and that which underlies the demand" (2000, 170). Although the nonrelational and autonomous desires women possess lack a cultural vocabulary and imagination in Turkey, they are the signs of the emergence of a less familial and relational desiring selfhood.

The Formation of a Desiring Self

I spoke with Nida about seven years after our first encounter in one of the budget sessions of Hamza Yerlikaya, to congratulate her on her entrance to university. I read to her some things she said during our interview in 2011:

> I have this thing, I am always hungry. I am hungry of knowledge. I want to learn, about everything and anything. I teach this to my children too. They have to learn everything, even if they won't need to use that knowledge right away. I want to learn. I want to learn languages too. Do you know why I want this? Because . . . there are free courses everywhere. One language equals one person. It means, progressing forward, always. . . . I can use Word, Excel. . . . And I never stop. After my third child, I did not stop either. I learned accounting, computer skills. I have never stopped learning. Because, you know why? Because nobody is indispensable. The day might come, and I should be able to let go of my husband, as he should be able to let go of me.[6]

We cried a bit together. It was an emotional moment.

Exercise was, in her words, "a way to start" back then. "When you go do sport, you have friends who are also into sport. You learn from them. You get energized by them. This [what I do] is important for myself and for my children too."

In one of her latest works, the great novelist and feminist thinker Ursula K. Le Guin tries to understand agency in realms that are less immediate but perhaps more radical in their transformative capacity—like those that have transformed the lives of many women I met during my fieldwork. Le Guin says, "There's a middle ground between defence and attack, a ground of flexible resistance, a space opened for change. It is not an easy place to find or live in" (2004, 216). For her, this is where hope lives. For me, women's ability to find that less-immediate realm to flourish is exciting, interesting, and humbling. In

---

6. Second and third ellipses indicate pauses in speech rather than omissions.

her own account, Nida used exercise as a way to get away from a life centered around others and to start forming her own relatively more autonomous sense of desiring self. Perhaps that was also what Selvi did when she later divorced her husband and married again. Indeed, desiring subjectivity is connected to an ability to imagine, aspire, and long. The connections I make here need to be explored further.

Lisa Rofel has developed the concept of desire as a way "to gloss a wide range of aspirations, needs, and longings" (2007, 3) and to denote the igniting of new lifestyles, new ways of being, new consumption patterns, and new ways of engaging with the world. Desire is seen to be associated with the human craving for new possibilities and to the ability to dream and fantasize. An object of desire—in the case specifically discussed here, *spor merakı*—is utilized to manifest desiring subjectivity as a step toward exercising other, much greater objects of desire.

Rofel argues that desire is formed through "a historically, socially, and culturally produced field of practices" (2007, 14), implying that behind the moment in which desire is felt and experienced stands a set of structures, processes, and practices. To get at these structures, processes, and practices, we must trace the historical and social routes whereby something becomes an object of desire and explain the unleashing of affect and agentive sensation around the desire. Istanbulite women use that object of desire, *spor merakı*, to bring into being a particular form of subjectivity linked to agentive imagination, aspiration, and longing. These latter forms of volition combine with elements of fantasy and anticipation, resulting in what we refer to as desire. That desire is then harnessed to selfhood in a specific manner.

According to Greek and Sufi ideas of personhood, desire is one of the core components of subjectivity. Finding its way to Latin in reference to longing or appetite, the ancient Greek word *orexis*, "desire," was derived from *orégō*, meaning "to reach or stretch" (Pearson 2012, 19). Giles Pearson notes that *orexis* conceptually "extends beyond action-prompting desires to hopes and wishes" (2012, 13). In his thorough analysis of desire in Aristotelean philosophy, he highlights two important points about desire that are relevant to my analysis of Istanbulite women's agency. First, desire is broadly seen as motivating almost every action in human life. Because of this broad application of desire to all willful action, some modern philosophers have charged the Aristotelean formulation with having trivialized desire (225), a conclusion Pearson does not share. This understanding includes fundamental parallels with how desire is perceived in the Turkish context as described earlier, albeit overlain with highly gendered norms whereby male desire is to be nourished and female desire is to be restrained.

Pearson's riposte, the second point relevant to the analysis of agency among exercising Istanbulite women, is that, according to Aristotle, the source of the motivation necessary for *voluntary* action is not desire but rather "the prospect of the objects of desire" (2012, 225). The crucial element is the human capacity to envisage the possibility of the object of desire—to hope, wish, dream, imagine, aspire, believe. This second aspect of desire works in complex ways in the case of *spor merakı*. Although *spor merakı* is an object of desire, it gains an instrumental value in women's lives because it enables women to maneuver through normative expectations toward the formation of a desiring subjectivity.

Influenced by his Greek predecessors, the theologian and philosopher Abu Hamid al-Ghazali of the eleventh century held that the human self (*nafs*) contains multiple faculties, one of which is *quwwa shahawiyyah*, the faculty of desire (Ad-Dab'bagh 2008).

Like the two faculties intellect and anger, desire is in constant interaction with the self because each faculty has the potential to go to either of two extremes. At the state of *ifrat* (excess), on the one hand, a person is incapable of any self-control and thus craves all physical and nonphysical desires. At the state of *tefrit* (the lowest minimum), on the other hand, a person loses all desire. Al-Ghazali suggested that either of these states would be the extreme and that the ideal state is *iffet* (chastity), where one desires what is permitted and despises what is forbidden. In the ideal state of *iffet*, rationality will develop control over desires (Ad-Dab'bagh 2008, 554).

Al-Ghazali articulated his idea that individuals' normative trajectory should be toward achieving the ideal state of *iffet* by formulating the human self in an interaction and process of investment with the faculties of desire, intellect, and anger.

Al-Ghazali did not present desire as a positive or negative concept. Rather, he referred to it as a driving force shaped by human agency that in turn shapes the self. Because in al-Ghazali's formulation self-making is an interactive process among the outside world, the self, and the faculty of desire, the way that the outside world and cultural setting respond to that interaction also determines the shape of the final desiring self. Women's desiring agentive subjectivities, then, are at least in part determined by multiple patriarchal mechanisms, an analysis in line with feminist formulations of desire and subjectivity that recognize multiple intersections with gendered, racialized, and classed cultural settings. In the case of Turkey, the gendered expectations and normative dynamics at play enable social recognition of particular desires over and above others, thereby influencing Istanbulite women's subject positioning.

Although the learned relational element involved in female subject formation has been addressed in Middle Eastern studies, what I am suggesting builds on more recent work by Suad Joseph (2005, 2012). In her work on the Arab community of Camp Trad in Beirut, Joseph (2005) captures how the relational selfhood and relational desires are learned and taught. And she states elsewhere that "desires, like subjects, are continually constituted in relation. The query I pursue is the shifting of wishes, needs, desires, claims, and demands to a vocabulary of relationality" (2012, 16). As she draws attention to the interactive processes that result in the formation of relational selves, relational desires, and relational agency, she formulates a theory that runs parallel to al-Ghazali's.

With followers of *spor merakı*, the desiring female self can be captured only through the pedagogies of desire that are informed by local constructs and relational selfhood. In an attempt "to develop a method and a language that situates desire at the matrix of relationships" (Joseph 2012, 16), I suggest a critical separation between the desiring self and the object of desire by means of a close ethnographic analysis of those elements that escape language.

Joseph's approach to the pedagogies of desire diverges from Freudian drive theory, wherein desire is defined as suppressed through social norms but present in the unconscious in its rawest form and unleashed in dreams. The early psychoanalytical approach to desire, observable across the social sciences of the late nineteenth and early twentieth centuries,[7] was limited by the researchers' inability to sever their privileged biases from their theoretical formulations. In contrast, the approach to desire exemplified in Joseph and Rofel's work reflects the latest poststructuralist feminist and queer interventions that call upon us to ethnographically study desire as something interactive, complex, and multifaceted.

Although desire has long been treated as a product of pedagogy, disagreements about how it is formed continue. It has been suggested that desire can be recognized only when it escapes from control, as when dreams reveal forbidden sexual desires, or that desire is defined through its foundational negation or "lack," again linked to systems of control. The same literature has also tended to associate the identification and experience of a person's purportedly authentic desires with the development of an autonomous self. My informants' process of using *spor meraki* to manifest a desiring self is simultaneously relational and autonomous, entailing the formation of an autonomous desire concomitant with a socially acceptable selfhood—for example, as mothers, grandmothers, aunts, daughters, or students. Over the past three decades, the scholarship on desire and the desiring female subject has become richer (see, e.g., Kristeva 1980; Butler 1987; Grosz 1994; Moore 2011), compelling us to think about desire beyond the concepts of sexual repression and "lack." In questioning the existing models of desire, Judith Butler wonders whether an oppositional relation within the Hegelian binary is enough to keep desire alive (1987, 15). In Butler's formulation, desire becomes more than just a

7. For the limits of early social anthropology, see Moore 1988.

relation of bound opposites: "Desire is *intentional* in that it is always desire *of* or *for* a given object or Other, but it is also *reflexive* in the sense that desire is a modality in which the subject is both discovered and enhanced" (25, emphasis in original). Since 2000, new work has emerged that addresses the pedagogies through which desire is learned, internalized, and manifested in the context of the Middle East (Allouche 2019; Hafez 2011; Osella 2012; Le Renard 2014; Canpolat 2015; Kreil 2016a, 2016b). Joseph has suggested that the term *relational individualism* has emerged among cultural feminists as a result of their attention to the relationality–autonomy dualism (2005, 103).[8]

With respect to Istanbulite women, if their desire lacks a local (Turkish) vocabulary and conceptual space, then how do they make it recognizable? It is at this point that we witness agentive work.

Feminist Agency and the Desiring Self

Women are able to manifest desiring selves without directly challenging the systems that objectify them through an interplay among three elements: the cultural ambiguity of independent female desire, the unpredictable nature of desire, and their own creative abilities. The binary conceptualization of Muslim bodies, where subjectivity beyond the secular–religious binary is immediately reduced to either/or/in between,[9] results in a gap much more problematic than a simple lacuna in research. Other sociologists and anthropologists working on Turkey and the Middle East have pointed out this problem in the context of domestic services, family, and how women use techniques alternative to direct speech to convey their emotional states, desires, and aspirations. In her book *Veiled Sentiments* (1986), Lila Abu-Lughod explores how the Awlād 'Ali Bedouin women of Egypt articulate their emotions in the form of poetry given that other public forms of expressions are

8. See in particular Ruddick 1980; Gilligan 1982; and Gilligan, Lyons, and Hanmer 1990.

9. For a critique of the literature that reduces religious Muslim women's complex subjectivity to a "paradox" or "self-conflict," see Sehlikoglu 2017.

governed by honor. Gül Özyeğin's ethnography *Untidy Gender* (2001) unpacks the complex dynamics of gender and class that exist between cleaning ladies and their female employers in Turkey. She details how the two sides negotiate their terms not through the social genre of *demand* but through requests made by their husbands. In contrast to these understandings, in the case of *spor merakı* Istanbulite women's avoidance of vocalizing their desires stems from the lack of local concepts and spaces afforded to their desiring selves rather than simply from the need for a negotiation strategy.

In her ethnography of desire in China, Lisa Rofel suggests, after queer theorists, that longings, desires, and aspirations are "partially unpredictable"; that is, they are determined not by their ontological nature but by "their ability to pave a path toward freedom beyond what was retrospectively portrayed as the constraints of the past" (2007, 23). Although I do not argue that women's desiring selves pave a path to freedom per se—I am not sure that freedom obtained via desires is ever entirely possible, ontologically speaking—what I observe is that the *objects* of women's desires are now more autonomously selected than they have been historically. Something that works against cultural norms and the mechanisms of power has intervened. The unpredictable nature of desire, the fact that desires can pave alternative paths, drives women to provide acceptable justifications for their pursuits, thus changing their fate.

The instability of gender norms (McNay 2000) reinforces the unpredictability of female desires precisely because managing that instability toward a relatively more autonomous self requires a creative capacity. Lois McNay defines agency in *Gender and Agency* (2000) as "the capacity for autonomous action in the face of often overwhelming cultural sanctions and structural inequalities" (10). This formulation takes a critical distance from the type of agency prevalent in Foucauldian analysis, which fails to recognize generative human agency because in this type of analysis "the process of subjectification is understood as a dialectic of freedom and constraint" (McNay 2000, 2). Thus, the conceptualization of selfhood remains passive with respect to discourse, and discursive practices and agency are left limited and partial. McNay therefore calls upon feminists to develop a generative framework that might reveal the creative aspects of agency (2000, 140–41; see also McNay 2003, 2008). She argues that recognizing the creative capacity of female subjectivity in creating change enables us to understand how gendered roles have developed through multiple as opposed to lone subject positionings. To avoid the risk of remaining within a *negative* paradigm of subject formation, McNay argues, we should not restrict our understanding of the history of human subjectivity to a one-sided analysis of the structures, rules, systems, and linguistic and discursive limits to which that formation is subject (see also Moore 2011; Long and Moore 2012). A negative concept of subject formation that focuses only on the workings of power risks creating a subject that "is understood, in essentially passive terms, as an exogenously imposed effect of language" (McNay 2000, 31). Seen in this light, the way individuals express and make themselves against, in relation to, or next to the workings of power while pursuing their desiring selves (Rofel 2007) is a salient aspect of human agency. The element of surprise in response to an unexpected encounter with veiled ballerinas, *hijabi* fashionistas, head-scarf-wearing *Playboy* cover girls, or desiring women is a reflection of the narrow formulations of subjecthood and agency that require women's desires to have emerged through a relation of resistance and only resistance.

I take issue with the conceptual boundaries that have been drawn in the study of Muslim women. By overemphasizing the role of religion in the lives of Muslim women, researchers in the *piety turn* have tended to minimize alternate forms of female agency that Muslim women use to navigate through multiple social structures, expectations, and daily pressures. Inasmuch as the ethical self-cultivation paradigm brought a long-ignored examination of pious Muslimhood into our scholarly orbit, in so doing it also served to bind Muslim women's agency to religion. Mahmood's (2001, 2005, 2011) struggle with secular feminist theory resulted in a thinning of anthropological approach. This result is curious given that Mahmood identified multiple patriarchal ideologies, including religion, that operate to objectify women's bodies. There were several conceptual tools available in secular feminist scholarship that could have helped Mahmood. With Deniz Kandiyoti's (1988) term *patriarchal bargain*, for instance, feminists had already been aware of women's ability to maneuver through multiple systems. Kandiyoti developed the term to identify women's and men's everyday negotiations and conversations to gain temporary benefits from various forms of patriarchy (see also S. White 1997; Pascoe 2011; A. Hart 2017).

Although the goal of Mahmood's project was to develop a critique of secular feminism by focusing on pious individuals and their project of self-cultivation, the application of her theory led to a generalized reduction of various forms of subject positionings solely to the ethical. This reduction, in turn, left almost no conceptual space in which to speak of the possibility of the female Muslim agentive capacities identified by an earlier generation of secular feminists. These agentive capacities constantly shift, working to escape control and falling outside of what is immediately visible as the ethical. In the case of the Istanbulite women followers of *spor merakı*, women at times act to divert patriarchal mechanisms; they provide acceptable excuses and take bargainlike attitudes toward the formation of a desiring subjectivity.

Rather than being resisted, as only an opposite does best, perhaps the theories of agency developed by previous generations of feminist scholars can provide a new impulse to breaking the binary. In my observations of Istanbulite women and in my stance from the perspective of Middle East studies, McNay's notion of *creative agency* may provide that impulse. By focusing on an object of desire, *spor merakı*, and by tracing the agentive capacities of religious Istanbulite women to manifest desiring selves, we see how the dualist religious–secular formulation can be troubled. In so doing, we can see how the gendered agencies of believing subjects can push beyond the paradigm of piety. Questioning the everyday desires of Muslim women as they unfold through self-making, creative agency, and negotiation enables us to understand women's fluid and shared subject positionings across diverse political, religious, and classed affiliations.

Conclusion

As discussed in the introduction to this book, Istanbulite women's *spor merakı* is less about what women actually do and more about how they use *spor merakı* as a tool to establish a new sense of self, which makes *spor merakı* an object of desire. Women objectify *spor merakı* in the making of their desiring selves; they turn it into a space where the social and the imagined intersect. Through *spor merakı*, women converse with the regimes of the body, such as religion, nation, and aesthetics, to articulate their desires to the extent that those desires are simultaneously downplayed and somehow also empowered. I delve here into the linguistic obfuscation strategies women use in order to better understand how they both direct discursive attention away from their desires and at the same time establish a more autonomous selfhood.

In this exploration of women's exercise in Istanbul, I identify two interrelated factors that limit our understanding of the complex subjectivities of women who also happen to be Muslim. The first factor is a habit of Eurocentric thinking that is conditioned to seek a fundamental difference between Western and Muslim lives. This determination to seek a contrast results from a second, more pervasive problem—an investment in dualist thinking. The Durkheimian sacred–profane binary continues to resurface in studies of Muslims in the form of associated dualisms, such as Islamic–secular, traditional–modern, and pious–mundane. The ontological and historical ground of Émile Durkheim's central definition of religion as "a unified system of beliefs and practices relative to sacred things, that is to say, things set apart and forbidden" (1915, 47), has been extensively critiqued within the social sciences as a foundation of secular thought inherent to Western academia. One of the most widely cited critiques of Durkheimian thought on religion pertains to its nonuniversality and its origins from within a Eurocentric ontology (Goody 1961). The problematic insistence on a religious–secular binary is often anthropologically irrelevant because it was built on a Christian and thus Eurocentric cosmology that features this distinction between the sacred and the profane. Given the Eurocentric ontological lens through which Western observers universalize these binaries, certain Muslim practices then unavoidably become incomprehensible.

In studies of Muslim women, this tendency to formulate binaries surfaces in even more problematic ways by reinforcing unquestioned categories and associations. More often than not, the phrase "Muslim women" seems to immediately refer to "*hijabi,* head-scarved, visibly Muslim women" both in the media (Samie and Sehlikoglu 2014) and in the anthropological literature. The same binary thinking most often fails to recognize non*hijabi* Muslim woman's Muslimhood or simply refers to them as "secular," thus dismissing their complex self-makings.

The dominant sacred–profane binary and its echoes across subsequent ideological pairings limit our ability to develop alternative discourses and conceptual tropes about Muslim women and their desires. When we end up either portraying complicated pictures with a vocabulary that cannot go beyond a composition of secular and religious life or discussing how interesting the marriage of the secular and religious is, we find ourselves working with a pallet of only two colors: black and white. As ethnographic work has demonstrated (Dağtas 2009), negotiating the secular and the religious is not an either/or question. Rather, it is a question of conceptual exiguity. But simply describing different types of gray reflects an inability to explore any colors beyond black and white; in other words, we continue to remain within the terms defined by a problematic dualism.

The tradition–modernity debate must also be read through this critique in that scholarly interest has been drawn to whether we can approach believing individuals as traditional or modern or a unique combination of the two. In her groundbreaking critique of the piety–everyday Islam binary, Saba Mahmood's (2005, 2011) strategy was to stress the multiple meanings and heterogeneity that motivate the lives of Islamic believers. This move, coupled with her adaptation of Pierre Bourdieu's notion of habitus, or how to inhabit one's life, introduced an emphasis on ontological piety to the literature, leading to what we today call the *piety turn* (Deeb 2006; Huq 2008, 2009; Gökarıksel 2009; Jones 2010; Heryanto 2011; Rozario 2011).

As happens in many analytical shifts, piety and the "focus on ethical self-cultivation through the inhabitation of Islamic norms" (Fadil and Fernando 2015a, 60) have become the paradigmatic lens through which to study Muslims, so that pious forms of subjectivity now dominate other possible subjectivities, especially those that are neither pious nor devout. The result is a scholarly lassitude that often proceeds as though Muslimhood were somehow pure, unified, and entirely consistent.[10] In a relatively short period of time, piety has become "an imperative obstacle" in studies of Muslim societies (Sehlikoglu 2018).

A small group of scholars of the Middle East and Muslim societies have resisted the allure of the piety turn. Among them is Samuli Schielke (2009, 2015; Schielke and Debevec 2012), who has suggested both a departure from the Asadian framework of Islam as "discursive tradition" and a critical examination of the scholarly tendency to centralize Islam in the analysis of Muslims. However, in drawing attention to the complexities of everyday life, Schielke's intervention has had the unintended effect of pitting *everyday Islam*—a term not of Schielke's making—against *pious Islam*, thus yet again invoking the tradition–modernity, sacred–profane binary (Deeb 2015; Fadil and Fernando 2015a, 2015b; Schielke 2015). The recurring concerns within the everyday–pious debate have shown how difficult it is to resist both the allure of these binaries and the temptation to find fault with others for thinking through them. Lara Deeb's response to the debate is important here, for she questions "why these bodies of work are so often constructed and read as diametrically opposed to one another, as though this is a zero sum game (aside from the academic practice of producing arguments against prior ones)" (2015, 93). For scholarship on the Middle East, it is far too easy to become ensnared in this dualism.

---

10. The recent call for a departure from the charm of piety and, as Amira Mittermaier (2012) calls it, "the trope of self-cultivation" may be a scholarly attempt to move away from Saba Mahmood and Charles Hirschkind (2006) and the way their work has *"been taken up more broadly* such that 'the pious Muslim' became *the only visible* Muslim" (Deeb 2015, 95, emphasis in original).

It is in part this dualism that renders my informants—Istanbulite women—and their desires unintelligible, almost ungrammatical. The same dualism leaves us baffled when we see snapshots of these new female Muslim subjectivities engaging with fashion, entertainment, and sport precisely because our binary places the pleasures and enjoyments at one end of the spectrum and the Muslimhood of the women who stand out in their *hijabi*s at the other. Recent examples of such binary-confusing snapshots include the Muslim Australian ballerina Stephanie Kurlow, the British fitness magazine cover girl Rahaf Khatib, and the fully clothed journalist Noor Tagouri in *Playboy* as the first head-scarf-wearing Muslim woman to grace the pages of this magazine of masculinist erotics.[11]

Although the assumption is that multiple unexpected encounters must have gone into making an image of a *hijabi Playboy* cover girl possible, perhaps the reality is that we simply do not know *what* to expect of these new Muslim women's subjectivities. A mundane, trivial act (such as exercise) may appear burlesque to the Western secular gaze if performed in *hijab*, leading us back to the question of epistemology, how our current analytical and conceptual tools limit our thinking and perceptions. In this vein, developing a new categorical repertoire that problematizes the binaries may be in order.

11. The Western gaze's perception of a sensual and even erotic quality in the veil has long been a focus in feminist postcolonial critique. See, for example, Yeğenoğlu 1998.

3

Mediating Desires

Viewers are bombarded with a new set of information and trends every minute. Fashion and beauty trends; health warnings such as the "bad milk" debate about the dangers of pasteurized milk; miraculous foods such as red tea, ginger, and physalis (known in Turkish as *altın çilek*, literally translated as "golden strawberry");[1] and inescapable beauty tricks such as drinking warm water with lemon or green tea with ginger in the morning for faster weight loss often emerge in daytime TV programs and then circulate in newspapers, magazines, and the evening news. Almost all radio stations allocate hours of broadcasting to advertorials and infomercials constantly promoting health products, natural herbs, holistic medicine, miraculous honeys, and more. The daytime programs have produced a new generation of celebrities and experts. Books written by celebrity doctors such as Mehmet Öz on taking care of the body, Canan Karatay on dieting, Ender Saraç on being religious and healthy, Osman Müftüoğlu on long life, Ahmet Maranki on medicinal herbs, and Ebru Şallı on fitness and Pilates are on the best-seller list year after year. These experts' names are common knowledge and important reference points for my interlocutors. In line with the new health milieu, new beauty- and health-product chains have been popping up on every corner of Istanbul. One realm of this new milieu is *doğal yaşam* (natural-lifestyle) products, often promoted by national or international direct-selling networks such as

1. This fruit is also known as "Peruvian ground cherry."

Amway and Migun. These networks sell a wide variety of natural-health products and services ranging from orthopedic shoes, massage equipment and beds, personal-care items, cosmetics, and dietary supplements to treatments targeting symptoms of ailments related to the sedentary urban lifestyle, such as backaches, knee problems, constipation, muscle loss, and weight gain. Considering the tremendous transformation surrounding women and their demands, it is not difficult to recognize in these trends women's ability to create a large market and genre. So how do women navigate this constantly changing and overwhelming information dynamic while manifesting desiring selves? The discursive register of "tips" and "secrets" provides an ideal context for studying this navigation further.

This chapter addresses the relational aspect of women's desires and examines how women's desires are mediated, articulated, and processed by interactions with media as well as how women's fascination with *spor merakı* is brought to light. By following the traces of women's *spor merakı* alongside interviews with popular media personalities, this chapter maps out *spor merakı* as an object of desire that is formed through a mutual, interactive process.

As introduced in the first two chapters, the sort of agency at play in the process of desiring self-formation requires careful mining. Women's agentive desires converse and negotiate with multiple normative systems, including multiple patriarchal mechanisms, often by escaping the latter's attention and seeking refuge in blind spots—spaces that fall outside of religious, nationalist, familiar, and even lingual limits.

What happens when we attempt to trace Istanbulite women's desires: How do they emerge, circulate, shift, redirect? To understand the operations of desire, we need to sketch the complex web of desires that produce *spor merakı*. We start this journey with the media figures and role models (a term I use cautiously) that inspired women in 2011 and 2012, such as doctors hosting daytime TV programs, Pilates gurus, and fellow sporty friends. I prefer to refer to these individuals as *mediating figures*, not *role models*, in order to encapsulate how women use them to mediate, tailor, recalibrate, and articulate their desires. The term *mediating figures* allows conceptual room to understand the ways in which women use media personalities and TV programs to mediate their existing desires. The mediating figures are one of many available options competing against each other to capture women's desires and to become significant to women (and consequently to their *spor merakı*). The term thus challenges the power dynamics typically assumed between so-called role models or trendsetters and their so-called followers.

Part of this investigation, therefore, requires attending to the role models' desires to be desired. As neoliberal market dynamics are established to prioritize demand, a mutuality between the object of desire and the desiring subject is often generated. It is more important, however, to ask whether these mediating figures are the ultimate objects of desire in this relationship or have a more compliant role in a web of relations of desire than we tend to give them credit for. In this vein, perhaps even the term *follower* is misleading, overshadowing the creative and agentive capacities of those who select particular goods or opt to follow specific trends or figures.

Mediated Desires and Daytime TV Shows

The webs of relations constructed by television create connections, belongings, physicalities, and subjectivities. To understand the complex ways in which desires are formed, I trace how television's mediascape interacts with the followers of *spor merakı* and outline women's interference in the mediascape in the process of making of their (own) desiring selves.

Daytime TV programs are remarkably important in creating any dominant market trend among women in Turkey,[2] in part owing to

2. There is a growing scholarly interest in the influence of Turkish soap operas on social life in Turkey and the broader Middle East (see Buccianti 2010; Salamandra 2012; Kraidy and Al-Ghazzi 2013; Yanardağoğlu and Karam 2013; Yesil 2015; Akınerdem and Sirman 2017). The actors and actresses on the soap operas have also become icons and idols of popular culture and are often featured in newspapers and on TV describing how they have lost weight and which diets they have followed to gain their charming looks. These urban and magnetic characters capture

the fact that 70 percent of the women in Turkey are *ev hanımı*, loosely meaning "housewives" but also referring to the female homemakers who spend considerable amounts of time at home and do not participate in any regular, full-time formal or informal work.[3] The TV is on when women perform domestic labor, including cooking and cleaning (Burul 2007). The daytime TV programs often begin at 10:00 a.m., which means they are specifically tailored to housewives' daily routines. It is the time after women have sent their husbands to work and children to school and begin to tidy the breakfast table and get ready for dinner— which might include gutting fish, kneading dough, marinating meat, shelling legumes, or picking little stones out of rice or lentils. Women often multitask and sit in front of the TV—which in some households might be in the kitchen—while completing their daily chores.

In different ways and at different levels, three daytime programs were significant (not just to women but also to trainers, gym owners, and anyone engaged in exercise, sports, or fitness) during the years 2011 and 2012. Two of them were health programs: Kanal (Channel) D's *Doktorum* (My Doctor) and Kanal 7's *Feridun Kunak Show* (*The FK Show*). Each had a different format, style, target audience, and rating strategy. The third program, *Ebruli* (Ebru-Style), was hosted by former fashion model Ebru Şallı, who also taught Pilates.

Many people involved in *spor merakı* pointed me in the direction of these programs and their hosts—not as simple characters appearing on TV but as reference points. These TV personalities' or mediating figures' names were constantly being dropped during my fieldwork, sometimes in the interviews when women described an exercise ("Concentrate on your core muscles when you breathe in and out, just

---

the imagination and appetites of the masses with the way they embed their physicality and urban lifestyles as they are projected onto the imposing and omnipresent TV screen at the center of the living room in every Turkish living room I have visited.

3. The employment rate of women in Turkey is 28.5 percent, the lowest percentage among Organization for Economic Cooperation and Development (OECD) countries, and excludes the women who are temporarily out of work owing to illness, maternity leave, and so forth (OECD 2013).

like Ebru does") or when they explained their choice of exercise ("The doctor [on TV] says swimming is better than walking"). At other times, fitness trainers would express their warnings with reference to mediating figures ("Don't overdo your breath, like Ebru Şallı does"), often with competitive implications. These mediating figures thus functioned as reference points for women to start conversations as they agreed or disagreed on which entrepreneurs to make investments or which personality threatens trainers the most. Mediating figures were often the tool or apparatus women used when knitting together their desiring selves. As a consequence, they stood somewhere between an object of desire (they are not the desired objects themselves but a means to an object of desire) and an everyday encounter, between sociality and the psyche.

As I explore in the following pages, my interlocutors, perhaps not very differently from many TV viewers across the world, selected the programs, media figures, and celebrities with whom they felt most connected. This connection was based in part on a sense of proximity and in part on other social signifiers. Proximity and the figures' ostentatiousness led to an affective and imagined intimate bonding.

The sort of relationship I am interested in here is, at one level, in conversation with Purnima Mankekar's (1999) and Lila Abu-Lughod's (2002) work on the multiple ways in which women engage with television discourses and reflect on them in relation to their own experiences and realities. I enrich the analysis of this interactive process (Kruse 2010) while tracking *spor merakı*, demonstrating how, just as part of women's desiring subjectivity is produced through interactions with media as social technology, mediating figures' subjectivities are likewise formed in part through interactions with their imagined audience: Turkish-speaking female homemakers.

The Making of a Pilates Guru: Ebru Şallı

Ebru Şallı's daytime TV show *Ebruli* begins with a forty-five-minute live Pilates class in which Şallı performs Pilates at the front of the studio with two trainers (one male, Kaan, and one female, Eren, behind her) on bright-colored exercise mats, all of them wearing tight exercise outfits. In every episode, Şallı informally interviews studio guests, discussing issues ranging from health to music to art and magazines. One of the distinctive features of Şallı's program is her devotion to a healthy lifestyle and regular exercise. In the third part of her TV show, called "Ebru's Kitchen," she shares a healthy, low-carb, low-glycemic-index recipe with her audience.

Ebru Şallı is *the* Pilates guru in Turkey. In her words, she has "taught Pilates to housewives."[4] She is proud of herself for being a flagbearer of the republican dream by reaching out to ordinary women and introducing sports to those with whom the republican project has long sought to engage (see chapter 1).

Şallı has also established herself as an entrepreneur with a vast commercial empire. She markets and sells Pilates DVDs, her own brand of exercise and Pilates equipment, cookbooks, and self-help books. From 2008 on, Şallı has focused on her career as a Pilates trainer, life coach, owner, host and producer of her own daytime TV program, as well as entrepreneur who produces Pilates equipment. Yet her career development has taken this new direction through an interactive process with the public that started the moment she signed in to Pilates classes for her own benefit.

Şallı was one of the few dozen Turkish women taking Pilates classes in 2004 when it was available only in exclusive sports centers in big cities. Her initial motivation, she explained to me, was to stay fit and healthy during her first pregnancy. In 2004, Pilates was just emerging as a global trend and was new even in North America. As soon as Ebru Şallı—one of the most popular and elite fashion models in Turkey—started attending Pilates classes, her involvement in this new trend immediately attracted the attention of Turkish media. At that time, Şallı was an established figure (she was Miss Turkey in 1995 and remains a rara avis beauty with beautiful green eyes). Her involvement in Pilates was presented as part of the "beauty secrets of models" register. Magazine journalists kept asking for interviews to

4. Interview, Mar. 14, 2012.

write stories about Şallı and her Pilates training, so this new type of exercise became associated with her name: it was "the exercise Ebru Şallı does" in the minds of the public, even before she started her own show. In other words, public interest paved the way for Şallı's series of investments in her career as a fashion model who was about to start a family and needed to retain her beauty and youthful appearance. In a way, Pilates allowed Şallı to stay fit into her late thirties and early forties (when models start retiring) and allowed her to emerge as a leader of the new "wellness" sector.

Ebru Şallı viewed Pilates as an opportunity because the public had already started linking it to her name when they talked about it. From this first step, her accelerated connection to Pilates in the following years made her the Pilates guru of today. By the time she was relatively advanced in Pilates in 2007–8, after she had her first baby (Beren, born in 2004), she was already investing in healthy eating both for herself and for her TV show. Incorporating Pilates into her TV show became the marker of her fame as a TV host, the symbol that allowed her to stand out among other daytime shows and their hosts.

Şallı as a Role Model

Seval was one of the few women I knew who talked about Şallı quite extensively. As a premium member of the Hamza Yerlikaya gym, Seval was not confined to exercising during the "free" hours available to others (two daytime hours a week). The modest amount she paid (60 liras or $20 per month) enabled her to work out in the evenings and during the weekend, which was very convenient in conjunction with her nine-to-five office job in marketing. She had a healthy, youthful appearance, bright green eyes, and brunette hair often tied with a hair bobble. She was born to a working-class family in the 1980s, so no one around her "had the mentality that children should do sport," she complained to me. She started exercising after she turned twenty-nine. As she grew up and entered middle-class Turkish society, thanks to her university education, she says, she began to gain new, middle-class habits. In January 2009, she quit her job to take another position in Erbil, Iraq. Seval described Erbil as a difficult place for a single woman. She narrated in detail her encounter with *Ebruli* in Erbil: "For three weeks, eighteen days, I watched Ebru Şallı's TV show called *Ebruli* on channel TV 8. She was teaching Pilates on the show. I thought I should give it a try. . . . I continued doing it regularly over the last three years."[5]

Seval's discipline to continue doing Pilates every day caught me by surprise. "You mean, every day?" I asked. She responded to my surprise with pride. Her face lit up: "Of course. By watching *Ebruli*."

When Seval first started doing Pilates, she was able to do only the floor exercises because she did not have any equipment. Gradually, however, she ordered all the necessary items, including a Pilates ball, band, and toning ring from Turkey: "We [the company she worked for] used to receive lorries full of merchandise to Erbil, Iraq, from Istanbul. I asked my boss's cousin to buy me Pilates equipment. He must have gotten them from Göztepe or something, from some sports market, I guess. He had put all the equipment into the lorry [that came to Erbil]. I even told him after a while that Pilates is not enough for me and I want to walk [i.e., jog]. He sent me his wife's treadmill."

Seval was highly influenced by the "energy" of Pilates and Ebru Şallı. In her words, "*Şallı is a role model for me.*" She ordered Şallı's Pilates DVDs from Istanbul because of the extra tips they provide. "She shows additional movements in those DVDs," Seval explained: "I bought the DVDs, but of course I followed the TV program mostly. There was a TV in my workplace that I could watch during the day. I used to watch the program in the morning. Then when I go home in the evening, I would repeat the movements. I knew most of them anyway since I spent three weeks [watching the program] before [practicing them]."

Seval was one of three women I interviewed who explicitly referred to Ebru Şallı, former fashion model and current Pilates guru, as her *rol model* (role model). The term they chose, *rol model*, struck me because of the apparent contrasts between her lifestyle and theirs. Neither

5. Interview, Jan. 8, 2012.

Seval nor Seda nor Sümeyra followed Şallı's footsteps in their career ambitions. In fact, being a fashion model or a contestant in a beauty pageant is something they would frown upon, as they explained to me. Şallı had other traits, though, that made her admirable. How and why women selected certain aspects of Şallı as admirable over other aspects of her identity intrigued me.

Seda, another admirer of Şallı, had followed *Ebruli* for almost a year and exercised with Şallı four days a week. By the end of that year, Seda started showing six-pack abs, or "baklava" in Turkish (referring to the square baklava shapes on the abdomen), "like *Şallı*'s." Like Seval, Seda also used Şallı's name as a point of reference for an achievable ideal.

Women pay attention to the details of Şallı's performance, from her body movements to her outfits, equipment, background music, and body shape. The Pilates section of *Ebruli* is aired at 10:00 a.m., a very "appropriate" time for Seda. Şallı herself explained to me how she calculated the correct time for her TV program: "Women like this hour because they can send their children to school or their husbands to work. Perhaps put a dish on the stove. I know they do this since sometimes they tell me they overcook or burn it while watching me [said with a smile]. That's how women organize themselves. The time should be 10:00 a.m., not 11:00 and not 8:00."

Yet Şallı's ability to capture her audience is not simply about tailoring the program to her target audience's schedule or to her own productivity.

Şallı embodies the ideal of the successful Turkish woman, which is why women mentioned her as a role model. With her career trajectory from elite model to Pilates trainer and host of a TV program for health and women's exercise and subsequently to entrepreneur with her own series of Pilates equipment, alongside her parallel "success" in family life, Ebru Şallı is an ideal female multitasker and overachiever. The demands of patriarchal ideologies on women are often contradictory, in conflict with one another, and sometimes humanly impossible to achieve. Şallı, however, is a mother of two who was married for eleven years (divorced as of July 2013); her physical beauty is internationally recognized; and she has managed to turn a short-term career and enthusiasm for a certain form of exercise into a business that will ensure that the aesthetic standards of her body will endure. In other words, women's use of the descriptive term *role model* in reference to Şallı reflects an admiration for her ability to make the most of the systems that objectify her and her body. Şallı stands for multiple things—successful mother, career woman, fashion personality, fitness guru, and modern individual. *Role model*, therefore, reflects more than a type of relation to *self* that one develops through exercise. It is a type of relation to this multiplicity of facets. This multiplicity is especially important, for it is one of the factors that make Şallı more real than any other celebrity or fashion model in Istanbulite women's worlds.

Bonding with the Audience

Şallı has established a successful channel or bridge between herself and her followers. She exercises live on air, sweats, gets tired, and with a televised desire to become a fitter and better-looking woman leads women who are watching her and repeating her movements. This human vulnerability makes her a tangible human being as opposed to an untouchable or impalpable celebrity. She does not inspire women to a hypothetical ideal body and beauty. For her admirers, Şallı is a person who works hard to achieve her fit body. She shares her imperfections (sweat, grit, fatigue) for women's reference. By revealing her "secrets," Şallı projects an authenticity that distinguishes her from the deception associated with TV beauties who are "hard to find in real life."

Şallı told me, "I enter into the lives of women and [in]to their hearts." Her followers enjoy her palpable presence in their homes, including her modest appearance with minimal makeup. When I asked Şallı to comment on the interaction she has with her audience, she said: "An energetic bond has emerged between me and my Pilates sisters. And it is all because I perform live Pilates. . . . I believe it has to be live. It brings reality to the life and forms an energetic bond, so that you breathe with women. You live everything there, and you reflect that energy to your audience."

The energetic bond to which Şallı referred is related in part to being present in a domestic sphere, on TV, in private homes and to the level of her follower's devotion to her program. Such a bond is better explained by Purnima Mankekar, who asserts that particular lifestyle programs perform affective work "on and through the bodies of spectators" (2012, 609). Mankekar defines this affective work as a category distinct from Althusserian ideological interpellation. In her analysis, it is something that is able to reach the presubjective realm (605) in the lives of audience members and thereby to inhabit a body. Echoing Şallı, Seda referred to this affective bond when she acknowledged that "it is enjoyable to exercise with Ebru." She felt Ebru's presence working out alongside her in her home.[6]

If one of the main questions we are trying to answer here is how desire is manifested, transformed, and shared, then provisionally we must also ask, How does the energetic bond Şallı referred to—which is visible to the researcher—produce a desire? I put this question in different words to Şallı herself: "What do you mean by the energetic bond?"

In response, Şallı gave an example of "creative solutions" to accessing Pilates equipment, which many women might consider exorbitant or see as an unnecessary expense. She offers these solutions to those who can't make this financial investment, such as using stockings as Pilates bands and innertubes for the big Pilates balls. According to Şallı, it is important to draw attention to these creative solutions because they signify women's willingness to overcome financial barriers in order to pursue Pilates and "keep up" with Şallı, too.

"The famous one [alternative solution]," she told me, "is the elastic garters of *culottes/pettipants* [that] women use as a substitute for Pilates/resistance bands." Her assistant, Özlem, intervened,

6. Interview, Dec. 1, 2011.

saying, "Yaratıcı Türk kadını [creative Turkish women]," with enthusiasm. *Don lastiği* is the Turkish name for these elastic garters. *Pettipants* are worn largely by middle-aged and senior rural women under their dresses and skirts for modesty. Because it is this demographic of women who wear *pettipants*, these garters have become one reference in popular culture for an unmodern lifestyle. "Modernness" (Deeb 2006) and Turkish imagination of modernity call for, among other things, a visual transformation, often of women's bodies (Kandiyoti 1987; Göle 1996; Alemdaroğlu 2005). This transformation embodies the desire to become part of Europe, not only in geographical terms but also in the personal terms of rejuvenating a European selfhood imagined as a timeless and enchanting subjectivity (Ahıska 2003). In the public imagination of this modern transformation, *pettipants* are a deriding yet intimate reference to a rural, old-fashioned, underdeveloped identity set up against the wished-for modern self.

In this particular imagination of physicality and modernity, the use of *don lastiği* as Pilates bands reflects an outreach, a transformative *stretch* from unmodern to modern, from rural to urban, from old-fashioned to fashionable, and from local to global. The physical and conceptual stretches are merged with the force of women's enthusiasm and creative aspirations. Although the women who watch Şallı's program and do Pilates with her remain in the same socioeconomic class they have been in, they are nevertheless engaging in an upper-class leisure exercise and sport, which alters the content and definition of that classed act. Meanwhile, they unsettle the modernization project. While not being submissive to the national project that aims to transform women from one end of the spectrum to another, women create their own middle-way solutions that inevitably shift and transform the very categories of modernization.

The current transformation taking place in Turkey is reflected in the scope of physical exercise, which is shifting from being an upper-class, exclusive club activity (chapter 1) to being domestic leisure for all classes, from something overwhelmingly associated with youth and men to an activity engaged in by a wider range of age groups and by women. In this changing milieu, Şallı feels and presents herself as *the* person who can make this change possible.

Her assistant echoed Şallı: "Ebru is the woman who introduced sport into women's homes." According to their perspective, Pilates is a form of exercise that reaches into women's lives and is responsible for a civilizing transformation. This perspective is likewise manifest in sports centers, reflecting early republican investment in sport (see chapter 1). Imposing a *civilizing* mission on women through exercise seems to create a new discourse of popular consciousness among Istanbulite women. Several mediating figures whom I met in the field, ranging from celebrities to gym owners and trainers, reiterated this point. They all mentioned how role models such as Şallı are raising the *consciousness* of ordinary Turkish women, who are envisaged as needing to be saved and civilized.

The point I want to underscore here, however, relates to Şallı's role in catalyzing this transformation. Her success is not contingent upon making this change possible but through recognizing the potential among ordinary housewives, who desire and fantasize about a new self. Once she recognized women's desire and ability to transform their selves, Şallı tailored the optimal format to capture this desire. Through her show and as both fashion model and mother of two, she created an intimate bond with women. In other words, Şallı is not the creator of (desire to) change or of new desiring subjectivities but rather the figure who *mediates* an existing desire. Moreover, when she refers to her followers as "Pilates sisters," she taps into a particular register already extant in the minds of Istanbulite exercising women.

The shared bond of "being confidants," a topic I develop in chapter 6, echoes Şallı's notion of a "Pilates sisterhood": sweating side by side and sharing with each other the "messy mystery" behind the "final product," whether fit tummies or slimmer arms. Through her live programming, Şallı's Pilates performance creates an affective bond whereby women can view the supermodel as a "confidant" who is willing to share her secrets with her "Pilates sisters," in a process similar to the "self-disclosure" that Laurie Haag (1993) notes is a key aspect of female bonding.[7] When Şallı was first caught in the "beauty secrets of the models" marketing trend in 2004 as she started attending Pilates classes, she had already started to become "ordinary" women's confidant. Her invention of the term *Pilates sisterhood* overlaps with this already initiated process of bonding and sharing secrets between herself and her (future) viewers.

Multiple Mediation of Women's Desires

Şallı has transformed the existing register of "beauty secrets of fashion models" into her new brand and successful TV program. As such, she symbolizes an important reference for women as a model who has sustained her physical appearance for almost two decades even after giving birth to two children. She states that her outlook is the result of a healthy lifestyle, which demands considerable time and energy in the form of two hours of daily exercise, disciplined healthy eating (enriched in grains and at a low glycemic index), and regular skin care. Such devotion requires a relatively sophisticated knowledge of nutrition and the human body, leading to a series of confirmed "beauty tips": masks for healthy skin, secrets for avoiding hair loss, exercise for better abs and better-shaped legs, recipes for detox, natural energizers with low calories, weight-loss secrets, and so forth. Şallı generously shares such tips in her TV program, books, DVDs, and interviews on TV and in magazines and newspapers. As Asiye, a woman I met in Hamza Yerlikaya once said, "These formulas are what attracts women." Sharing tips and secrets is one of the main components of women's health and lifestyle magazines, TV programs, and even TV news, and they come from all kinds of sources, including different types of specialists, doctors, nutritionists, and celebrity personalities.

---

7. In her work on Oprah Winfrey, Laurie Haag (1993) discusses the ways in which Winfrey as a public figure is able to construct intimacy with her audience, and she underlines the importance of Winfrey's female-friendship style, meaning that her self-disclosure on intimate matters, including her wage, her childhood traumas, and family matters further connect her with her followers.

This stream of daytime Turkish celebrities includes Seda Sayan, Gülben Ergen, Melek, Ebru Şallı, and Saba Tümer, who share their secrets for and tips on beauty, health, and fitness on daytime health programs. The women I talked to constantly invoked these personalities and programs in interviews and casual conversations. These programs and their hosts (as well as the experts hosted by them) are in constant competition with each another to reach the audience and be followed by them by creating an imaginary bond with them and by sharing as many important or useful tips as possible. As a consequence, these programs are locked in a perpetual endeavor to influence women and shape them based on the programs' *desire* to be significant in women's lives. The significance of this endeavor is measured not only by the programs' ratings but also by the extent of the programs' influence. The information, tips, secrets, and miraculous formulas they share are attempts to claim importance in women's everyday lives. Hence, the tips they share are not only too numerous but also in constant contradiction with each other. An expert guest on one program tells women to avoid running because although it results in fast weight loss, the weight is quickly regained when one stops running, whereas another expert may strongly recommend running as an optimal cardio workout. Suggestions on health (i.e., diet and exercise) also change over time. As a consequence, experts often end up recommending what they formerly cautioned against, thus making nutritional and fitness advice confusing for many women. A common example is the older warning that all types of fat lead to inevitable weight gain. After decades of constantly rhapsodizing about zero-fat foods, women are now told there are different types of fats and that certain types are in fact good for the human body and may even help one lose weight.

As a result, secrets and tips register as noisy, confusing, crowded, and often self-contradictory, yet they nonetheless mediate women's desire. In a way, this multiplicity overstimulates desire that is always ready to escape from forms of regulation. Istanbulite women's desires are polymorphous; they are influenced by multiple factors and figures, including TV with its many channels and programs, and printed text, as well as their friends, neighbors, and other women—often all at once. In such polymorphous circumstances, some desires may be in conflict with each other; others may be inchoate, not explicitly articulated. Still, they work together to refashion attitudes toward the formation of desiring selves.

Women's abilities to compartmentalize, select, filter, and translate their desires is crucial in the making of *spor merakı*. The effect of public mediating figures, however, does not always enter women's lives without a filter. Despite celebrity appeal, women fine-tune their expectations based on individual knowledge of their own bodies. This filtering process can be better understood if this chapter is read side by side with chapter 6. As discussed in that chapter, women employ an even more active form of intimate encounters with other women in homosocial spaces. The homosociality and screening of each other's performances, bodies, and progress often reflect women's ability to make sense of mediating figures and their tips and secrets. In homosocial interactions, women translate their longings, aspirations, and desires into everyday life.

Women do not judge the fact that Şallı performs in tight activewear that reveals her hypersexual body, despite the fact that Şallı's performance (on TV, YouTube, and DVDs) has caused a sensation among male spectators with her stretching, gasping, sweating, and deep breathing.

Regardless of Şallı's visible hypersexuality, women share an intimate bond with her because they perceive her as a confidant, allow her into their domestic spaces, and invite her to become a mediating figure of their desires. I saw this most clearly in the case of Seda, who dressed modestly in plain colors, a small scarf that covered her hair, and flat shoes. Seda compartmentalized her desires; she was aware that Şallı is a "role model" to her only as someone who became a Pilates guru after having two children.

The intersubjective aspect of self-formation, as Lieba Faier (2009) points out, is formed at an intimate level. Faier uses the term *intimate encounters* in her analysis of Filipina brides in Japan and how their position in Japanese social life is transformed from belittled sex workers to ideal brides in the eyes of the public. Faier maps their transformation through the term *encounters*, which "is regularly invoked[, although] the dynamics of cultural meetings are rarely explored" (5), and underlines the importance of "the messy, inter-active, and sometimes surprising ways that people create cultural meanings and identities through everyday relationships with oth-ers" (5). Those intimate interactions or encounters signify multiple levels of crossings, go beyond interpersonal encounters, include cul-tural, historical, and social relations, and are able to connect "differ-ent discourses, genealogies of meaning, and forms of desire" (1). In a completely different setting, I have observed a similar transforma-tive force enabled by encounters. Those encounters often tend to escape from language, like anything intimate would (Moore 2014; Sehlikoglu and Zengin 2015), and to create zones where the desires of mediating figures and Istanbulite women intersect. In the context of Istanbulite women, the encounters are also intimate because of their proximity to the self.

In the lives of Istanbulite women, the desire for public mediat-ing figures (celebrities on TV programs, experts offering health and beauty news or trends through various media, social media icons) to become significant enables these figures to carefully craft themselves in order to remain at the crossroads of women's desires. In this vein, the health register emerges as a new stream through which mediating figures become significant.

Health Register

In 2011 and 2012, among all programs aired on Turkish TV channels, ranging from famous soap operas to talk shows, the "health" register involving exercise and healthy diet was gaining rapid popularity, high ratings, and wide reach. Daytime Turkish television is dominated by the popularity of these shows that propagate healthy and slim bodies, a popularity owing in part to the alarming rise in obesity and diabetes in Turkey (Çayır, Atak, and Köse 2011; Buyukbese and Bakar 2012).

The Turkish Ministry of Health circulates public-information films on TV highlighting the dangers of obesity, one of which tells the success story of Demet and shows before and after photos of this cleaning lady living in Ankara who lost forty-five kilograms (one hundred pounds) in a year and a half. The video starts with the former minister of health, Recep Akdağ, issuing warnings against obesity and continues with Demet telling the audience quite poetically how she did very little to achieve weight loss, simply "shrinking my [food] portions and expanding my life." She adds: "What we all need are determination and will; both are given to us by God."[8]

The "weight problem" is often presented as a matter of health, not aesthetics. Yet public attitudes to health issues are often aesthetic. In the media, diabetes and obesity are often portrayed and discussed as a women's issue, despite the fact that a higher percentage of men (39 percent) were reported to be overweight in Turkey in 2012, but only 30.4 percent of women qualified as obese. Yet most of those who seek medical help from endocrinologists and nutritionists at private and state hospitals are women (62 percent) (Çayır, Atak, and Köse 2011). Although being overweight is not exclusively a women's problem, women in Turkey appear more eager than men to solve it.

Partly related to the culture of aesthetics that pressures women to seek medical advice and a global trend that valorizes "wellness," "fitness," and thin bodies, Turkish TV stations have pioneered a new stream of health programming. The most popular health programs are *Doktorum* and the *FK Show*.

Doktorum: Women's Actual Doctor

Health and weight-loss advice circulates significantly in gyms, especially in changing rooms and tea parties, where women bring teas and pastries to consume after a tiring exercise session. Tips shared are perceived as more valuable when they are scientifically supported; thus, women often back up their statements by referring to their doctors' advice. Sometimes they say, "This is what the doctors say," as in the

---

8. The program entitled *Demet'in başarı hikayesi* (Demet's Success Story) is available on YouTube at https://www.youtube.com/watch?v=PqOcCmaKqvI.

case of Sacide, a fifty-one-year-old woman attending the Hamza Yer-likaya gym, who mentioned bad-milk warnings while we were talking about unhealthy foods. Sacide provided a very detailed account of bad milk and the process by which milk is pasteurized. When I asked her, "Which doctors are you speaking about?" she responded, "The ones on Channel D."[9]

Women talk about *Doktorum* the way Atiye, a forty-seven-year-old housewife, did. Atiye was explaining to me how she had chosen Pilates for her back pains when she said, "My doctor advised me to swim or to do Pilates for it. This gym does not have a swimming pool, so I started Pilates."[10] In the first couple of weeks of my fieldwork, I did not realize that women like Atiye, whose comments seemed to refer to advice from their family doctors, were in fact referring to TV figures, hosts of daytime health shows. It turned out that these women were not passing on suggestions from a doctor they had consulted in person but suggestions broadcast by the host of *Doktorum* (My Doctor), MD Aytuğ Kolankaya.

The Turkish language is excellent for making ambiguous statements, and, like many other women I interviewed, Atiye was playing with this lingual ambiguity. Although she could have said "the doctor on *Doktorum* [Doktorum'*daki doktor*]," she instead made an ambiguous statement, perhaps desiring to hold onto a feeling of proximity by making it sound as if she had been advised by her own doctor. This appearance of proximity enabled her to avoid considering alternative suggestions, such as walking, instead of Pilates.

The program to which women feel so connected and have accepted into their lives is broadcast on Turkey's highest-rated TV channel, Channel D. *Doktorum* airs on weekdays from 8:00 to 10:00 a.m. Sharing parallels with the type of health program started in the United States by another Turkish doctor, Dr. Mehmet Öz, *Doktorum* covers a different health-related theme in each episode, including not

9. Field notes, Oct. 18, 2011.
10. Interview, July 29, 2011.

only health problems but also preventive medicine. Reflecting Dr. Kolankaya's personal health view, each episode promotes the importance of a healthy diet and a physically active lifestyle. Unlike the state-promoted public-information film of Demet's success story or the *FK Show*, *Doktorum* features an MD with a degree in biological anthropology who bases his view of contemporary health on an evolutionist perspective.[11] When I interviewed him, he backed up his medical views with examples from various recent scientific studies: "The human body is designed for movement, not immobility. Why is that? Ever since the time of cavemen, humans have been seeking for food or surviving against nature, migrating from one place to another, in constant movement."[12]

This evolutionary perspective reflects Dr. Kolankaya's awareness of the latest scholarly debates in medicine; he keeps himself well informed in order to maintain his viewers' trust and consequently high TV ratings. After explaining to me how Pilates is one of the best options for women to improve their health and well-being because it is an exercise that does not isolate or abandon selective muscles that humans have evolved to use, he then talked about Turkey's obesity problem with the most recent numbers:

> There is scholarly work done in Turkey. In the last ten years—you would find the numbers if you do research—in the last ten years women gained five kilos [eleven pounds] and men gained six kilos [thirteen pounds] in Turkey. The belly fat has worryingly increased. That is the case for all societies, and there is an obesity map from the United States which is quite striking if you would like to use it in your work. The map is spread through three decades—the first in

11. Dr. Kolankaya does not explain on the air that he is informed by an evolutionist perspective, however. Evolution was removed from the high school curriculum in Turkey in 2012 and is seen by the majority of believers as a challenge and threat to Muslim belief—that is, despite the evolutionist perspectives in classical Arabic and Islamic scholarship and sciences before modern times.

12. Interview, Mar. 13, 2012.

1991, if I am not mistaken, then another in 2001, and the third in 2010. It shows the obesity ratios of the states. The first map [shows] between 10 percent and 14 percent [obesity rates in states], and it is completely blue. In 2000, around one-third of the states have obesity rates higher than 30 percent. And in 2010, all states are above 30 percent.

This scientifically supported approach uses multiple strategies both to ensure ratings and to maintain a populist feature. *Doktorum*'s format is developed specifically to connect with housewives, and the program makes tremendous effort to invest in this connection. As Dr. Kolankaya says, "We always aim for the techniques or remedies people can prepare in the comfort of their homes." On one of the days that I visited the program at Channel D, the endocrinologist Dr. Ayça Kaya, presented as an obesity specialist, informed the audience about the medical aspects of obesity and the significance of the hormone ghrelin in causing eating disorders. After a visual presentation (an animated video) and a segment in which an obese young woman was offered free treatment, the cameras then moved on to part of the stage that is set up as a kitchen. There, Dr. Kaya revealed five "miracle foods," one by one, each in a separate copper serving plate with a lid: *leblebi* (roasted chick peas),[13] quince, oats, green tea, and white coffee. As she opened the lids one by one, she explained the calories of each and the ideal amount, time, and way to consume them. While she was giving this information, the studio audience was taking careful notes for future reference. Dr. Kolankaya and cohost Zahide Yetiş's next studio guest was another doctor, an optometrist, who likewise promised full treatment of a teenage girl's eyes and shared a home-made remedy for sties.

This format is designed specifically, as Dr. Kolankaya put it, "to inject awareness [*bilinç aşılamak*]." This "awareness" register shares several parallels with "sport consciousness" (chapter 1) and Şallı's mission to civilize women through Pilates. Ms. Asuman Oruçoğlu,

13. A popular snack in Turkey.

the production editor of *Doktorum*, explained that the format is tailored with role plays, short videos, animations, and simplified details by imagining and targeting "a woman in a village of Hakkari" (the farthest east end of Turkey). This gendered, classed, and geographically bounded description simultaneously captures the program's urban and upper-class tone.

This upper-class republicanist register creates a class barrier that the producers strive to solve and is reflected in the daily ratings. *Doktorum*'s ratings have always been higher among skilled workers and the upper class than among any other group, which highlights the fact that no matter how hard the producers try to target a lower-class audience, the program attracts middle- and upper-class viewers more. On the days I visited the program set, March 12 and 13, 2012, the hosts and the producers were discussing strategies to increase their total ratings and to capture lower-class housewives as viewers. Their search for home-made, easily accessible, and inexpensive ways for the audience to solve health problems was in part related to that concern. On previous occasions, however, the solutions the producers had developed for lower-class housewives did not achieve the popularity they were seeking.

In late 2011, *Doktorum* trialed new exercise sessions on TV, following the trend Ebru Şallı had started. Zumba, a new style of fitness that combines Columbian-style dance moves with rhythm was popular among upper-class women in Istanbul at the time, and *Doktorum*'s producers decided to stream it live on air. Their challenge was to customize this highly effortful and difficult-looking exercise for their target audience, the woman in the village at the far end of Turkey. Exercise equipment such as dumbbells or fitness sticks was often replaced by bottles of water and mop sticks to make Zumba look as if it would be easy to do at home. At the time, I was watching TV and enjoying an after-breakfast Turkish coffee at Zeliha Abla's home, and together we watched the Zumba training they taught. Zeliha, a forty-five-year-old housewife and a member of "free classes" at Hamza Yerlikaya, could not afford the fancy Vileda (mop brand) the trainers were using on the show. In fact, the brand of mop used made the entire performance look fancier in Zeliha's eye. Even these ostensibly "friendly" solutions did not seem to speak to the lives of everyday Turkish women. While we watched *Doktorum*'s Zumba, it did not look intriguing to Zeliha Abla, not like something in which she felt included. Rather, she felt as if she was watching a foreign movie, something fictional and non-native.[14] Indeed, despite the *Doktorum* producers' efforts, Zumba did not reach the popularity of Pilates among diverse classes of women even after three years, nor did it prompt women to seek creative solutions to the obstacles they encountered in exercising.

Despite the class barrier that the producers need to overcome to reach a wider audience and their desire to reach the "woman in a village of Hakkari," *Doktorum* does not sacrifice quantity for quality. It works with a large team of specialists and MDs who are often popular media "brand names" known for treating celebrities. The program is purely professional, polished, proficient, and broadcast in a Western style with a team of more than a hundred people, including the production team, interns, and a network of specialized physicians in the Channel D building in Istanbul. Even the studio audience is arranged professionally by third-party organizers and brought to Channel D by private shuttles. The *Doktorum* technical team consists of two dozen people, and an agent carefully selects the studio audience so that it will look "modern." Audience members are often *ev hanımı* (housewives) like the target audience at home, but unlike the target audience the studio audience is not allowed to come to the show in traditional clothes, such as *şalvar* (wide pants bound by elastic at the ankles, often known as "harem pants") and the *başörtüsü* (head scarf, *hijab*).

Doktorum regularly holds two meetings for each episode of the program. The first meeting is at noon, after the program, to discuss the details of the next day's show. The next morning at 7:00 a.m. the team meets with the studio guests, and they go over the program one more time. Every little step of the program is thoroughly planned by a

14. Field notes, Oct. 3, 2011.

large team of coproducers, assistants, technicians, cameramen, and so on. This hard work pays off in high standards, but because these standards are determined by an urban, upper-class taste, following them often compounds the problem of reaching out to rural and lower-class audiences.

Women's references to the program host are an extension of the class dynamics operating between the audience and the show in that they are in a mode similar to the hierarchical relationship between patient and doctor at hospitals in Turkey. The program's high standards, Channel D's secular ideology, and the pedagogic tone of the show and its hosts all work to establish a particular relationship with the audience. That relationship is an affective bond that intimately works at the level of the psyche, but it is not a bond between equals and feels hierarchical. This hierarchical dimension is even more visible when the show's relationship to its audience is compared to the audience's response to another daytime health program, the *Feridun Kunak Show*, which airs on an Islamic pro-government network, Channel 7.

The *FK Show*

The *FK Show* appears considerably dilettantish when compared to *Doktorum*. It is led by a team consisting of Dr. Feridun Kunak's family members and employees from his private clinic, and Dr. Kunak often adds impromptu elements to the daily program, as was the case when I visited his studio. On that day, for instance, Dr. Kunak had read news of an electroshock accident that morning and shared information on his show about how to respond to such an accident. The team often throws things in at the last minute, which occasionally leads them to make "unprofessional" mistakes on air. Yet the audience perceives this "less-professional" ethos as more "friendly" or even "familial."

I first saw the *FK Show* when I was sitting in Fevziye Teyze's large kitchen. Fevziye Teyze, sixty-one at the time, lived in Istanbul Gaziosmanpaşa, a working-class district, and although she was not enthusiastic about being interviewed, she was happy to invite me into her home and talk to me about various things, including her limited exercise life. Fevziye Teyze did not attend any gyms, but we became friends through her daughter-in-law, Sevilay (twenty-eight), who was a member of Hamza Yerlikaya. Instead of going to a gym, Fevziye Teyze occasionally went for a walk and followed the exercise suggestions on the *FK Show*, which eased her neck and joint pains. She told me that doctors recommended swimming for her pain. She then suddenly shook her head, as if she was changing her mind, and said, "Walking is the best." Fevziye Teyze was also a very religious woman and thought that watching TV weakens one's spirituality. She proudly told me that she did not know anything about any of the soap operas but occasionally followed the live sermons on TV channels. She heard about the *FK Show* from a relative, who had heard a recommendation for joint pains on it, and she "trusted" she could watch it since it is on Channel 7, which is known as an Islamic channel.

Fevziye Teyze and I started watching the *FK Show* together with her daughter-in-law, Sevilay. It was May 1, International Workers Day, an official holiday in Turkey, so Sevilay did not have to work, and the three of us could spend time together. Before going to Fevziye Teyze's home, I had already been informed about the *FK Show* by other interlocutors, who told me that several elderly women they knew were pleased with the exercises promoted on the show. We had breakfast together, *menemen*, a pepper-and-tomato omelet in Turkish style, and moved to the sofa to drink our postbreakfast Turkish coffee when the program started.[15] Fevziye Teyze turned the volume up, and I first heard the show's theme tune, adapted from a famous Turkish folk song, "Doktor civanım, doktor doktor civanım [Oh dear young doctor, oh dear young doctor]," followed by a summary of the issues that would be covered during the episode.

The episode we watched focused on babies and their nutritional needs. After the short summary, we saw a young girl of around eleven or twelve years old dancing and singing "The show is beginning with Dr. Feridun Kunak" as she welcomed the audience. I was informed

---

15. In Turkish, breakfast is called *kahvaltı*—literally "precoffee."

that she was the daughter of the two hosts, Dr. Kunak and his wife, Mrs. Serap Kunak. This element of the show, like the unprofessional factors mentioned earlier, is one of the reasons why viewers seem to find Dr. Kunak's program friendly, familiar, and even familial. In other words, his relatively less professional style is translated into proximity.

After Dr. Kunak welcomed the guests to the studio and greeted viewers with his wishes and prayers for the studio workers and for the well-being of his studio guests, he started the program with a series of suggestions about daily health. Then he asked the studio guests to follow his lead and repeat the suggested exercises. The studio guests of the *FK Show* looked significantly different from those featured on *Doktorum*: they were dressed in head scarves and traditional outfits rather than in the modern attire worn by *Doktorum*'s carefully picked guests. Dr. Kunak slowly and very clearly described how to perform each exercise movement, so that his lead could be followed by an elderly audience and he could avoid misunderstandings that might lead to an injury. It was obvious from watching his movements that he had been in conversation with elderly patients for years on a daily basis. From Fevziye Teyze's comfortable sofa, I watched as Fevziye carefully repeated Dr. Kunak's movements with the serious face of an attentive student. Fevziye was utterly dedicated to following his advice—almost as if Dr. Kunak were in the room with us, giving direct orders to her. While slowly performing the exercises, Dr. Kunak also explained the significance of each movement and its benefit. He then completed his exercise with the following grace: "I am thankful to be up today, thankful to your benefactions, to your sun, to your rain; I owe infinite gratitude, O my Lord! May you let our bliss and happiness persist. Give us good days and keep us away from bad days. O Lord, keep us on your way and on the path of the prophet!"

Finally, Dr. Kunak reminded the audience to "never ignore the exercise of your soul." His prayer was accompanied by the voices of the studio audience, mostly elder women, calling "Amin" all together. Sitting beside me, Fevziye Teyze likewise joined this voluntary chorus, adding her own "Amin." Dr. Kunak calls this final prayer *şükür egzersizi*, an "exercise of gratitude." In his view, by performing this *şükür egzer-sizi*, we also perform our gratitude for having a body to move.

Dr. Kunak's program and his *şükür egzersizi* are immensely appealing to Istanbulite viewers. The movements are very easy to follow, and Dr. Kunak is skillful in tuning in to the age and style of his audience. He gives clear instructions in a tone that manages to be simultaneously commanding and compassionate. Dr. Kunak explained to me his popularity in relation to his manners and familiar style:

> I call them [his female patients] *ablacığım* [my dear elder sister], and it is very important in the clinic. If I ask [a patient], "Ma'am, what is your complaint?," what would she understand from that? I went to Denizli, for instance, and—apologies for saying that—but this woman who came had a large tummy. I told her, "Sweetie, how come you came to me chubby chubby [*tombiş tombiş*]?," and she hugged me right away. If I had used a formal language, she would have felt uncomfortable.

Dr. Kunak employs an informal, personal strategy that he has developed over years in clinic to gain permission from women to examine their bodies, minds, and aspirations, and he now uses that strategy in public on an Islamic channel that is sensitive to issues of modesty and gender segregation (see chapter 5). On TV, this same strategy gains him virtual entrance to women's homes, such as Fevziye Teyze's. Dr. Kunak's warm and patient demeanor on the *FK Show* conveys these familial codes to studio guests and viewers, building a connection through comfort, which enables him to gain their trust and respect.

Despite the dissimilarity of the styles *Doktorum* and the *FK Show* display, both shows prioritize exercise as a core part of their health discourse, whether from an evolutionary perspective (Dr. Kolankaya) or as a form of embodied religious gratitude (Dr. Kunak). Both health programs and the ongoing health register that celebrity doctors and well-being trends evoke reflect a new Turkish understanding of the self and the body in relation to the world and the physical environment.

Indeed, the popularity of health programs among exercising Istanbulite women[16] is related to the latter's desire to take an informed position toward their bodies and toward the changing conditions that may threaten their health, including rapid urbanization (Cavill, Kahlmeier, and Racioppi 2006; Vatansever et al. 2008; Kurt-Karakus 2012) and the rise in the availability and consumption of industrialized and fast food (Pekcan and Karaadaoglu 2000; Baş, Ersun, and Kıvanç 2006; Tuzen and Soylak 2007; Unusan 2007).

Most of the other daytime TV shows, however, tend to host celebrity doctors rather than design an entire show around health and have it cohosted by a medical doctor. The popularity of these two TV shows, *Doktorum* and the *FK Show*, may be related to cardiothoracic surgeon Mehmet Öz's influence on popular health culture around the world and particularly in America. This boom in medical, family-friendly shows is also known as the new "Oz effect" (Bootsman, Blackburn, and Taylor 2014). Yet it is important to avoid reducing Turkish examples to a global–local binary analysis so that we can instead capture the dynamically interconnected nature of the contemporary world (Moore 2004, 2011). What I find especially interesting about the Turkish equivalents of Dr. Öz is the way my interlocutors connect themselves with global health trends (like Dr. Öz's program) by means of their own agentive desires. It's worth taking a closer look at the way women interact with some of the mediating figures of these global trends to better understand their engagement with developments in Turkey.

Intimate Bonding and Intersubjectivity in the Formation of the Desiring Self

As desire moves through particular configurations, women's aspirations coincide with those mediating figures' desire to stay in the spotlight, to be followed, and to be significant in women's lives. Şallı,

---

16. The significance of health programs in the lives of nonexercising, non-Istanbulite women (and perhaps men as well) may also be subject of research but is beyond the focus of this work.

Dr. Kunak, and Dr. Kolankaya mold themselves as celebrity doctors or Pilates gurus based on women's expectations of them so that as mediating figures they remain at the core of the excitement and affective milieu of the celebrity health world. It is impossible to dismiss women's desires as an agent in the making of celebrity figures and Pilates gurus like the three figures I have discussed in this chapter. Thus, agency works both ways: celebrity health influencers create and promote particular forms of desire while simultaneously responding to their viewers' or fans' desires.

Desiring subjectivities require an intimate connection with mediating figures to unleash the imaginative capacities of the psyche. And it is this intimate connection that determines the centrality of those mediating figures in women's lives.

The basic premise of this chapter is related to Arjun Appadurai's (1996) formulation of imagination and reality in relation to modernity. According to Appadurai, acts of imagination mediate operations of consciousness and its engagements with the world. Through such mediated processes, new modes of realism are generated. Having said that, the mediation that we observe here involves an active self-making. In order to form a more or less steady self and make sense of multiple tips and trends, women need to invest in a series of interoperations and negotiations. The intimate connection that results from this investment becomes evident in the way women address program hosts as their "own" doctor or in their friendly interactions with Şallı and Dr. Kunak, one of many strategies that women develop in relation to their desiring bodies and selves.

An intimate connection forms when women pay attention to and form a bond with a selected public figure. This connection entails aligning their desiring selves with the trends they wish to translate into their everyday lives. These multiple desires work together to refashion a relationship with the self and with significant others.

Conclusion

Any trend that receives a high number of followers can be defined in terms of the actors whom the public follows: role models, fashions, and the social conditions that enable the emergence of such role models and the enchantment of these trends for their audience. Even something quite political, such as following a charismatic leader, can be seen as almost mindless. The followers of trends are rarely described in terms of agency; they are typically depicted as irrational or even unthinking. Yet that is not the picture forming here. Women's *spor merakı* is located at the center of changes in Istanbul's social life. While women interact with social circles and networks in everyday life, they simultaneously and fluidly navigate multiple attachments, thereby combining and recombining desires, aspirations, and relations in new ways. Therefore, at the core of women's desiring subjectivities is a pursuit to establish an intimate connection with mediating figures. It is this intimate connection that determines the centrality of figures such as Şallı and Dr. Kunak in women's lives. Nonetheless, Istanbulite women live in a complex web of relationships, and it is impossible to fully understand the content of their desires without accounting for the complexity and "dynamism of the relational matrix in which humans are embedded" (Long and Moore 2012, 43).

Istanbulite women's connection with the mediating figures discussed in this chapter is not mindless; it is dynamic, temporal, selective, and fluid. As women's desires move through particular configurations, their aspirations coincide with the desires of mediating figures, and this meeting becomes significant in their lives. In other words, Şallı, Dr. Kunak, and Dr. Kolankaya position themselves as a Pilates guru or celebrity doctors by responding to women's expectations; they do so in order to remain at the core of this affective milieu, preserving or promoting their popularity and therefore their success. It is thus impossible to dismiss women's desires as an agent in the making of celebrity figures and Pilates gurus. Nevertheless, the significance and perhaps the success of the mediating figures arise from their ability to stimulate women's interest in exercise, which requires connecting with women at an intimate, affective level, especially as the stimulation they trigger enables women to navigate their own *selves* by locating those desires at the center of global trends. As a consequence, each mediating figure is located in an interconnected and interactive relationship with the desiring Istanbulite women. As the mediating figures seek ways to connect with women, they place women's demands, aspirations, and longings at the center of actions that will cultivate their media register.

The ethnographic vignettes in this chapter help us understand the relational dynamic of desire. Relationality and intersubjectivity are key dimensions of forming desiring selves, not only by stimulating and triggering pleasures and possibilities but also by creating frustrations and limitations. Relationality and intersubjectivity have two key aspects: self and space. For this reason, in the next part of this book, "Space," especially in chapter 6, relationality takes another turn. I look more closely at the interactions between women at gyms and especially in changing rooms as spaces where homosociality shapes intersubjective encounters.

I follow Henrietta Moore's suggestion that "intersubjectivity plays a key role in maintaining forms of identity and belonging through establishing new possibilities for connection that are animated and propelled by hopes, desires and satisfactions" (2011, 29). Such an analysis requires a closer look at the space where women *encounter* mediating figures; a second axis of this approach is understanding how the individuals process those encounters in forming their selves as desiring subjects. Within a women-only sphere, women can more easily evaluate the "idealized" imagery available in the media. This homosocial environment provides a safe space for them to check, reexamine, and evaluate the "reality" of the idealized bodies it is suggested they become. In this process, women develop a complex yet intimate bond with mediating figures, another important dimension of women's desire-making process.

Space

4

Leisurely Istanbul

"You do not take a minibus in Kayseri [an Anatolian city] very often. You mostly walk. And the distances are not close either. So you have to walk to everywhere. Now, here [in Istanbul], no one walks. Sometimes I want to walk here as well. After starting to walk for a short while, I then have to take a bus because I cannot continue walking for long. [There's] too much car exhaust. The air we breathe here is not clean. There [in Kayseri], the air is clean. If you are not in rush, you can just walk for the pleasure of it. There [in Kayseri], you start walking and don't want to stop till your legs are tired."[1]

At the time I interviewed her, Firdevs Teyze was living in an Istanbul suburb called Sultançiftliği, an area inhabited by many first- and second-generation residents of Istanbul (Istanbulites). Its residents come from different parts of Turkey and the Balkans. In the neighborhood, there are walking tracks, outdoor gyms, and the very large Hamza Yerlikaya Sports Center.

Hamza Yerlikaya is one of thirty-five sports centers established and run by Spor AŞ (Sports Inc.), a company owned by the Istanbul Metropolitan Municipality and responsible for providing sports facilities for the city's residents. Firdevs Teyze attended Hamza Yerlikaya during winter, one of the "free sessions" that target and reach low-income residents. In the summer, she would join her relatives and neighbors on walks in a nearby park. She felt trapped in the city, and

1. Interview, May 10, 2012.

so her *spor merakı* took her outside the home. She tried to deal with the claustrophobic effects of the city by walking in the grids of her neighborhood or by going to her gym.

When I started this research on exercising Istanbulite women in 2008, the presence of exercising women such as Firdevs Teyze had just started becoming conspicuous to the public eye. The number of women-only gyms was rising, and although women were walking on the streets and in parks in small groups, wearing large scarves and cheap sneakers, the phrase *sporcu teyzeler*, "sporty aunties," had not emerged yet. The municipal governments had started installing Tartan walking tracks to respond to the "needs" of the women marching through the city every morning. The simple act of walking by auntlike, middle-aged women much like Firdevs Teyze had gained the city these Tartan walking tracks. Tartan is a rubberlike, polyurethane material that is resistant to weather conditions and improves the athletic performance. The playgrounds in public parks were losing their charm for children. Safety was also an issue in some parts of the city, such as in Cumhuriyet Park, one of the parks where I conducted research. "Fifteen years ago," Fahriye explained to me," "this park was not a safe place for a woman to spend time alone, let alone to take her kids."[2]

Discovering the appeal of Tartan walking tracks to the city's women led municipalities to think of alternative uses of the city parks, which brought about the idea of outdoor gyms. The municipal governments decided to open the parks to the use of the middle-aged women walking in the city and installed the first outdoor gym equipment in various corners of Istanbul in 2008. As of 2012, there were 311 public parks in Istanbul: 128 on the European side, 126 on the Asian side, and 57 in the town of Şile. And there were 468 outdoor gyms with a total of 4,502 pieces of sports equipment.

Without knowing it, women were shaping the city as the municipalities' neoliberal concerns became tuned to respond to women's moving bodies. Just as Jane Rendell famously puts it, walking in

2. Interview, May 10, 2012.

Istanbul became "a way of at once discovering and transforming the city" (2006, 153). Women's *spor merakı* slowly started marking the public sphere more visibly and thus could be traced in numbers more and more easily. In the years 2008–11, the municipal governments spent more than 150 million Turkish liras ($45 million) on Tartan and outdoor exercise equipment.

The municipal governments' investment in women's *spor merakı* was not independent of their political ambitions for the city. Recognizing the public's interest in anything, especially sports, which had already been used as part of colonial and nationalist political projects for longer than a century (Di-Capua 2006; Sehlikoglu 2017), was an opportunity not to be missed for the populist neoliberal political actors (Bayraktar 2011; Aksoy 2014; Özbay 2014).

The years between 2010 and 2014 witnessed a series of events that reflected Istanbul's crowded, vibrant, cosmopolitan, energetic, and vigorous yet equally draining and crippled character. These changes demonstrated the Istanbul governments' ambition to lead. Increasing Istanbulites' involvement in exercise has moved to the center of municipal governments' agenda and has been seen and presented as part of an "Istanbul dream." In 2012, Istanbul was the European Capital of Sports. During this year, the Istanbul Metropolitan Municipality's company Spor AŞ raised its annual budget by 20 percent and received 250 million Turkish liras ($75 million) from the Istanbul Metropolitan Municipality for the sports activities it organized in Istanbul. In 2013, Istanbul was disappointed for the fifth time in its bid to host the Olympics, yet it had never felt itself so close to reaching this long-held dream.

Istanbul is not only a metropolis that longs for a place in the global world but an embodied opportunity for the Turkish government to prove that it can excel at anything and everything. Such ambition requires continuous construction across the city, including tunnels, highways, and residential areas, as well as urban transformation projects featuring cultural and shopping centers.

Just as concrete physically absorbs humidity and the tall buildings block the winds, turning the formerly humid Istanbul summers into dry desertlike ones, it affectively sucks up the positive energy of its inhabitants, blocks the pace of life, traps the living bodies. The people I talked to were in constant interaction with the city's entrapping physicality, to the extent that they were transforming the city to fulfill their own desire, *spor merakı*.

This chapter focuses on the main shared subjectivity of the interlocutors of my research. It focuses on what it means to be an Istanbulite as a hook to understand and map out *spor merakı* as a spatial object of desire—something that has carved out Istanbul in the contestation between the desires of the city's authorities (municipal governments, investors, and so forth) and the desires of the city's women. It lays out the multiplicity of desires that are molding Istanbul with new walking tracks, parks, gyms of all sorts in the middle of political battles and neoliberal susceptibilities. Although it is relatively easy to observe the municipal governments' ambitions simply by tracing the literally concrete changes, women's desires are less apparent to the public gaze. However, the desires of the municipal governments and the desires of the Istanbulite women as the city's gendered residents are often interconnected. In this chapter, I elaborate on this dynamic and interactive relationship between women's desire as explored here through their *spor merakı* and the political ambitions of the rulers of Istanbul.

Istanbul: The City of Desires

As I was about to submit this book to my publisher one last time, I read the brilliant book *Istanbul: A Tale of Three Cities* (2017) by Bettany Hughes. It reviews the life of Istanbul from ancient times. Hughes begins her book by locating the city at the intersections of dreams and reality: "This is Istanbul incarnate. A place where stories and histories collide and crackle; a city that fosters ideas and information to spin her own memorial. A prize that meant as much as an abstraction, as a dream, as it did as a reality" (xxvi).

Istanbul comprises one-fifth of the entire population of Turkey, with residents from various parts of rural and urban Turkey, the Balkans, Circassia, and now Syria. Istanbul has significance to Turkey in stimulating trends and in shaping desired and desiring subjects, and the city itself is desired by the folks and the elites alike.

Istanbul is an eight-thousand-year-old desiring city, a beast that multiple desires—those of its government authorities, of its residents, and of its visitors—have attempted to tame. The descendants of its former residents and rulers still mourn over the loss of the heart of the city, Constantinople, making Istanbul an object of longing for many Greeks. Meanwhile, the city's current residents and authorities have new aspirations for the city's meaning and topography.

The struggles and violence among Istanbul's residents make the emotive elements of belonging and the desirous attachments to it especially contested. On the one hand, there is always an ongoing discussion in everyday life that no "Turk" would belong to the city, along with an automatic assumption that everyone is from somewhere else. Yet, on the other hand, after decades of attacks and discriminations against Greek, Armenian, and Jewish minorities (e.g., the Istanbul pogrom of 1955), not many non-Turks are left in Istanbul either. Their absence has turned Istanbul almost into a city of nonbelonging, where the outsiders find other ways of attaching themselves to the city. Yael Navaro describes the fragmented accounts of the current inhabitants of formerly Greek, Armenian, and Jewish neighborhoods (Fener and Balat): "The pieces of the puzzle emerge like debris gathered from the rubble without being put into any complete assembly or whole" (2011, 236). Indeed, everyday interactions between the city and its residents sometimes seem to be attempts to piece a puzzle together.[3]

In Istanbul, a casual conversation between any two random strangers meeting on a bus or at the gym or coffee shop is also informed by this nonbelonging and usually attempts to trace the roots of each

---

3. There is a very large literature on Greek, Armenian, and Jewish legacies of Istanbul. For those who are looking for a start on piecing together Istanbul's scattered past, I would recommend the following work: Vaka 1971; Türker 2000, 2001, 2003, 2004, 2006, 2008, 2016; Bali 2004; Kıvılcım 2009; Baronyan 2014; and Örs 2018.

person, who, it is assumed, must have migrated from elsewhere. The first encounter almost always starts with the question "Where are you from?" or "From which Anatolian city or which Balkan country did your family come to Istanbul?" "Istanbul" or a "neighborhood in Istanbul" can never be the right answer to either question. Anyone who claims that she is from Istanbul will be questioned about her (paternal) origins ("Where is your father from? How about your father's father?") or about her "Turkishness" ("Are you Armenian or Greek?"). No Turk can be Istanbulite because almost every Turkish person—or her father or her father's father—must have come to this city from somewhere else.

The inhabitants' sense of nonbelonging is established on the violent separations of those who once belonged. Their desires for the city and for themselves through the city are affected by this violence and thus are built on a dismissal. Several scholars' attempt to respond to the question of how one belongs to this city of nonbelonging reflects this dismissal, too. Take, for instance, Ayşe Öncü's formulation of myth. Starting her powerful article "Istanbulites and Others," Öncü writes that Istanbul "is a city of immigrants, with three-quarters of its population born elsewhere. In this sense, the question of who is an Istanbulite is a rhetorical question. A true Istanbulite is a 'myth'" (1999, 96).

What Öncü calls "myth" corresponds to the fact that belonging to the city requires a certain amount of imagination, storytelling, and fantasy. The fantasy, Öncü points out, is designed to fill the gap that has resulted from lacking the human link to the city's oral and affective traditions and knowledge. The new inhabitant needs to go through an actual physical struggle to establish a life despite the missing pieces, or "fragments," as Navaro calls them, and establish a myth in the process.

Perhaps one can read the accounts of Istanbul by Ayşe Öncü, a prominent sociologist, and Orhan Pamuk, a Nobel laureate novelist, side by side. I find Pamuk's book *Istanbul: Memories of a City* (2005) to be one of the most comprehensive and relevant works on what it means to belong to this city of nonbelonging and what it means to be an Istanbulite. Öncü and Pamuk's accounts of Istanbul share several commonalities. First, both scholars highlight the transition and transformation in the changing face of the residents of Istanbul. Second, both claim that residents of the city are connected to one another not by any economic, homogenizing, ethnic, or class factors but instead by only an affective element. Pamuk suggests that this element is *hüzün*—a particular, shared, and communal type of melancholy that haunts the city and is taken up by its residents, and Öncü focuses on humor and how it constructs a sense of belonging to the city.

Third, both Öncü and Pamuk use the word "İstanbullu," the Turkish version of "Istanbulite," rather than the English or Arabic/ Ottoman "Istanbuli."[4] Öncü discusses how being İstanbullu is both an object of desire and a classed self-reference. She says, "İstanbullu is a myth . . . in the sense of a discursive construct that transforms the formless void of everyday experience into meaningful reality, and informs practices of inclusion and exclusion" (1999, 115–16). The inclusion–exclusion dynamic, as she explains in her work in detail, is about middle-class Istanbulites' references to "the migrants," which also forms a unique hierarchy between the urban and the rural and has formed the foundation of the power struggle in the city, as I discuss in subsequent chapters.

Being an Istanbulite might be determined by two types of relationships the residents have with the city: a desiring relationship and a physical relationship.

The desiring relationship comprises the meanings and fantasies one attributes to the city to fulfill one's own desires. It includes an element of imagination, although it is not like the desiring in Arusha, Tanzania, where, Brad Weiss (2009) argues, inhabitants fantasize

---

4. "İstanbullu" is often used in works that are about urbanization as a modernist project and about the tension between that project and migrants in the city. Arabic (also Rum/Greek and Farsi) "Istanbuli" is used as a cosmopolitan Ottoman reference to signify those who have been living in the city for several generations. I prefer "Istanbulite" to denote the sense of belonging and subjecthood in today's Istanbul as a gigantic site of construction.

about being in America and adjust these fantasies to the materiality available to them. The imagination at stake in Istanbul is not determined by media representations of a distant place and culture that is perceived to be better than what is immediately present. The imagination that shapes the desiring relationship between Istanbulites and their city is built on whatever is materially left in the city. The inhabitants fill the gaps between what the city offers and what they can acquire from those offerings through fantasies.

It is impossible to capture and live in Istanbul in its entirety, so its residents and visitors look at selected faces and areas of the city and imaginatively locate their selves in that part vis-à-vis the imagined rest. For instance, one might live in Sancaktepe on the Asian side of the city—as Betül did, for instance—an area nine miles from the nearest seacoast that was not even a residential area thirty-five years ago but instead a shantytown next to the city's garbage landfill. Betül would not mention how the area was near the city landfill just a few decades ago. She did, however, picture herself drinking tea in Haliç (Goldenhorn) when speaking of herself as an Istanbulite to her in-laws in Çankırı, even if she hadn't had a chance to see the sea or cross the Bosphorus for the past eight months. She wanted both her *self* and the city to meet her expectations and aspirations: (1) belonging to an old Ottoman city as opposed to a former landfill and shantytown, (2) having leisurely time to cross the narrow sea, (3) living closer to the sea, (4) living on the European side of Istanbul as opposed to the Asian side.

The physical relationship is about the space and the actual physicality of the city, as experienced on the roads and streets, at shops, parks, and shopping malls, among the inevitable traffic, and on the crowded pavements. The physical relationship is about the moments one attempts to walk from the bus stop to one's destination, changes public transport in various locations, or stands squeezed in a packed *metrobüs* or fights for a seat or the moments one attempts to find a parking space and keeps one foot on the clutch because of the extended traffic jams, making only little advances, centimeter by centimeter. One always feels trapped and hopelessly struggles to go from one location to another.

The desiring and physical relationships one has with Istanbul are rarely in harmony. Betül might want to enjoy the Bosphorus, but she would suffer in traffic just to gain the pleasure of the sea breeze. Everybody desires green areas in the city, but the most green they see on a daily basis is the grass and the sickly shriveled trees near the highways, grayed and suffocated by the ever-present car exhaust.

All these elements shape the very fabric of the desiring relationships, marked with gaps and ruptures, physical limitations, feelings of being trapped and suffocated. When I study Istanbul as a desiring city, I map out its topography through the ways in which women's desiring selves surface, often in battle, in negotiation, or conversation with the municipal government officials' desires. I also explain the formation of Istanbulite women, a heterogeneous body of individuals who connect to one another through their desiring subjecthoods, desires, and the city.

Topography of Desire

The most important component of the changing topography of Istanbul is the migration from rural Turkey and East Europe to Istanbul, which increased the city's population sixfold from 1950 to 1990 (see table 1). It was a migration marked by aspirations: "Taşı toprağı altın İstanbul [Istanbul, of golden land and soil]," the new migrants used to say, a phrase that was popular in the 1970s and 1980s. The issue of migration was quite central to the city also in terms of the rising number of buildings and *gecekondu*s (shantytowns) erected to accommodate the new settlers.

For the newcomers, Istanbul was also a site of battle: these new settlers would find themselves in a fight against the city in which they would aim to win over their opponent, Istanbul. In the minds of the public, the city space often had an agency—a perception that can be traced back to Ottoman times.[5] "Seni yeneceğim Istanbul [I will beat

5. Ottoman writings told of good and evil neighborhoods that would make their residents good or evil (Kalender 2013; Tanyeli 2013). The neighborhoods had

Table 1. Population of Istanbul between 1950 and 2010

Year	Population
1950	1,166,477
1960	1,802,092
1970	3,019,032
1980	4,741,890
1990	7,309,190
2000	10,072,447
2010	13,255,685

Source: Data compiled by the author from Devlet İstatistik Enstitütüsü (State Institute for Statistics), n.d.

you, Istanbul]" was another renown phrase signifying the migrants' relationship with the city. Istanbul was full of promises and fantasies, yet it was simultaneously a rival against whom one needed to fight for one's desires.

The municipal governments were reorganized in 1984. Istanbul was established as a metropolitan municipality and was already facing the usual difficulties of a metropolis: complex infrastructure and traffic problems.

Becoming a Metropolis

For visitors, tourists, and a small percentage of lucky residents, Istanbul is a city with a beautiful sea breeze—something that the majority of Istanbulites do not experience. More than 60 percent of the population needs to beat traffic for a minimum of one hour to reach and enjoy the sea, which both surrounds (Marmara Sea and Black Sea) and runs through the middle of the city (Bosphorus Sea).

---

a personality, and residents' interaction with the neighborhoods would transform the residents, too.

The parts of the city that were suburbs in the 1970s have now become more central. The blistering transformations have forced city authorities to consider a new municipal governing system. In 1984, Istanbul was established as a metropolitan municipality, and Bedrettin Dalan became the first mayor of Greater Istanbul in the same year. He was the first person to attempt to give meaning to what a metropolis in Turkey might represent. What kind of a metropolis should Istanbul become? Dalan was able to address politically diverse aspirations and merge them with the new migrants' desires (to "beat" the city and find the metaphoric goldmine). He invested in the ideal of becoming modern and Western by permitting skyscrapers in the city (pledging to build a Manhattan-like district in Istanbul), and he promised to revive abandoned Ottoman legacies (famously declaring that Haliç would once again become as blue as his eyes).

During Dalan's time, the sea view that was once enjoyed by the old Istanbul mansions, *yalı*, facing the Bosphorus, the narrow sea that both connects and separates Asia and Europe, was blocked by sea bridges running parallel to the coast for faster access to and lighter traffic on the shoreline. In urban sociology classes, the editor of the renowned collected volume *Istanbul between the Global and the Local"* (1999a), Çağlar Keyder provided references to Marshal Berman's concepts to point out the dangers of leaving decisions about public spaces to technocrats. After all, pace was quite essential in achieving modernist or what we today call neoliberal ideals, and Dalan was talented in marketing neoliberal aspirations. According to the lower-class residents of the northern suburbs abutting the Bosphorus, those who objected to the installments of the sea bridges were "the rich," infuriated that their view was blocked, and so according to the lower-class residents' story Dalan was the knight fighting for the benefit of the poor.

With a discursive investment in both nostalgia and aspirations, Bedrettin Dalan's populism belied his ability to address the issues of Istanbul. His famous promises are tattooed in the memories of Istanbulites: he would turn the road that connects the Bosphorus to Taksim (Büyükdere Caddesi) into a Manhattan (which he in part did), and the polluted Haliç, Istanbul's historic peninsula, would once again be blue (which he never succeeded in doing).[6] As Rıfat Bali has brought to our attention, Dalan's projects were seen as fantasies; Dalan didn't see Istanbul itself but rather a make-believe version of it (2012, 83). He promised not only to transform select parts of Istanbul but also to revive "this tired city," "drag its glory from past to today," and "turn it into a city of 21st century, filled with promises" (quoted in Keyder and Öncü 1994, 391; Aksoy 2014, 28; Bali 2012, 121).

In this period, Bedrettin Dalan became the poster boy for transformation, and several studies have critiqued the destructive traces he left on the city (Ekinci 1994; Keyder and Öncü 1994; Keyder 1999b; Bezmez 2008; Kuyucu and Ünsal 2010; Aksoy 2014; Özbay 2014; Zengin 2014; Zeybek 2014). Dalan's legacy in defining and rebuilding metropolitan Istanbul by constructing new buildings and roads and spreading concrete throughout the city would later also mark the spatial contours of *spor merakı*.

Becoming an Istanbulite: Between Urbanite and Villager

Although Bedrettin Dalan had a vision of how to transform Istanbul into a global metropole, which simultaneously led him to invest in a number of controversial ventures and to change its topography irreversibly, he invested little in a shared Istanbulite identity among its inhabitants. That "honor" would later be given to his social-democrat and republican successor, Nurettin Sözen, mayor of Greater Istanbul from 1989 to 1994.[7] A flagbearer of the nationalist project of his and

6. For further information regarding Dalan's neoliberal investments in forming Istanbul as a metropolitan city, refer to Keyder and Öncü 1994, Keyder 1999b, Bezmez 2008, and Özbay 2014. For a detailed account of how the intelligentsia and the politicians in Turkey embrace and promote a particular form of American lifestyle, I strongly recommend Rifat Bali's book *Tarz-ı Hayat'tan life style'a* (From an Ottoman Life Style to a European One, 2012).

7. Nurettin Sözen's party was the Social Democratic Populist Party, whose leader was Erdal İnönü during Sözen's mayorship. İnönü was the son of İsmet İnönü, who was the second president of Turkey, a close associate of Mustafa Kemal Atatürk,

Dalan's ideological predecessors, Sözen invested in the well-being of Istanbulites (Bezmez 2008) as a civilizing mission.

Sözen aimed to find a way to integrate the large migrant population into Istanbul. The rural–urban distinction had been a crucial indicator of class hierarchy. With their clothes, accents, and manners and in numerous other ways that emphasized the contrast, the migrants were bringing the rural lifestyle to the city. The urban elites used the term *köylülük* (villagerness/peasantry) to refer to the rural migrants who failed to become *kentli* (urban), to integrate. In the urban discourse, anything the migrants did, said, and wore that reflected their hometown and their *köylülük*, rural background, was frowned upon. The everyday interactions between the new rural migrants and the urban middle class (Özyeğin 2001) were marked by the differences and tensions, and these tensions would later mark the rural migrants' self-making processes.

Whereas some of the migrants attempted to find ways to be proud about the aesthetic signifiers of their rural backgrounds, others adapted their manners, vocabulary, outfits, and accents to urban life. Serpil's mother, Fatoş, was one of the latter type of migrants. She was proud of how she had changed her once thick eastern Turkish accent to a clear Istanbul accent. "That was when I first arrived in Istanbul in early '70s," she remembered her progress in integration with nostalgia and pride. She worked on her accent, and during her teenage years she also made a small alteration in her name, changing it from "Fatma" to "Fatoş," a more urban-sounding name.[8]

In contrast, the former type of migrants, instead of removing all the markers of their peasantry (some markers were inevitably lost), found ways to embrace their rural origins. Two major references, *hemşehrilik* (colocalism) and religion, became the underpinnings of their migrant pride. *Hemşehrilik* was formed as a shared pride among

---

and one of the founders of the Republic of Turkey. Several intellectuals speculate that Turkey owes several secularist principles to Ismet Inönü.

8. Field notes, Apr. 17, 2012. "Fatoş" is one the few real names I use, with her permission, to emphasize her transformation for the Turkish-speaking reader.

those who came to Istanbul from the same city, region, or town (Tugal 2009). During the 1980s and 1990s, religion gained recognition and became the hallmark of both tradition and the class struggle taking place between the urbanized locals and the rural migrants in the city. An excellent example of this was highlighted in an interview I did in 2008. Nuray, a thirty-one-year-old woman, told me how when she was young, she never wanted her head-scarf-wearing mother at her school: "Our teacher used to tell us to stop and ask the *örtülü* [head-scarf-wearing] women why they cover their head. *Örtülü* women wouldn't be able to provide an answer, she used to say, [and] that women cover [their hair] out of ignorance. I was afraid she would treat me differently if she knew my mother was *örtülü*."[9]

As a response to similar everyday encounters, *örtülü* women were increasing their Islamic knowledge and the articulation of it to prove that they were not ignorant. This class struggle to strategically hold on to discourses of religion against derogatory urban (*kentli*) encounters would later trigger the Islamic revivalism in cities. In time, a large number of migrant Istanbulites invested in Islamic knowledge and Muslim "consciousness," *bilinçli Müslüman*, which later dominated the political movements in major cities (Tugal 2009; J. White 2002).[10]

Just before Islamic revivalism surfaced, Nurettin Sözen addressed the issue of integrating migrants into Istanbul. Building on the republicanist mission of integration and civilization, during his mayorship Sözen revived the Kemalist populist idea of creating a healthy nation and reapplied it to the inhabitants of the newly rising metropolitan Istanbul. Following in the footsteps of his predecessors, he invested in one of the most obvious venues for achieving this goal: sports. Sports would create new, healthy, strong, fit, and Western Istanbulites.[11] To

9. Interview, Aug. 7, 2008.

10. For a discussion of how investments in religious consciousness turned into a political struggle during the Islamic revivalist period of the 1990s, see J. White 2002, 23.

11. For a more detailed discussion of sport as a republicanist project, see chapter 1.

achieve this aim, in 1989 a Sözen-led municipal team established a corporate body dependent on the municipality that would provide sports centers for youth teams in various branches of amateur sports in the city—Spor AŞ, which would later become a major player in Istanbulite women's *spor merakı.*

New Populisms and the Gyms in Neoliberal Times

Like many other establishments that contemporary Islamist neoliberal politicians inhabited and restructured to reach out to the greater public, which in the long run also further enhanced their political power, Spor AŞ initiated projects for suburban neighborhoods shortly after the election of Recep Tayyip Erdoğan in 1994 as the mayor of Istanbul (he is now the president of Turkey). One of those projects was to finalize the construction of the largest sports complex of the day in an industrial district of Istanbul, Okmeydanı, which was populated by underpaid, working-class Istanbulites—most of them first- and second-generation migrants from rural Turkey. The sports complex was named the Cemal Kamacı Sports Center after a Turkish boxing champion of Europe who was also known for his religious, working-class family background, because of which he was looked down on in elite sports and other circles, according to the rumors of those days. Giving the name "Cemal Kamacı" to a sports complex that would not only be the largest in Istanbul but also be accessible to lower-class families and children quickly turned it into a monument of the new right-wing political project. This gesture, of course, later brought Kamacı and Erdoğan even closer, letting Kamacı become one of the founders of the Justice and Development Party (Adalet ve Kalkınma Partisi, AKP)—he was still listed as a founding member as of 2019.[12]

Toward the end of the 1990s, while the postmodern coup was taking place (precipitated by the memo issued by the National Security Council on February 28, 1997, after which many religious

12. See the AKP website at http://www.akparti.org.tr/site/yonetim/kurucu -uyeler.

schools, nongovernmental organizations, and political parties were shut down and a number of Islamic politicians, Erdoğan included, were either imprisoned or banned from politics), women-only gyms were also emerging, often to teach step exercise, aerobics, and martial arts to women. These new women-only facilities were signifiers of the rising number of conservative women in the city. The investors, most of whom were Islamists, assumed that such spaces would be preferred only by head-scarf-wearing women, and so they marketed their investments accordingly. Their aim was to provide space for the religious women. Located in the basement of a building in Üsküdar, Buhara Sports Center was one of these newly emerging places.[13] It specialized in martial arts, and female users needed to walk through the men's section to access the women's section. A martial arts gym required a smaller budget than a fitness gym because it needed only exercise mats and padded gloves (for kickboxing and taekwondo, the two sports for which Buhara had female trainers). The name of the place also reflected the romanticism of Islamic revivalist tendencies of that time, when corporation names would highlight their Islamic sentiments: "Buhara" (Bukhara) is the name of an Uzbek city that was once a medieval center of Islamic theology. With one exception, all the female attendants of Buhara Sports Center were head-scarf-wearing women. It was in the 1990s that head-scarf-wearing women started demanding and receiving opportunities both in education and in leisure equal to those of their non-head-scarf-wearing counterparts.

As my interviews in 2008 reveal, women attending women-only gyms, most of whom wore head scarves, explained their everyday enjoyments vis-à-vis the secular prejudices about them. Their responses to my questions about their choice of women-only gyms were marked with a sense of battle against prejudices—which made these interviews significantly different from the interviews I held in 2011 and 2012.

13. "Buhara" is the Turkish spelling of "Bukhara," a historical city in Uzbekistan known for its centuries-old legacy of Islamic higher education. This sports center's name reflects the Islamic revivalist aspirations of the 1990s in Turkey.

In 2008, women kept telling me how they "can be modern *too*" (their emphasis) and "have the right to enjoy sports" and to demand spaces tailored to their modesty standards (Sehlikoglu 2010).

Visibly Muslim (i.e., head-scarf-wearing) Turkish women as modern subjects have been discussed quite vastly. What has almost never been acknowledged, however, is that these "researched subjects" often perceive the researcher as a "Kemalist": a middle-class secularist person, just like the ones that look down on Muslim women on a day-to-day basis on the street. Head-scarf-wearing women's discourse on how they "can be modern *too*" is a continuation of their everyday struggle in public, wherein they are assumed to be ignorant about both modern life and religion and are treated accordingly in their everyday encounters with middle-class Kemalists. The interviews I conducted in 2008 revealed these women's subaltern pride about being referred to as "unmodern." A Cemal Kamacı Sports Center customer, Melahat, thirty-two at the time, said in 2008 that "they want to see us ugly and fat. It doesn't mean that I will not look after my body since I'm covering it. We do stuff like swimming, exercise, or aerobics just like they do."[14] Several of my interlocutors in 2008 perceived their membership at gyms as a "right" (to be beautiful, to do sports, to enjoy modern facilities). More interestingly, the reference to some hypothetical "they" was reiterated, meaning those who looked down on my interlocutors. The head-scarved female customers such as Melahat would constantly assert "modern-ness," an ideal they were seen to be unworthy of (Deeb 2006).

A head-scarf-wearing aerobics trainer, Ayşe Akbaş, emphasized this notion of "modern-ness" in an interview in 1997: "It is still possible to see people surprised when they hear about a head-scarf-wearing woman doing aerobics or even training aerobics in a gym" (quoted in Yılmaz 1997).

Akbaş was working at the Altunizade Cultural Center, one of the first cultural centers established by the middle-class Islamist entrepreneurs on the Asian side of Istanbul. The center had started aerobics

14. Interview, Aug. 13, 2008.

and self-defense courses shortly after Buhara did. It is important to see how Akbaş, like the head-scarf-wearing journalist who conducted the interview, Meral Yılmaz, talked about sports as something that head-scarf-wearing women "can do too."

It was in this context that Cemal Kamacı Sports Center opened the doors of women-only fitness rooms in 2001. Although its manager highlighted in an interview how the center did not prioritize head-scarf-wearing women as its clientele, the fitness room was tailored to keep the male gaze out: the windows were covered, male trainers and cleaning staff were not allowed in, and no male relatives or friends were allowed to accompany the female members.

Secular feminists have suspected that the AKP-run municipality's investments in segregated sport spaces were meant to promote traditional ideas about women and their bodies and therefore were proof of the AKP's Islamist agenda. However, even my initial interviews in 2008 suggested a more complex set of dynamics that included not only the (undeniable) Islamist agenda but also neoliberal and financial concerns. Women's own engagement with each of those elements should not be ignored, either, because women's desiring selves have managed to intervene in political projects.

At this intersection lies the populist and lower-middle-class content of the Erdoğan-led Islamism. Jenny White (2002) discusses the success of Islamist political actors in the Turkey of the 1990s as resulting from their ability to tap into existing traditional, religious, and even rural codes. Her approach is also useful in understanding the ways in which populist politics are established and maintained. In this vein, the emergence and spread of women-only gyms are situated at the intersection of heteronormative conventions in an Islamicate[15] context and neoliberal economics.

15. The historical term *Islamicate* refers to the contexts where Islam is lived as a religion, although it may or may not be devoutly followed by each and every individual. Coined by historians, the term allows scholars, including me, doing research

The relationship between Istanbulite women and exercise centers has been a contentious one. Istanbul has been both the hub and the substratum of divergent desires. Women's experience in and endowment to this desiring and desirous city have been shaped through their pecuniary circumstances and social conditions. Different types of gyms and exercise centers have emerged, often tailored to capture the desires of their particular potential clientele.

Spor AŞ: Making Privileges Accessible

Cemal Kamacı's women-only hours and fitness rooms gained popularity quite quickly after the gender segregation was launched in 1996. For the women of middle- to lower-class financial backgrounds, most of whom were also first-generation migrants to Istanbul, it was thereafter easy to convince their immediate family members (parents, husbands, and in-laws) that this inexpensive gym was not a "frivolous" leisure activity.

The new Islamists managed to tailor a metropolitan project, Spor AŞ, to the conservative and traditionalist subtleties. Spor AŞ started using the city's resources to increase the residents' involvement in sports. In contrast to their Kemalist predecessors, the Refah Party and then the AKP did not present the sports facilities as a civilizing project but used a more populist discourse and presented them as a way to make sports accessible to the lower class.

By 2011, Spor AŞ had developed multiple sessions and projects mostly for women out of the workforce, offering them either free or almost free of charge. The free sessions were subsidized by private events hosted at the sports centers and by advertisement income raised by Spor AŞ and the municipal governments.

---

on contemporary sexualities to locate the values associated with Islam within its historical and geographical boundaries while avoiding the essentialization of those values at the center of the lives of the people who are living in this context (see, e.g., the essays in Babayan and Najmabadi 2008a). I elaborate on this concept more thoroughly in chapter 5 on pages 141–42.

During the process, the entire project of Spor AŞ was tailored to the desires of a particular class: the new migrants of a lower-middle-class background. The idea was to make privileged enjoyments, including sports, exercise, fitness, and Western music,[16] accessible to the lower class. In a setting where carrying the signifiers of the *köylülük* was seen as low class and inferior, any urban enjoyment became an object of desire. Thus, for a new migrant of Istanbul, getting a membership at a sports center was an immediate signifier of becoming urban. It meant taking several steps away from the *köylülük*. Gender segregation, in this vein, had political significance in that it meant making sports and exercise accessible to a wide range of people with modesty concerns (without necessarily challenging traditional norms), including both religious and traditional families and those who had concerns about sexual harassment.

Even after two decades, upper-class enjoyments are still financially accessible, although they do not come in abundance. Free and budget options are currently either scarce or highly regulated. Budget exercise sessions, for instance, require heavy management to prevent overload. The absolutely free "early-bird" public sessions are held as early as 7:00 a.m. and take place in the public parks and stadiums. Whereas "paid" classes that cost 60 liras ($18) a month or 1,200 liras ($360) in more expensive places are regulated only by gender segregation (for instance, women-only classes are given three times a day and two evenings a week), the budget sessions are monitored closely for regular attendance.

Budget sessions cost 10 liras ($3) for two and a half months, and payers are allowed to participate in any of the available budget classes but not more than twice a week. The membership fee is mainly symbolic and basically covers the cost of the digital card, which is why such budget sessions are also referred to as "free." Attendance

16. Spor AŞ was a continuation of the Istanbul Metropolitan Municipality's new populism under Erdoğan's mayorship. Bogazici Konserleri (Bosphorus Concerts) are another example of his populist projects tailored to lower-class citizens.

is highly regulated, so members must swipe their cards when entering the building. If a member misses three classes (or two sequential classes) in one session, then the membership is revoked. This regulation is not meant to motivate members to exercise but simply to make room for those on the waiting list. The demand is quite high, and another attendance sheet is filled by the trainers during the session to detect any attendance fraud—I was told that in earlier years some members used to swipe their friends' cards so they could keep their membership.

Women attending the budget sessions have to go through a series of procedures to determine their dedication to exercise. For a limited privilege, they need to calculate layers of cautions. Because the budget sessions are almost free, and there is a long waiting list, the contract they sign does not roll over automatically. It has to be renewed at the end of each two-and-a-half-month session. The budget members need to be careful so they won't lose their membership privileges. Once a member loses those privileges, reapplying means being put on the waiting list. Gym members inform each other about the specifics of the free-membership options, such as when they will be eligible to switch to another session and the ideal time to switch so that they won't lose their budget privileges and still manage to gain a spot in the desired session. Sometimes they keep going to the less-popular session just so they won't lose their budget privileges or get put back on the waiting list.

Being put back on the waiting list poses a nuisance in that the member is once again regarded as a new member, which means providing a new medical report, including blood and urine tests for certain contagious diseases—tests that can be done for free but only after one waits in long queues in state hospitals or for 25 liras ($7.50) in faster-track clinics. Women with a limited income are thus constantly maneuvering their way through these highly regulated free sessions.

The regulation continues once the members enter the gym. Only clean training shoes that are not worn outside can be worn at the gyms, which is Spor AŞ policy. Proper branded sports shoes are too expensive for the attendants of such gyms, so they often purchase fake brands at street bazaars for as low as 10 percent of the actual market value.[17] Sometimes members borrow each other's shoes so that they will be allowed into the facilities. After entering the fitness rooms, they have to queue up for the use of the equipment and cannot use the treadmills for longer than fifteen minutes—or ten minutes if the session is too crowded, as it often is during winter and school term.

If desire is one of the fundamental elements that forms the subject, what sort of desiring subjecthoods are constructed through the constant regulations that lower-class Istanbulite women must follow?

The regulations mark low-income Istanbulite women's attachments to leisure.

On the one hand, lower-class families always go through regulations to obtain "free" services: medical aid, financial aid, and other state services. The free gym membership is also offered only after similar regulations. So all the paperwork, approvals, and other restrictions are considered only a small price to access this middle-class object of desire. On the other hand, women often share with a sense of pride their stories of easily handling such regulations. Enjoying access to a gym is an accomplishment. This sense of accomplishment also contributes to their process of self-making.

An Object of Desire and the Neoliberal Market

By 2005, women's *spor merakı* was no longer an ambivalent occurrence but an established aspiration. The budget sessions available across Istanbul shaped the way *spor merakı*, as an object of desire, gained market value.

---

17. A large number of my interlocutors preferred *markasız* (non-brand-name) training shoes. The word *markasız* refers to those products produced with the lowest-cost labor and material by unregistered companies. Even the least-expensive consumer product, if it has any brand name, is called *marka/lı* (brand/ed). *Markasız* products can also be knock-offs, with names such as "Nikke" and "Adibas." For an elaborate discussion of the impact of knock-off brands sold in Istanbul bazaars on self-making, please refer to chapter 5 of Magdalena Crăciun's book *Material Culture and Authenticity: Fake Branded Fashion in Europe* (2013).

Neoliberalism has been studied in the anthropological literature in three main ways. One group of scholars has critiqued the global operations of neoliberal market dynamics as homogenizing, reducing, and carving out local differences. The second group has taken a skeptical approach to the use of the term *neoliberalism* and has pointed out that it lacks a coherent definition and thus that anthropologists need to approach the concept with caution. The third group has developed a more nuanced approach via an ethnographic examination of East and Southeast Asia. In studying these contexts, this group has demonstrated how the neoliberal system has become a new form of governmentality as state policies adapt it and thus has shaped the way citizenship is constructed in those contexts.

The literature on desire and neoliberalism has also evolved from that third group's scholarship. Both Lisa Rofel (2007) and Aihwa Ong (2006) establish how neoliberalism and desire are historically produced and culturally situated fields. The scholarship on desire in the global South (Tadiar 2004; Ong 2006; Rofel 2007; Weiss 2009) has focused on neoliberalism in relation to global structures of power. In particular, drawing on the works of Carl Schmitt and Giorgio Agamben, Ong (2006) has cogently argued that neoliberalism is not to be reduced to an economic doctrine. Rather, it should be approached like a form of governance, of *exception*, that is able to agentively adapt itself to different regimes.

In the context of Turkey, from late-Ottoman and early republican times exercise and sports had already been established and presented as a tool for transformation and had already been accepted as a narrative of self-making projects. In the context of Istanbul specifically, three factors were added to this already existing object of desire: (1) women's reduced physical mobility, (2) women's desire to engage with leisure activities and become urban, and (3) homosociality. It is in this context that the neoliberal management of the city enabled the recognition of women's desires and turned them into a currency. Starting in the 1990s, various types of women-only gyms started popping up across the city, which led to an enormous increase in the number of women-only gyms—a whopping twentyfold increase between 2005 and 2012.

The gyms serving upper-class clientele also started women-only sessions, and new types of gyms attempting to capture this new women-only exercise trend started emerging. In a neoliberal context where women-only exercise was initiated by the neo-Islamist groups and was almost immediately seen as the signifier of an Islamist agenda, secularist entrepreneurs' investment in this newly emerging industry resignified that agenda's neoliberalist aspect. Small gyms were seen mainly as a good investment, and various class subjectivities started being shaped around the new gyms.

Secular and Feminist Enterprise: B-Fits for the Middle-Class Woman

Selma, unlike Firdevs Teyze, was born in Istanbul. She used to live in Fıstıkağacı, a small neighborhood on the hills of Üsküdar, when she was little. Her parents moved to Ümraniye after the rents in Fıstıkağacı got higher. Married and the mother of two young children, Selma was living near Libadiye by 2012. Libadiye is almost midway between Fıstıkağacı and Ümraniye, where her parents still lived. She attended a gym in her neighborhood, which was not free, like Hamza Yerlikaya, but not expensive either. "We sit and we sit and we sit, and it is not going anywhere," she complained to me. "You cannot really take a walk here like we used to in Üsküdar. When you don't move, after a while, you feel tired of not moving."[18]

The most notable of the women-only gyms with no Islamic agenda is the one Selma attended, a B-Fit gym. Founded by a secular feminist entrepreneur, Bedriye Hülya, B-Fit has more than thirty branches across the city and has won Hülya a series of awards and scholarships for women's entrepreneurship since 2005. Hülya got the idea of such gyms during her studies in the United States, when she discovered Curves, a women's fitness club franchise.

B-Fit's success, according to Hülya, is related to the fact that it is sensitive to women's needs: fast weight loss, short workouts, and

18. Interview, Mar. 22, 2012.

a designated women-only space. For the fast weight loss, B-Fit gyms use special exercise equipment. The equipment looks not too different from the exercise machines that work out abs, legs, or arms at other gyms, but B-Fit machines operate with a hydraulic system instead of with weights. This system provides resistance training, which develops lean muscles, making weight loss more visible to the naked eye. The entire workout can be completed in thirty minutes, which means spending less time at the gym. Last, all the trainers and franchise owners are women, which makes attending gym acceptable to both women and women's family members (partners, parents, in-laws, etc.) Although B-Fit addresses proud secular women, it informs its customers how it is careful about gender segregation and assures its members that no man, "not even the doorman," is allowed to see inside the gym while women are working out.[19]

At a gym where no man is allowed at any time, like the B-Fit gyms, only women can become managers. This aspect has contributed to B-Fit's success as female entrepreneurship. B-Fit gyms are known as spaces by women and for women. The more than thirty B-Fit branches in Istanbul are very popular among women.

The New Middle Class in Altunizade and Bulgurlu

Three of my interlocutors, Selma, Tuğçe, and Zerrin, were members of the Bulgurlu B-Fit, the most popular branch in 2011. What made Bulgurlu B-Fit the most popular branch and the most popular place to work out in the neighborhood was a combination of multiple factors. First, middle-class religious families have been living in Bulgurlu since the late 1990s, soon after Recep Tayyip Erdoğan moved to the neighborhood with his family. It was a new residential area and an alternative neighborhood for those who wanted to be close to Üsküdar but could not afford to live in that more prominent area. Within about ten years after 2000, estate prices in this relatively less-expensive area

19. Casual conversation with potential B-Fit member Sima after breakfast, May 19, 2012.

rose, and Bulgurlu became a middle-class neighborhood. The Bulgurlu B-Fit was affordable for those middle-class women, the hours were not regulated, and the thirty-minute workout time was adaptable to the unsteady routines of both working and stay-at-home women. Branch manager and minor celebrity Özlem Yeprem's name has also worked as free advertisement for the branch among religious middle-class women, contributing to the branch's popularity.

In my first visit to a B-Fit, I spotted two bizarre objects on the manager's desk, a light-gray, chunky plastic item and a smaller, round plastic item. They stood out among several motivational and weight-loss-related items that decorated every corner of her office. The manager explained to me that the large object represented the color, mass, and shape of one kilo of body fat, while the smaller one represented the color, mass, and shape of one kilo of muscle. "You need to choose which one you want to have in your body," she told me, moving on to tell me her own weight-loss (success) story and the activities they organize at B-Fit, including award nights (awarding the women who have lost the most weight) and picnics.

The manager and owner of this branch was Özlem Yeprem. Özlem Yeprem and her husband, Reha Yeprem, were small-scale celebrities, especially within Islamic circles, between 2000 and 2014 for transitioning from a secular life centered around modeling to a religious life in the late 1990s, when an Islamic revival was taking place in Turkey (Gülalp 2001; Saktanber 2002; Altınay 2013b). Following this change in their lifestyle, Reha continued his career, both in modeling and working as a TV host on various programs—although he was employed almost exclusively by Islamic companies—while Özlem partly retired from public life.

In early 2012, Özlem became more popular once again when she was featured on the cover of the seventh issue of *Âlâ* magazine, the new lifestyle magazine for head-scarf-wearing women, with a green *pashmina* around her head. The *pashmina* was the latest head-scarf trend in Turkey, and green is the color of the B-Fit logo. In chapter 3, I discussed how various media figures have been working to gain women's recognition in *spor merakı* by becoming women's role models. Özlem Yeprem was also trying to find ways to become significant in this trend.

For the attendants of the B-Fit Bulgurlu, their involvement at this particular gym is about all of the aforementioned factors. It is about becoming the person who addresses a celebrity on a first-name basis, goes to a gym within walking distance, and makes friends with other women who share similar desires and have a similar socioeconomic background. "Getting results" is also about physically transforming into that person who does not carry around excess fat, presumably unlike a woman from the lower class.

Upper-Class and Elite Yeşilvadi

Istanbul is also where Turkey's contemporary Islamic ruling elite have thrived. The rising interest in the women-only gyms resulted in a demand for a separate, special gym for upper-class clientele. The majority of the middle-class Islamist families of the 1990s—once called the *yeşil sermaye* (green capital) by the Kemalist media—are now the upper class. As they have moved up the class ladder, they have started developing the leisure habits of their newly achieved status, which include the women's demand for both gender-segregated and upper-class service.

The Yeşilvadi (Green Valley) gym is located in a high-security, gated residential community, Yeşilvadi Sitesi. This residential community is located in one of the fastest urbanizing suburbs of Istanbul, Ümraniye Tepeüstü, within ten minutes' walking distance of two large shopping malls (BuYaka and Meydan), the Ümraniye Anafen private school,[20] and an immense mosque built in an avant-garde architectural style. The market value of the houses in this residential community ranges

20. Ümraniye Anafen is one of the many branches of the Gülenist education foundation. The Gülen movement is the largest Islamic movement in Turkey, known for its national and international initiatives in education. Wealthy religious families prefer its private schools for their Western training program. For a better understanding of the movement's entangled relationship with the wider Turkish society and the state, see Turam 2007 and Tee 2016.

from $600,000 to $4,500,000, an amount large enough to buy a *yalı*, an Ottoman-era house on the shores of the Bosphorus— the marker of wealth for hundreds of years. Many people in this class, however, prefer to live in Ümraniye Tepeüstü rather than by the sea in an old house with historical value. Living in Yeşilvadi locates its residence in close proximity to the rising Islamic bourgeoisie of Turkey. Those who do not live in the residential community can nevertheless connect with those who are privileged enough to live there by participating in the activities that take place in it, such as attending the gym. The gym was initially intended for the exclusive use of the community's residents, but it was later taken over by Spor AŞ, which designed the Yeşilvadi gym for what the company described as "VIP" customers.

In the years 2011 and 2012, the Yeşilvadi gym was the new "trendy" spot for upper-class women who wished to exercise in a homosocial space. The annual membership fee was as high as 2,000 liras ($600), four times more than a regular, municipal-owned gym membership would cost (although a family discount is given to Yeşilvadi residents). Members can train on equipment with a view of the pool or watch their choice of TV channel on the screen embedded on each elliptical trainer, exercise bike, and treadmill. Women also can see their children playing in the day-care section via a nearby CCTV monitor while they swim. The facilities also include a sauna, a steam room, and a spa offering massages. The gym provides courses such as Pilates, spinning, step aerobics, and yoga. One of the trainers, Nazan, a forty-year-old professional trainer at the time I interviewed her, occasionally appeared on various TV channels to provide on-air training. Nazan always finished her training sessions with a short prayer: "Şifa olsun," meaning "May it lead to healing." The word *şifa* signifies both physical and spiritual healing in Turkish, so her choice of words was not a coincidence. Nazan was beloved by the religious Yeşilvadi gym members because "although she is a sportswoman, she is *maneviyatlı* [spiritual]," they told me.[21] Nazan indeed offered the

21. Field notes, Sept. 6, 2011.

members what they wanted: a spiritual link to what they did in their free time, to something they enjoyed, and to something they did for their bodies.

The contrast between Yeşilvadi as an upper-class gym and the budget sessions in other parts of the city goes beyond the greater benefits it offers. An overwhelming majority of the followers of *spor merakı* (more than 65 percent) attend either such budget sessions or the free morning sessions offered in different parts of the city. Whereas the Yeşilvadi clientele are served and their needs are satisfied before they demand them (e.g., CCTV monitors connecting the daycare to the fitness room and pool, a trainer who is both fit and spiritual), the attendants of the budget sessions must put in an effort to maintain the privileges they have acquired through hard work.

These two positions shape and reflect the ways in which an object of desire, exercise, is experienced and how the desiring self is formed differently by women of different social classes. An expensive gym is designed to capture the pleasure and comforts its members have not even discovered yet. The gyms offering the budget sessions, in contrast, must work to keep an overflowing demand under control and to contain an already existing aspiration.

Conclusion

Istanbul is a city of desires. On billboards across the city, on TV programs and dramas, and in newspapers, Istanbul is never depicted or presented as just any metropolitan city but as a global leader, the "capital" (of Europe if not of the world) in almost everything: culture, finance, fashion, sports, science, health, city planning, cinema, tourism, art, and design.

Fantasy has been seen and read as a central part of human agency, something in which individuals seek refuge against reality. In the context of Istanbul, the city is where desires become an object of fantasies and reality is appropriated to serve those illusions. The city is filled with fractured longings, dreams, ambitions, makings and remakings, and so are its residents. Istanbul embodies possibilities for the leftovers. The hopeful aspirations of new Istanbulites are connected to each other. Erecting and owning new buildings in the city have some-how become the fastest way to achieve those aspirations, to capture the city's dreams. Concrete is the glue that can permanently seal these newcomers' ambitions. Yet this very same concrete has created a feel-ing of claustrophobia among its residents, and in turn this claustro-phobia is one of the forces that have driven women to *spor merakı*.

Most of the accounts one finds in written material on Istanbul is how the city transforms people and shapes their very beings, their souls, through interactions between the subjects and themselves as well as among its subjects (whom it enchants, shapes, and subjectifies) (Mesutoğlu 2014). However, in the case of *spor merakı* Istanbul is also a venue where multiple desires are in contestation. In their political ambitions to make the city a metropolis of highways, tall buildings, and concrete, the city's governing officials have trapped the bodies of its inhabitants. Women's *spor merakı* has in turn been triggered by the city's entrapping physicality. Yet their desires have in time managed to transform the city as well.

The transformative effect of Istanbulites' desires on the city's smothering cement is observable. In 2013, the young urban residents responded to the changing shape of their city during the Occupy Gezi movement by taking over Gezi Park in Taksim Square, at the heart of the city, defending it first against bulldozers, and then defending themselves against water cannons, teargas, and rubber bullets. In the aftermath of Occupy Gezi, the city council poured something unbear-ably familiar to the city's inhabitants: cement. The area long occupied in protest by the flesh of young Istanbulites was instantly flattened by the municipality—with the same speed at which cement dries and becomes concrete. Just as human flesh marked the park with resis-tance and aspirations, the concrete then blocked up every other urban landscape possibility (park, Armenian cemetery, Gezi monument) (Parla and Özgül 2016).

The women who participated in my research for this book are living in the affective milieu of a longing and dreaming metropoli-tan city. They are striving to become a new kind of woman who is Istanbulite, urban, mobile, *and* Muslim. As Istanbulite women, they negotiate for the spaces to exercise, and they transform both the city and their selves interactively. They alter the structure surrounding their mobility. Their bodily movements are slowly changing the city. More importantly, their exercise is challenging the borders that enable and maintain the social structures that objectify women's bodies.

In his work on boxing gyms in Chicago, Loïc Wacquant asks, "On the surface . . . what is more banal and more self-evident than a boxing gym?" (2004, 13). Istanbulites also see Istanbul's women-only gyms as deeply banal. However, the women-only gyms in Istanbul offer a significant tool to unpack the relationship between the city and desire and between the simultaneous and confronting desires of women and of the city's governing authorities. As this chapter investigates, women's desire for exercise is constantly engaged with neoliberal actors' desirous projects. Through that engagement, women-only gyms are shaped and marked by femininity, and *spor merakı* is formed as an escapist object of desire. In this struggle and encounter over multiple desires, the women-only gyms are established as bubbles of desire and sociality that bump up against the concrete, the construction, and the highways.

5

Men-Free Exercise

Bending, stretching, raising my legs are within my *mahrem* boundaries. I won't do them in public.

—Belgin, interview, January 26, 2012

Rahat (comfortable) was the word women kept repeating as they struggled to describe their feelings behind their choice of men-free environments in which to exercise.[1] Referring to the choice of women-only gyms, the diverse body of people I met during my ethnographic fieldwork cited the option to exercise in a *rahat* environment as their central concern. My interlocutors kept telling me that they wanted to exercise *rahatça* (comfortably). This comfort is achieved by multiple techniques: segregation, the company of female friend(s), control of behaviors in public, and avoidance of anything that will make them feel *rahatsız* (uncomfortable.) Depending on the context, *rahat* may refer to a place where men do not disturb women (*rahatsız etmek*) or to a state in which women feel comfortable (*rahat hissetmek*) and do not fear being perceived as a *rahat kadın*—literally, "comfortable

An abridged version of this chapter appeared in the *Journal of Middle East Women's Studies* 12, no. 2 (2016): 143–65. The revised version is published here by permission of Duke University Press.

1. In contrast to a non-Muslim context, women-only gyms in Istanbul are spaces completely freed from the male gaze—suggesting the centrality of the gaze to privacy concerns—which is not necessarily the case even for the women's gyms in the United States or Europe, where there are male janitors, trainers, and security guards.

woman," a Turkish expression referring to a seductive or promiscuous woman.

In a context like Turkey where sexual harassment can take multiple and mundane forms, ranging from staring to physical abuse, women use daily techniques to self-control their public sexuality. "Public sexuality" here does not designate an act of sex in public but the making and remaking of women's and men's (hetero)sexed bodies in public. Depending on the social setting, that self-control might range from maintaining skirt length at a certain level to wearing a shirt or top that covers the hips, putting on a tight shirt under a décolleté blouse, and keeping a jacket on. At other times, women's self-control might include small adjustments—for instance, as they carefully pull their shirt down while reaching to an upper shelf or under the table (to cover their belly) or strategically keep their handbag pressed to their legs to prevent their skirt from blowing up. However, exercise makes these types of control impossible. Women-only gyms are an easy solution to this complex issue of self-control.

What is particular about exercise that complicates women's experience of public sexualities?

In this chapter, I link this seemingly simple choice, a women-only gym over a mixed-gender one, to the broader systems of public sexuality in Turkey. I explore Istanbulite women's demand for segregated exercise spaces to control their public sexuality in relation to the larger institution of intimacy and sexuality that I refer to as the culture of *mahremiyet* in Turkey. *Mahremiyet* is the Islamic notion of privacy and intimacy and acts as a boundary-making mechanism. The culture of *mahremiyet* is constituted through cultural scripts, normative spaces, and gendered acts in the Islamicate contexts of the Middle East.

In the preface to their edited volume *Islamicate Sexualities*, Kathryn Babayan and Afsaneh Najmabadi define the term *Islamicate* "as a complex of attitudes and practices that pertain to cultures and societies that live by various versions of the religion Islam" (2008b, ix). Approaching Istanbul as an Islamicate context fits well with how the culture of *mahremiyet* operates to influence even those who do not necessarily believe or observe religion at the same level as others. Despite the diversity among them, women share similar concerns about public sexuality that have led them to seek modesty and women-only spaces in which to exercise. The techniques they use to meet certain social expectations in relation to public sexuality and institutions of intimacy are part of their everyday lives and often take on complex and changing semblances. I call for a shift away from the dominant focus on the head scarf and suggest exploring what is often referred to as "modesty" in Middle Eastern studies as part of a larger normative mechanism. I join Asma Afsaruddin's call to "re-examine the notion of one grand paradigm of gender relations and gender exclusivity in cultures dominated by what are generally perceived to be Islamic/ate values" (1999, 4–5). More importantly, I believe that it is impossible to disentangle women's dynamic, complex, and multiple gendered subjectivities without addressing the larger mechanisms women encounter on a daily basis.

Feminist scholarship has often overlooked this type of control over *unruly* public sexuality and has either called it "modesty" or over-focused on the politics of the head scarf without necessarily thinking about how both head-scarf-wearing and non-head-scarf-wearing women have to negotiate with the norms embedded in public sexuality. However, the everyday techniques women employ to control their public sexuality provide a lens through which to view the broader institutions of intimacy and operations of heterosexuality.

In this perspective, what women mean by "comfort" when explaining their choice of women-only gyms is related to several broader questions. What are the mechanisms that enable, define, and differentiate particular forms of "comfort" in homosocial settings for women? What is particular about segregation in an Islamicate context from women's perspective? How do women shape, reshape, and negotiate with the culture of *mahremiyet* in their everyday lives when they exercise? These questions also compel me to ask how the historical, cultural, religious, and linguistic particularities of Turkey as well as the global visual interactions enabled by media tools influence and shape women's privacy, specifically the interaction between women's bodies and public space.

Answers to these questions are interwoven with language, history, and culture as constructing forces of sex and sexuality (Moore 1994). This chapter's analysis of *mahremiyet* as a reference point to "comfort" revolves around women's own conceptualization and imagination. This analysis does not involve theology or law per se, however, because when it comes to understanding and analyzing gendered norms, centralizing religion or law runs the risk of ignoring the complex makings of those norms. The ethnographic complexity I witnessed and the way women explained or often failed to articulate their concerns, all aggregated in the single word *rahat*, "comfortable," steered me away from Qur'anic or hadith-based explanations of segregation and rather toward treating it as a mechanism that inhabits, informs, and controls everyday life.

I aim to understand the relational mechanisms used to maintain the limits and boundaries between gendered bodies, to construct femininity and womanhood through space making, and to regulate the relationship between the sexes. I argue that the "discomfort" women refer to leads them to choose segregation and to use multiple strategies to establish distance from the opposite sex. This choice is related not only to normality and (hetero)sexuality in Turkey as an Islamicate context but also to the ways women need to deal with the fragility of their privacy in public in an era when the institution of intimacy (Berlant 1998) is undergoing change.[2] This chapter, therefore, also demonstrates the ways in which women's everyday enactment of the culture of *mahremiyet* is changing its content.

Mahremiyet as an Institution of Intimacy

Intimacy, as discussed in this chapter, is not necessarily tied to romantic coupling but involves boundaries and borders of the gendered female body and the ways female heterosexuality and femininity are built and rebuilt, made and remade in everyday life, and produce

2. For other work examining changing forms of sexuality in Islamicate contexts, see Smith-Hefner 2006 and Özyeğin 2015.

gendered knowledge and meaning (Yanagisako and Collier 1987; Moore 1988; Strathern 1990). I consider the culture of *mahremiyet* an institution of intimacy (Berlant and Warner 1998). Lauren Berlant and Michael Warner discuss sex and sexuality as always "mediated by publics" and argue that heterosexual culture creates privacy to preserve its own coherency: "Heterosexual culture achieves much of its metacultural intelligibility through the ideologies and institutions of intimacy" (1998, 553). In another article, Berlant defines the institution of intimacy as something "created to stabilize" and "normalize particular forms of knowledge and practice and to create compliant subjects" (1998, 286, 288). Such an approach illuminates the roles of unspoken assumptions, techniques, expectations, and nonverbal cues that draw the lines of intimacy observed in the multiple heterosocial and homosocial settings where women engage in an activity—such as exercise—loaded with sexual appeal. In other words, in this framework segregation and the culture of *mahremiyet* are inherently public.

The word *mahremiyet* is not easily translatable into English. It suggests multiple meanings, including "privacy," "secrecy," and "domesticity." Derived from the Arabic root *h-r-m*, *mahremiyet* simultaneously refers to forbiddenness and sacredness. It relates to a notion of privacy and confidentiality, which the insider is expected to preserve and an outsider is expected not to violate. In her in-depth analysis of the term, Nilüfer Göle (1996) points out that the insider–outsider binary in *mahremiyet* does not fit into the customary theoretical framework of public–private. *Mahremiyet* is a mechanism that creates boundaries between spaces and individuals as well as within the body of the individual. The question of *mahremiyet* and the prerogatives to infringe upon such boundaries is the focus of this chapter.

There are times when the interior of those unspoken boundaries is so private and confidential that it cannot be easily vocalized, mentioned, or described. Proprieties of confidentiality forbid it to be enunciated. *Mahrem* is a voiced yet nondescriptive reference to the *intimate*. The ineffable nature of the intimate is precisely why the word *mahrem*, too, is not easily translatable and can therefore have multiple references: one's home, wife, bedroom (*mahrem* space); a secret (*mahrem* information); familiality; domesticity; confidentiality; and even sacredness. *Mahrem* refers to anything and everything one might avoid enunciating.

Mahremiyet, as a boundary-making mechanism, marks certain acts and people as *mahrem*s, "insiders," and others as non*mahrem*s (*na-mahrem*), "outsiders." The regulatory and boundary-making nature of *mahremiyet* is embedded in Islamic jurisprudence that regulates marital relationships, a core part of culture entangled in everyday life. According to Islamic marital law, it is forbidden for two relatives of the opposite sex to marry, and the word *mahrem* refers to this ban on an intimate heterosexual relationship between relatives. The proximity of these two individuals of the opposite sex is formed either by blood (i.e., father and daughter), by marriage (father-in-law and daughter-in-law), or by breast-feeding or milk (i.e., a woman and a man breast-fed by the same woman). Yet although they are forbidden to marry, these relatives are nevertheless *mahrem*s to each other and thus have fewer boundaries. In other words, forbiddenness also denotes and creates proximity and a familial intimacy.

In this sense, two non*mahrem*s of opposite sex are expected to establish distance and follow codes of invisible boundaries, such as segregation, veiling, a limited gaze, and controlled behavior. By delineating basic principles of marriage, *mahremiyet* creates heterosexual barriers and regulates proximity and gendered intimacy at multiple levels. In this way, Islamicate sexualities are created and normalized in the everyday lives of observant and nonobservant Muslim individuals, and to a certain extent, non-Muslims (Sehlikoglu 2015c).

Gazing Produces Sexual Scripts

The boundaries created in the culture of *mahremiyet* are signified primarily by regulating who can see whom and how. In their everyday lives, women become aware of their sexed bodies in relation to different types of gazes: the male gaze, the female gaze, the foreign (non-*mahrem*) gaze, the envious gaze, and so on. *Mahrem* boundaries are regulated to help one avoid attracting a foreign gaze, which produces sexual scripts in public settings.

The gaze as a producer of a sexual script is an expansion of the psychoanalytic approach that considers gaze a love object, a notion Sigmund Freud first argued and Jacques Lacan (1981) later expanded. To Freud's partial list of love objects (breast, face, phallus), Lacan adds two other objects: voice and gaze. It is therefore by no means accidental that gaze and voice are love objects par excellence—not in the sense that we fall in love with a voice or a gaze but rather in the sense that each is a medium or a catalyst that sets off love.

In the culture of *mahremiyet*, however, the gaze produces a sexual script that is more than a mere medium. As the term *sexual script* suggests, gazing is entangled with larger cultural meanings enabled by historical makings and maintained by intersubjective displays (see Simon and Gagnon 1986). Furthermore, the gaze has a clear and almost physical embodiment in the everyday life of the Middle East. In Turkey, the gaze has nonhuman agency with the capacity to bring misfortune or illness through *nazar*, "strong eye," which is able to touch people (*nazar değmesi*).[3] The significance of this kind of gaze is not fully reflected in Western theories, such as Lacanian *le regard* (almost exclusively translated into English as "gaze"). Lacanian *le regard* refers to looking or staring, often with desire, yet it does not encapsulate the physicality of the gaze in the particular context I discuss here. In the following pages, I revisit the ways my interlocutors negotiated different types of gazing in various spaces in daily life. Because the gaze is imagined to be physical and concrete, powerful and ambient rules, emotions, and beliefs are created around it.[4] As

3. *Nazar* is often misunderstood and mistranslated into English as "evil eye." In the Turkish context and in several other Middle Eastern contexts, however, *nazar* does not have to be *evil* to bring misfortune. *Nazar* is a *strong* gaze. Because of its strength, it can "touch" or "hit" the person gazed at if it is directed with heightened emotions, such as envy or love. For instance, a mother's loving gaze on her child is believed to be one of the strongest *nazar*s.

4. The Middle Eastern and eastern Mediterranean concept *nazar* originates from Arabic but also exists in Turkish, Urdu, and Farsi and their wider cultures. The rituals surrounding it have only minor variations in different ethnic and geographic

such, in everyday life the sensation of the gaze is experienced as tactile rather than simply visual.

In a culture that envisages (and regulates) the gaze as a physical object, the one who is looked at feels a "discomfort" because the *mahrem* boundaries have been crossed, violated, and even penetrated. The curious, penetrating gaze is therefore an intrapsychic reflection of the heterosexual active male. Aside from the sensorial dimension of intimacy, the female is also positioned as penetrable, marking women's privacy with fragility. The tangibility of gazing takes a masculine penetrating position against the *mahrem*.

In his work on the heterosexual culture in Ottoman society, Dror Ze'evi (2006) lays out the normative binary as female/passive/penetrated versus masculine/active/penetrating. What I witnessed in Turkey does not immediately correspond to the binary Ze'evi describes, however. First, I am cautious about using the feminine-versus-masculine binary so hastily. I suggest that we use a more complicated distinction instead: *mahrem*/penetrable/hiding versus non*mahrem*/penetrating/gazing. The power dynamics between these two positions are more complex than a simple passive–active dynamic, so I have not put "passivity" or "activity" at either end. Although women are considered to be *mahrem* in general, other bodies and acts (e.g., kissing, sexual intercourse) are and have been considered *mahrem* and thus are juxtaposed with the non*mahrem*. For instance, recent queer historiography on the Ottomans suggests that the beardless boys were "protected" against harassment by the use of a face veil (Delice 2017). In the use of the veil to actively avoid the non*mahrem* penetration

---

contexts. According to Timothy Mitchell ([1988] 1991), in Egypt *nazar* refers to a certain kind of power that makes the object of the gaze more vulnerable. This belief system is referred to as "superstition" in early sociological and ethnographic works (Johnson 1924). In one of the earliest works that connect beliefs about the eye, gazing, and the eye's power, the psychologist Richard G. Coss (1974) suggests that the overall "evil eye" interpretation stems from particular cultural behaviors regarding staring and gazing. After the mid-1980s, closer examinations of *nazar* emerged in ethnographic works (see, e.g., Brav [1908] 1992).

by the gaze (or other forms of harassment), beardless boys' bodies were treated as *mahrem*. As discussed throughout the chapter, the avoidance of the penetrating non*mahrem* male gaze requires rigorous work and a series of calculations, which is why I avoid associating the *mahrem* position with passivity in this chapter.[5]

Harem: A *Mahrem* Space for Leisure

The culture of *mahremiyet* has adapted to new habits as particular leisure practices have become established in Turkey. To stay within the boundaries of the complex social rules regarding the gaze that *mahremiyet* demands, various regulations regarding space and social distance have emerged and been adapted as the solution to that complexity. Although androgenic fantasies predominantly stimulated colonial interest in the harem (Alloula 1986; Yeğenoğlu 1998), the harem was in fact one of the main ways of regulating *mahrem* boundaries.

As opposed to the common misunderstanding, the harem (*harem-lik*) was a socialization zone of *mahrem*s, those who remained inside the borders created by the culture of *mahremiyet*. Thus, if the place in question was a household, the insiders who had access to the harem were not only women (as the common stereotype suggests) but also male relatives, such as fathers, sons, and brothers. The households with harems were predominantly of the upper and ruling classes during Ottoman rule (Peirce 1993; Booth 2010; Brown 2011), and the uses of those spaces were aimed at regulating the gaze (Lad 2010). A harem was often situated where those inside it could see other parts of the house (garden, main room) or outside but also so that outsiders could not see inside it. In sum, as Marilyn Booth (2010b) brilliantly

---

5. By doing so, I also slightly diverge from my own earlier suggestion that was assuming a female/penetrated/passive versus masculine/penetrating/active binary in this normative sociality (Sehlikoglu 2016). I now call for a more nuanced approach, as discussed in this chapter. The *mahrem* is not necessarily passive, for the discussed reasons, but can be active in navigating normativity. It is also not necessarily a female position alone because a *mahrem* can also be a young (beardless) male.

points out, the idea of the harem was in fact a border-making mechanism that still exists in Islamicate contexts.

I agree with the call in Booth's edited collection *Harem Histories: Envisioning Places and Living Spaces* (2010a) for closer attention to the ways those borders are established, maintained, and threatened. "Islamic" rules are not enough to understand the culture of *mahremiyet* fully because the culture's historical, temporal, spatial, and intersubjective dimensions complicate individuals' (and in this case women's) relationships with it. Moreover, even when individuals have the interest in and ability to apply particular Islamic interpretations of *mahremiyet* and its regulations, they sometimes choose to ignore those interpretations. For instance, it is permissible for women to breast-feed in the presence of women and male relatives (i.e., brothers or fathers), yet it is a highly unusual practice. In contrast, despite the prohibition against women seeing other women's genitalia, this does often occur, as when women visit a waxing salon. The ways women regulate their bodies cannot be understood outside the culture of *mahremiyet* because their sexed bodies have been constructed through it. However, there are ways they also negotiate these regulations.

The Living Borders of *Mahremiyet*

> Do you know what *mahrem* is? It is a secret and a seal. It is private.
> —Feray, interview, May 22, 2012

Sibel was a single woman in her late twenties who was working toward a doctoral degree in dentistry during the time I did my research. As a young single woman with a respectable job in higher education who lived in a suburban area of Istanbul (Beşyüzevler), she considered herself a more *aydın* (enlightened) woman compared to her family members and her neighbors. Indeed, Sibel was the "perfect" modern Turkish woman: she was tall and skinny, with natural-looking blond hair, often clothed in tight pants and miniskirts, and sporting an academic career. She was by no means a traditional or religious woman, according both to her own accounts and to circulating stereotypes in Istanbul.

The way Sibel explained her choice of a women-only space to do aerobics and take a fitness class is worth a closer look:

> Well, in the end, you stretch your legs, spread your legs, lie down, and raise your feet. Your body may be revealed. In the end, you would be surrounded by people you don't know, which is discomforting in my opinion. I mean, I wouldn't feel comfortable. For instance, your trainer tells you to spread your legs, and I wouldn't want to do that; I would be uncomfortable. Or, for instance, you wear sweatpants and do the cycling movement with your feet up, and you will have to worry about your T-shirt coming off, and you will have to worry about your sweatpants coming off, and you will try to stuff it into your socks. Why should I have to have all these concerns? . . . I don't feel comfortable at all. I don't want to do aerobics movements when I am with people I don't know. . . . Why would I do such bedroom movements? I don't want to.[6]

Sibel's statement elaborates on the shared aspect of the culture of *mahremiyet* that embodies three layers. The first, most obvious level corresponds with the bodily movements she avoided in the presence of foreign (non*mahrem*) men. Her concern was not about all men or just any men, but about men she did not know. What she referred to as "bedroom movements" is the resemblance between the body movements of a woman during an act of sexual intercourse and those of a woman exercising. Her reluctance to exercise with people she did not know was based on this resemblance and the way it might appear to an unknown man. She wanted to elude the risk of anyone imagining or fantasizing about her body. She avoided exercising in public to be able to preserve her control over her public sexuality (and over the heteroerotics of the movements in exercise).

The second level of *mahremiyet* is in her choice of words: her depiction of aerobics as "bedroom movements." She did not directly say that the aerobic movements resemble body movements during sexual

6. Interview, Jan. 27, 2012, with first ellipses indicating a pause in speech.

intercourse. She instead referred to the closed-door space (bedroom) in which such body movements (e.g., opening legs or moving hips) often occur. She used a symbolic reference to the heteroerotics of her body and avoided enunciating the intimate.

Sibel revealed the third layer of *mahremiyet* when she explained very vividly that what pushes the boundaries of sexuality is not limited to the content of the bodily movement. Despite the wearing of proper clothing, through movement that clothing can become less controllable and reveal the body. Sibel complained about her uncontrollable sweatpants. This third layer highlights the possibility of losing control through movement, which for Sibel was exemplified through clothing, and she described how in exercise the loss of control of clothing may expose sexualized body parts.

Gül, another interlocutor, also provided a detailed description of controlling her outfit when exercising and how women-only gyms saved her from having to make these calculations. She was a forty-one-year-old married woman with two children who worked as a manager in an international corporation. Gül was a member of two gyms, a women-only one and a mixed-gender one. In the gated community where she lived at the time, she had access to a gym (Yeşilvadi) that has separate hours for women and men. If she was free to exercise during the time of the day when Yeşilvadi was open for men only, she went to a mixed-gender gym not far from her home. When I asked her to compare the two gyms, she first compared their services, such as towel provision and swimsuit-drying machines. She then described levels of "comfort" and discomfort:

> There is an advantage here [at Yeşilvadi], which, of course, is a disadvantage for some others: men and women are segregated. You are more comfortable. For instance, when you need to exercise, you don't go all, "Oh, have my underpants gone between my hips? Oh, has my underwear appeared over the top [of my sweatpants]? Oh, did the neck of my top show my breasts when I bent over?" You have to check each and every one of these things [in a mixed-sex gym]. "Oh I'm sweating, is my shirt sticking to my body too much?" So,

yes, you need to have a certain level of *mahremiyet* between men and women. You don't have to worry about these when there aren't any men around.[7]

For work, Gül usually preferred to wear sleeveless shirts under jackets and knee-length skirts. Yet her body's movements during exercise made the clothing she wore to the gym uncontrollable and thus "uncomfortable." She then felt obliged to pay attention to whether her bunched-up T-shirt exposed her back and tummy.

Neither Gül nor Sibel wore a head scarf; both considered themselves modern, secular Turkish women. Yet the culture of *mahremiyet* goes beyond covering and segregation. It is more broadly a multilayered, boundary-making mechanism of privacy and sexuality that women live through and in and with which they negotiate. Women in several Euro-American contexts may have similar concerns. However, the particularity of the Istanbul context is not only about the different ways the link between the public and the intimate is constructed through sociality and relationality but also about the significance of the gaze, particularly the non*mahrem* gaze.

The significance between the gaze and the culture of *mahremiyet* can be captured in a term from popular culture: what both Gül and Sibel tried to avoid is giving a *frikik*, a "free kick" in football, a highly masculine zone. In football, a free kick allows the player the chance to score directly. This term is often used in and applied to everyday life—for instance, when a woman loses control of her outfit and reveals parts of her body that she normally tries to keep concealed (i.e., her upper legs). At that moment, she also loses control of her (guarded) sexuality, leaving her with a feeling of shame and unwanted public nudity. This movement allows a potential (foreign, non*mahrem*) male gaze to see something he was not supposed to see—or something the woman was supposed to guard. So he figuratively "scores" against the woman who is trying to guard (part of) her body.

7. Interview, Dec. 21, 2011.

By avoiding certain body movements, both Gül and Sibel disallowed victory to the opposite sex. In a way, the cultural *frikik* is more about the everyday power game of hiding and revealing. Both Gül and Sibel wore knee-length skirts at work. Neither of them was especially concerned about men seeing their legs in other spaces, such as the pool or public beach. However, certain body movements in non-sex-segregated exercise spaces caused them to worry about losing control in this power game.

One of the conceptual barriers anthropological inquiry encounters in relation to intimacy is its ambiguous relationship with language. During my research, my interlocutors were often unable to describe their discomfort. In fact, unlike Gül and Sibel, very few women were able to describe the actual measures they took to control their public sexuality.

Another woman who was as able in her descriptions as Gül and Sibel was the thirty-year-old Meziyet, who had stopped wearing her Islamic head scarf four years prior to our interview and after wearing it for longer than a decade. Her experience allowed Meziyet to compare her years wearing a head scarf with the years she hadn't worn one and how her attitudes toward public sexuality changed. She said: "Many women, veiled or not, already prefer to cover their *mahrem* body parts and protect them from men's eyes. When you are running, you do not want your tits to be jumping around in front of men. This is also a cultural thing."[8] The *mahrem* body parts can be a woman's upper legs, tummy, and upper chest, depending on the person and the context. Because the content of "comfort" is, as Meziyet called it, a "cultural thing," it was often inexplicable for many of the women I interviewed. This sense of comfort was so deeply embedded in their lives that explaining their discomfort often seemed unnecessary to them—something that goes without saying.

Seval was another young career woman. She was in her early thirties and single. She came from, in her words, "a traditional family," reflecting the way traditional discourse is tied to religion and rural

8. Interview, Sept. 16, 2011.

culture, and referred to herself as *çağdaş modern,* "progressive modern." "It's something you learn from your family and on the streets," she said about her discomfort in exposing herself through certain bodily movements and about dressing in a particular way in the presence of men.[9] Seval's reference to "the streets" concerns highly intersubjective relations in the public sphere, where interactions are built through multiple means but overwhelmingly through the gaze. This is what Alev Çınar terms the "public gaze," arguing that because public space is loaded with meanings, interactions, debates, contestations, identities, and subjectivities, the public gaze dominates that sphere at multiple levels of encroachment (2005, 34).

I asked Seval to explain her discomfort in relation to gaze:

SERTAÇ: Do you restrain yourself because men look at you? Or because you are used to [doing] it?

SEVAL: That [being used to restraining oneself] can be a reason too. I mean, we are raised to behave properly as women and girls in the presence of men, like subconsciously. It doesn't really matter if you look *açık* [open, uncovered] and comfortable; you are careful because it's engrained in your culture. That's why I am content to exercise with women.

Head-scarf-wearing women in Turkey are sometimes called *kapalı,* "covered" or "closed." Women who do not wear a head scarf are called *açık,* "uncovered" and "open" (to seduction and flirtation too). This particular normative terminology reflects the culture of *mahremiyet* as something beyond wearing a head scarf or not, and women negotiate with this culture on a day-to-day basis. Seval did not say "if you are *açık*" and did not refer to herself simply as a non-head-scarf-wearing woman. She said "if you *look açık*" to highlight her position that she is not less modest than those who wear a head scarf.

Seval's everyday concern to regulate her sexuality in public echoes Afsaneh Najmabadi's analysis of the transformation of Iranian women

9. Interview, Jan. 8, 2012.

as they moved from all-female homosocial spaces to heterosocial spaces (1993, 513). During Reza Shah Pahlavi's (r. 1925–41) mandate for compulsory unveiling in 1930, women began to develop strategies to discipline their sexuality by other means to maintain cross-sex barriers. Najmabadi provides the example of "walk[ing] to work facing the walls" (513) as one of these strategies. Thus, she argues that "in its movement from a homosocial female-bounded world into a heterosocial public space, the female body was itself transformed," including women's voluntary adaptation of an "invisible metaphoric veil, hijab-i'iffat [veil of chastity], not as some object, a piece of cloth, external to the female body, but . . . [as] a disciplined modern body that obscured the woman's sexuality, obliterated its bodily presence" (489).

Unveiled and yet pure, the new Turkish women of the early republican period were expected to be "modern" in appearance and intellect but still required to preserve the "traditional" virtue of chastity and to affirm it constantly (Durakbaşa 1988; Parla 2001). Seval's everyday negotiations and strategies reflect how she maneuvered through the demands of patriarchal mechanisms. She stated that despite her looks she in fact maintained the *mahremiyet* norms of public sexuality.

Other women, regardless of whether they wore a head scarf or not, echoed Seval's concern. This suggests that in Turkey's cultural expectations of public sexuality, women need to learn how not to look "accessible" or, in their words, *açık* or *rahat*. I met Mübeccel, a head-scarf-wearing woman who was single and a freshman at a local university, at the municipally run Hamza Yerlikaya Sports Center. She was one of the many respondents who shared long lists of details regarding how they regulated their bodies and attitudes *dışarıda*, out in public. During our conversation, Mübeccel pointed out these limits:

MÜBECCEL: In the end, I am covered [by a head scarf] and should know where to draw the line.

SERTAÇ: So how do you know where to draw your line? How do you do that?

MÜBECCEL: With my attitudes and behaviors. . . . Sure, I do everything when I'm surrounded with women. I mean, everything, like I wear low necklines and do this and that. But when I go out, I pay attention to my behavior, for instance. When I walk or talk, for instance, I don't laugh *dışarıda*. There's this thing, like my character. I am never too close to men, for instance. [Stopped to think for a moment.] Actually, I have a tough character *dışarıda*, did you know that? People who see me *dışarıda* usually think "What a tough girl" about me.[10]

The term *dışarıda* refers to the nondomestic sphere that is both nonfamilial and heterosocial. *Dışarıda* indicates mixed-gender public spheres, such as streets, public transportation, and school campuses, perhaps with the exception of special occasions, such as weddings, where people are known and familiar to a certain extent.

Mübeccel was from a lower-class background, and so *dışarıda* referred to the neighborhoods of her class, where she encountered foreign males all the time in various proximities. Her experience differed from that of upper-middle- and upper-class women I talked to. Mübeccel took public transportation to school and walked on the streets of the lower-class suburbs of Istanbul, whereas women from the upper-middle and upper classes told me that they walked only in "sterilized" public spaces, such as upper-class neighborhoods and shopping malls. Thus, to rebuild the boundaries Mübeccel needed in a heterosocial public space (inhabited predominantly by lower-middle-class people), she developed a certain body language and a certain public attitude. Her *dışarıda* lines were invisible boundaries. She avoided looking "easy" or *rahat* and donned a "tough" look. These lines were there to prevent complications. She explained: "I am not tough in my real life. I need to appear as serious [*ciddi*]; that's how it's supposed to be. Time and environment are corrupted [referring to the rising incidence of sexual harassment]. I mean, what would they think if I laugh? They could derive multiple meanings from that laughter."

10. Interview, Dec. 30, 2011.

Mübeccel knew not only what kind of message she needed to send through her public appearance and performance but also how to manifest it. Her control of her behavior in public was shaped with reference to an imagined gaze that not only monitors but also judges, evaluates, criticizes, and approves. It is also worth mentioning that Mübeccel's head scarf, her *kapalı* look, did not save her from having to make any of these calculations.[11] She still had to calculate the effects of her acts and her looks, which demanded that she continuously and self-consciously evaluate what was appropriate for her to say and do *dışarıda* and any potential threats or misunderstandings in that space. Thus, the culture of *mahremiyet* works almost exclusively against women's privacies, so women feel obliged to ensure that their fragile privacy boundaries are not violated.

The Intimate Paradox and Fragility of Women's Privacy

What is it that makes the position of the *mahrem* (in this case a woman) so fragile? The very culture of *mahremiyet* is structured in a way both to sanctify *mahrem* bodies and to allow room for random violations of those borders. It is crucial to understand this structure because the culture of *mahremiyet* not only operates in public life in Turkey but regulates the political scene as well (Sehlikoglu 2015c).

In the last stage of my fieldwork, a strange incident occurred at a formal reception when in the presence of the press a minister told a newly wed female professional athlete, within earshot of everyone present, including the media, "I want a child from you." He apparently was saying this to show his support for the latest pronatalist policies, but, quite amusingly, the sentence has the same double

---

11. Several women who wore a head scarf told me that they needed to be more careful because they are still exposed to the gaze even with a head scarf, which, they highlighted, was not the case twenty years ago. Recent work suggests that the culture of sexuality in Turkey is changing (Özyeğin 2015; Sehlikoglu 2015b; Şahin 2018; Ünal 2019), and this change should be considered when evaluating women's everyday worries.

meaning in Turkish as it has in English. It is unclear whether he wanted to father her baby or was just encouraging her to become a mother. Despite this awkward articulation and public address of a private matter, nobody in the room showed discomfort at the minister's comment.

What are the current conditions that render women's theoretically more sacred and secret bodies an easy target for public, random intervention? Of course, the familial versus nonfamilial distinction makes the *mahrem* position more vulnerable than the non*mahrem*. In other words, any outsider (non*mahrem*), such as a minister, can claim a familial position (e.g., brother) to comment on a private matter. By adopting such a familial position, the outsider presents himself not as a disrespectful harasser violating another person's privacy but as a rightful insider. However, what might be seen here as a twisted use of the language of *mahremiyet* often remains unrecognized locally. Women's bodies (otherwise defined to be sacred and honorable) can easily be turned into public objects, and women often try to act in ways that prevent a violation of their privacy—for instance, acting tough, as in Mübeccel's case.

One might ask, What are the dynamics that prioritize certain privacies, secrets, and intimacies over others? Most importantly, how do they become reified as norms and gain public intelligibility? In another article (Sehlikoglu 2015c), I discuss these questions in relation to the "intimacy paradox." The fragility of women's privacy (*mahrem*) in public is a result of the paradoxical nature of intimacy in the culture of *mahremiyet*: the significance of *mahrem* is embedded in its silence or invisibility; it is recognized as private when it is not enunciated. The moment the intimate (*mahrem*) is openly addressed or enunciated, it is no longer private but public. Even being present in public space (e.g., a spice shop) might make a *mahrem* body a target for intervention. Thus, female bodies, which are formulated as *mahrem* and passive in Islamicate heterosexual duality, hold a more fragile privacy.

The fragility of the privacy of *mahrem* is the distinctive feature of its public mediation. Quoting Laurie Anderson's lyrics, "It is not the bullet that kills you (it is the hole)," Rosi Braidotti reminds us how the "boundaries between the inside and outside are not a one-track sequence. Their meaning, consequently, cannot be restricted to a one-way mode" (2013, 28). In other words, the fragility of the privacy of *mahrem* is not about the porous boundaries reified by the culture of *mahremiyet* but about the easy reversibility of the *mahrem*'s otherwise private and sacred position. This paradox is also the very mediation of intimacy.

Morning Exercises in the Parks: Public by Nature, Private by Culture

Although a ten-week gym membership at 10 Turkish liras ($3) might sound financially feasible, open-air exercise with no fee was still preferable for several women I talked to, both for financial reasons and because they enjoyed outdoor exercise. I wondered: If women's privacies are so fragile, then what sort of strategies do these women use both to guard their boundaries and to establish comfort while they exercise in a public park? How does the culture of *mahremiyet* take shape in mixed and public spaces?

Middle-aged and senior women walking in sneakers and exercising at outdoor gyms in public parks in the early hours of the day are a familiar scene to most residents and even visitors in Istanbul. The trend has become mainstream.

The immediately obvious difference between women exercising outdoors in North America, the United Kingdom, and continental Europe and women exercising outdoors in Istanbul is appearance. Rather than tight-fitting athletic clothing, women in Istanbul exercising outdoors often dress in casual, loose-fitting clothing and sometimes wear robes or even black veils that cover the whole body, along with their sneakers (figures 3 and 4). But there are less-visible differences as well.

Spor AŞ's early-bird training sessions are part of a project called Morning Sports in thirty-one locations across the city, with multiple sessions for some of these spots. For instance, in Fatih, a majority-Islamic neighborhood of Istanbul, there are two outdoor exercise sessions—at 7:00 a.m. and 8:00 a.m.—owing to high demand among women for them.[12] Spor AŞ employs and sends trainers (mostly women) who are graduates of sports academies to sports centers in various neighborhoods.

The early-bird exercise sessions require bodily movements that immediately trigger issues related to heteroerotics: running that involves the movement of hips and breasts, stretching that may emphasize the contour of the body, and leg movements that draw attention to the genitalia. As such, my interlocutors often considered them highly sexual, even erotic. The eroticization of exercising female bodies can be observed in Turkish popular culture. Women's volleyball has long been perceived as a "leg show," for example. In the 1970s, all-male audiences regularly harassed female volleyball players on national teams (see Harani 2001 and chapter 1 in this book). Indeed, in Sultançiftliği, where I conducted my ethnography, morning exercise sessions were eventually moved, at the request of women participants, to an indoor facility because men were watching. In other words, the discomfort caused by the foreign male gaze resulted in a demand for a segregated indoor space. Given Mübeccel's everyday calculations in a nearby (equally lower-middle-class) neighborhood, women's demands for indoor spaces for exercise in Sultançiftliği came as no surprise.[13]

Besides the sessions Spor AŞ offers, women walk and do light exercise in small groups in public parks. This emergent trend is not a privately initiated project. The practice has become so popular in recent years that municipal governments have redesigned many public parks to accommodate it, installing walking paths and outdoor gym equipment (see chapter 4).

Outdoor gym equipment in these public parks include cross trainers; leg, shoulder, and chest presses; benches; and equipment to work arms and shoulders, such as hand bikes and shoulder wheels. These

12. Selim Terzi, vice president of Spor AŞ, interview, May 18, 2012.

13. In some Istanbul neighborhoods where more privileged residents live (e.g., Caddebostan, Bebek), both women and men exercise regularly and often in typical sports outfits.

3. Women using outdoor gym equipment in Cumhuriyet Park, May 21, 2012.

machines are heavier, water resistant, and less sophisticated than indoor gym equipment. The spaces for such equipment look like playgrounds for adults, with seesaws and swing sets replaced by adult-size exercise equipment. In a park near the Hamza Yerlikaya Sports Center, women almost take over the park as early as sunrise—the time of morning prayer—until 9:00 or 10:00 a.m., depending on the season. By "take over," I mean not only that they outnumber the men in the park but also that they dictate the ways male patrons of the park behave during that time.

Even though women avoid "bedroom movements" during their exercise in public and do not stretch, run, or (for the most part) dress in tight clothes, they can still be targets of harassing oglers, even though the oglers may be limited in number. Responding to an imagined (if not actual) foreign male gaze in public, women's sexuality is rebuilt and internalized daily to reproduce normative boundaries.

4. Women in loose outfits walking in a public park, May 21, 2012.

Figen, a woman in her forties who regularly exercised in this park, revealed in an interview that in her mind the looks given by "everyone" and the looks by "men" were in fact interconnected:

SERTAÇ: What bothers you in a mixed[-gender] environment?

FIGEN: [Slightly surprised by the question, almost finding it irrelevant and the answer too obvious.] To be out in the open [*Öyle açıkta olmak*]! I don't know, I would be spreading my legs and raising my arms while men are passing by, out in public [*dışarıda*], in the middle of the street [*sokak ortasında*]. Everyone would turn and look at you. It would bother me if everybody were to look at me!

SERTAÇ: When you say "everybody," do you mean men?

FIGEN: Yes, men.[14]

14. Interview, Feb. 13, 2012.

Figen's few sentences are haunted by boundaries, outsiders, discomfort, and openness. Her reference to "everybody" as a source of discomforting gazes is not hollow. On the contrary, when Figen said "everybody," she referred to the possibility of a male gaze evaluating her public acts. Evaluation and judgment of this kind are independent from the gender of the looker because no matter whom they come from, they mark Figen as a woman. In other words, the gaze, whether by a man or a woman, places judgment on the person who is its object, making her a woman who exercises in the (potential) presence of an actual foreign male gaze. Like Mübeccel, Figen referred to the opinions and judgments about herself that lie behind the gaze. She felt uncomfortable exercising outside of her *mahrem* zone—in her words, "out in the public, in the middle of the street," sites loaded with unpredictable, foreign, and violating interventions.

Likewise, Kamile, a thirty-six-year-old, lower-class housewife and mother of two, decided to become a member of a women-only gym a couple of weeks after she began to exercise in her neighborhood. She lived in Cumhuriyet Mahallesi, a suburban part of Istanbul that is home to primarily middle- and lower-income families, most of whom are first-generation migrants from other parts of Turkey. The park there is very small, about twenty square meters (sixty-six square feet), with five outdoor exercise machines. It has no trees and no rubber walking paths, so Kamile needed to walk on the streets circling the park and use the equipment where any passer-by could see her. She felt she was visible in public and therefore more vulnerable. She complained to me about the actual male gaze staring at her moving body.

KAMILE: We used to start and continue for one or two months and then take a break. And maybe we would start again. One naturally hesitates when there's no one else [to accompany one when one exercises]. Also, Sultançiftliği [her former neighborhood] is more rural [*kırsal*, referring to the area's mostly rural immigrant population] compared to here [Cumhuriyet Mahallesi].

SERTAÇ: How so?

KAMILE: You go out to exercise alone in the morning, and every-
body gawks at you like a moron [*bön bön bakmak*], men and all.
You cannot do it alone. There's nobody [doing sports] there.
It's not like here.

SERTAÇ: Yes, you are right, you need to have someone to accompany you.

KAMILE: Exactly!

I asked her to further describe her discomfort. She explained:

At the beginning, I did not feel comfortable while I was walking in
the park. Your hips move, and there are men around you. I especially
cannot be free with the equipment where you should open and close
your legs [referring to the inner-legs exercises]. Men look, especially
when we are on the trainers in the park. I hate them! Women have
to argue with men who sit on purpose right across women to watch
women. Actually, security deals with them, but they return again
after an hour.[15]

The gender segregation draws a boundary between women's bodies and gazing male strangers and regulates both verbal and nonverbal
(i.e., the gaze) cues. This same boundary also turns women's bodies into strange objects in the public sphere. Particular types of exercises—in Kamile's case, opening and closing her legs in the sitting
position—include bodily movements that cannot be performed without concern in the presence of the non*mahrem* male gaze because they
resemble movements in sexual intimacy. The "penetrating" aspect of
the gaze is a result of a combination of factors, including the looker's attitude and the tactility of the gaze. Therefore, the discomfort
caused by the penetrating foreign male gaze parallels the feeling of
harassment. Moreover, this gaze, unlike physical or verbal harassment,
is not a concrete act of violence and cannot be prevented, stopped,
or reported, despite the disturbance it causes. So Kamile needed to
develop strategies to negotiate it.

15. Interview, Jan. 10, 2012.

Kamile's discomfort and initial impotence in the face of street harassment (by gazing) expose how easily and randomly women's bodies can be turned into public matters and the fragility of their privacy. Because of the power dynamics embedded in the very fabric of heterosexual duality in Turkey, women's privacy is always more fragile than men's (Sehlikoglu 2013a, 2015c). For women, the fact that their bodies can be made public at any moment is experienced as risk. This fact is the nexus of the problem for women when it comes to exercising in public. Whether they are followers of the Islamic faith or not or are veiled or not, self-identification as modern or traditional does not necessarily change this experience of risk. In addition, oddly enough, this problem cannot be reduced to being subjected to the male gaze or patriarchal control. Although these two factors may be aspects of the larger felt problem, what women really worry about on a day-to-day basis is the instability of what may occur at any moment during exercise because of the fragility of their privacy. A woman can be at any moment caught by that instability and troubled by it through violation of her privacy. A word, an insistent gaze that touches, or in some cases a physical touch leaves room for potential instability and thus harm.

Like Meziyet's, Seval's, and Sibel's experiences, Kamile's experience also draws attention to the bodily movements or "bedroom movements." However, owing to her limited income and the fees at a women-only gym, Kamile exercised outdoors from time to time, and her "bedroom movements" encountered the (non*mahrem*) male gaze in the public, heterosocial sphere. A man would sit across from Kamile to watch her as she opened and closed her legs. She was performing a *mahrem* act, meant to be private, in public, and the man was taking advantage of its public performance. As Kamile described this incident, all three adult women present had a clear idea about the look in the harasser's eyes. Kamile mimicked the erotic pleasure of his gaze. "When it first happened, I felt so angry. . . . I was ashamed. I couldn't do anything," she explained. She initially tried to confront the situation by calling security, yet this did not seem to provide a solution. She shrugged her shoulders and added: "Then

I learned to ignore it. . . . Now I think that we do not know each other, so never mind!"

These words reveal a process in which she actively unlearned the *mahrem* borders and the feeling of privacy that comes with them. Instead of maintaining and guarding her *mahrem* borders, she began to ignore them. In the culture of *mahremiyet*—which situates males as active and penetrating, females as passive and penetrated—ignoring this penetrating foreign male gaze is not a simple act, but the ability to do so enables a woman to steal the power of penetration away from her harasser.

Kamile underwent a personal transformation evinced by her ability to ignore a significant and powerful male gaze. When she moved from Sultançiftliği, a more suburban ("rural," in her words) neighborhood, to a less suburban, more citylike, and "progressive" neighborhood, she changed her attitudes, her body movements, and her exercise routine. By using the gaze as a gauge, she evaluated her new environment and coordinated her body accordingly. She was aware of the pedagogic aspect of her environment but also of the stakes of the "ethico-aesthetics of a body's capacity for becoming" (Gregg and Seigworth 2010, 14). What I would like to highlight here is not how she evaluated the conditions in her new neighborhood or how she negotiated them but rather her creative use of all of the possibilities and options as part of her transformation and her self-formation without directly challenging the culture of *mahremiyet* and while indirectly blurring the borders within it.

Exercising in Public Parks

When women take over a park, however, the situation changes, and the culture of *mahremiyet* starts acting against male patrons, who thereby feel obliged to control their own public sexualities. They start worrying about how they will be perceived if they visit the park, ordinarily a heterosocial space. In Cumhuriyet Park in Sultançiftliği, for example, which two of my interlocutors frequented during the summer because it was financially difficult to access an indoor gym in that season, a curious spectacle took place. The photo in figure 5

5. Women's exercise often begins with a fast walk, followed by working out on the equipment. There are only two men in this photo of women walking in Cumhuriyet Park, May 21, 2012: one is walking against the stream (the man in the blue T-shirt), and the other is walking with his spouse.

was taken in Cumhuriyet Park. As it illustrates, very few male patrons come to the park simply to watch women's moving bodies or to meet women. More often, men come to exercise either with their wives or by themselves, but this is also quite rare. Thus, because of men's rare presence, it is easy to spot men who are there to ogle and who are a frequent subject of women's disdainful conversations. As such, there is a public consensus about the "intentions" of male patrons present in the park early in the morning. Women refer to the males who are in the park only to exercise—not to watch or harass women—as those with "pure, untainted intentions [*saf, temiz niyet*]."[16] Yet those with "untainted intentions" also need to demonstrate them in a public manner. I observed two strategies that a small number of men used to display their "untainted intentions," that they were in the park solely to exercise and not to watch women's moving bodies. In the figure 5

16. Focus-group interview, May 11, 2012.

photo, the gentleman with the cap walking with the lady in black had come to the park with a female relative and, facing away from the camera, walked against the stream so that women could see where he was looking. That is to say, he felt obliged to prove that he was not there to stare at women's moving bodies (from behind), and to do so he adopted this practice of facing them. In a way, he proved that women are "safe" from his gaze. One aspect of performing proper public Islamicate sexuality necessitates limiting the *mahrem* body. Another, however, necessitates limiting the penetrating gaze. This is what this retired high school teacher was doing in Cumhuriyet Park.

Conclusion

The daily techniques women use to build boundaries between themselves and the "foreign" opposite sex are pivotal elements of public sexuality and its culture of segregation. The call for a feminist investigation of women's daily gendered negotiations with respect to cross-sex relations fits nicely into Asma Afsaruddin's attention to the gap in feminist studies. Afsaruddin calls for a more diligent study, "a dispassionate, nuanced look," that does not overfocus on women's attire, which inevitably overlooks the ways women "appropriate public space and assert their presence" (1999, 14). Afsaruddin's call for a nonessentialist gender analysis is influenced in part by Lois McNay's interrogation of Foucauldian theory and feminism's nondifferentiated remarks that neglect cultural, historical, temporal, and geographic shades, which leave women's experiences "either not understood in their full complexity [or] devalued or . . . obscured altogether" (1992, 64). This problem exists in scholarship on Turkey, which includes an impressive number of studies on the issue of veiling, the head scarf, and visible Islam. Although there are significant and groundbreaking works among them, this dominant interest and obsession have obfuscated alternative probes regarding Islamicate gender practices in the public sphere and women's appropriation of public space.

Henrietta Moore (2014) refers to the awkward relationship between language and intimacy as one of intimacy's components. Recent studies show that the culture of *mahremiyet* as an institution of intimacy has an uneasy relationship with other senses. Gazing, for instance, has a physical power in this culture owing to its ability to penetrate (Sehlikoglu 2015a). Affect theory has helped us to grasp the unspoken aspects of intimacy, intimate relations, and intimate bonding in human and nonhuman life. It is equally crucial to address the systems that operate in the making of the intimate—that is, what makes the intimate intelligible. Indeed, there are multiple forms of intimacy, and it is important to recognize the distinctions between those multiple forms (Rubin 1975), including the pre-, peri-, and postlingual ones. The way the institution of intimacy operates in multiple realms of everyday Turkey suggests, as this chapter tries to demonstrate, that this awkward relationship between language and the intimate is in fact the very foundation of intimacy's public intelligibility.

Multiple factors lie behind the ways women organize their bodily movements in multiple spaces, which constitutes a multilayered process of building privacy, heterosexuality, and intimacy. These layers are established through cultural scripts (heteroerotics), structural fixations (class and religion), normative spaces, and gendered acts (Ze'evi 2006). Through analyzing women's management of their bodies in relation to public sexuality and public visibility, I have aimed to shed light on the ways selfhood, gender, and body are linked in Islamicate contexts.

Women's strict management of their bodies is connected to larger schemes, such as the culture of *mahremiyet* as it operates in various aspects of life. Women's relationship with this culture, as *mahrem* bodies in it, involves several layers of calculation and risk because of the instability and fragility of women's privacy. In this context of "approachability," women employ various techniques to avoid the instability of *mahrem* zones, often also avoiding the foreign male gaze altogether and sometimes confronting it. Thus, women reimagine, re-create, and negotiate their privacy through everyday forms of contestation. Their privacy is so fragile that at any random moment it might be made public, and they will feel violated. Their privacy can be violated not only by sexual harassment but also by any other type of harassment—including remarks on their weight gain, the shape of their arms, their height or questions about their marital status, family relationship, even reproductivity. In this context, one of the points we need to make about the culture of *mahremiyet* is that it concerns the very fabric that produces normalcy, or "comfort," defining the boundaries between private and public and illustrating the penetrability of those borders.

However, women are far from docile objects in the culture of *mahremiyet*, no matter how fragile their privacy is in its operations. Challenging the power dynamics in the culture of *mahremiyet* is possible in multiple ways. I focus elsewhere (Sehlikoglu 2015a) on headscarf-wearing cover girls in *Âlâ* magazine and on the kissing protest in Ankara and read them as daring performances of the *mahrem* that reverse the gazing/hiding dynamics in the culture of *mahremiyet*. Daring *mahrem*, I argue, takes the penetrative power away from the non*mahrem* gaze, stealing its masculine position and leaving it impotent, disabled, and eunuch. The daring *mahrem* not only underlines the masculine position of the foreign male gaze but also publicly averts the gender binary and pushes it to the end of this very spectrum.

The outdoor exercises performed by women who seek comfort do not necessarily become an act of daring *mahrem* or immediately challenge gazing/hiding dynamics so immediately. However, they work in subtle ways even as they do not risk the fragility of women's privacy. Instead, they loosen and stretch the borders. As Kamile's case demonstrates, by taking arbitrary risks, women exhibit agentive responses and often create ruptures in this culture. The rupture is even more visible in the case of Cumhuriyet Park, where women have reversed the power dynamics of *mahremiyet* by "taking over" the park. As such, *mahremiyet* operates in their favor. Although women may not be taking bold risks or directly challenging or resisting existing systems as they avoid random violations of their privacy, they nevertheless test the limits of the culture of *mahremiyet* and negotiate these boundaries.[17]

***

17. Although my interlocutors were not activist feminists, their everyday negotiations regarding the fragility of their privacy spoke to the frequent antiharassment

They indirectly change the dynamics when they ignore the power of the male gaze or when they take over a park during a certain time each day. This argument, in fact, parallels the conclusions of recent work focusing on homosociality and women's agency in other Middle Eastern contexts, such as Iran (Shahrokni 2014) and Saudi Arabia (Le Renard 2011, 2014).

An analysis of Istanbulite women's self-control and of their bodily movements in public spaces provides us with a perspective on how these movements are, in fact, parts of a multilayered process of building privacy, heterosexuality, and intimacy. I have argued that the demand for privacy (*mahremiyet*) has created regulated spaces and institutions that have elements of intimacy. At one level, Istanbulite women's concerns and demands for segregation shed light on discussions in social studies about Muslim women's visibilities, modesty concerns, dress codes, and public sexuality. Different forms of modesty are established in the community through various techniques (Antoun 1968; Werbner 2007), including veiling, segregation, language, and behaviors such as using only certain body language, sitting and walking in certain ways, laughing appropriately, and having a certain posture. These techniques are related to the ways *mahremiyet* is defined, made, and remade in daily life as part of what Berlant terms "institutions of intimacy" (1998, 281). Such a perspective is particularly crucial in developing conceptual tools to identify the ways normalcies are created and reinforced through institutions of intimacy, which extend beyond female-bodied persons (Zengin 2011) and may also include young or gay men (Özbay 2010). It also contributes to an important recognition of similarities with other, non-Islamicate institutions of intimacy (Lazaridis 1995; Agathangelou 2004).

Finally, it is no surprise that the intimate is able to manifest itself across multiple realms of everyday life, political and social alike. In her

---

campaigns in Istanbul. One example is the dispute in 2005 over the term *müsait* (available), translated in the official Turkish-language dictionary as describing "[the woman] who readily goes out or flirts."

groundbreaking work *The Erotic Vatan* [*Homeland*] *as Beloved and Mother* (1997), Afsaneh Najmabadi demonstrates how national communal bonds are established through domestic and familial norms and through the desires attributed to those norms. In a similar vein, Joane Nagel (1998) shows how the nation and the modern state can implicate subjects through masculine, emotive attachments. In this understanding, intimacy is entangled with boundaries, privacies, proximities, insiders, outsiders, and secrecies. It constantly shifts, formulates, and reformulates itself.

6

Homosociality and the Female Gaze

I arrived at Hamza Yerlikaya Sports Center at 12:00 p.m. as four women from the morning session were leaving. Three of them, all wearing head scarves, walked past me. We smiled at each other. I tried to remember whether they were related (no, they were not.) The fourth one, the one with pale bleached hair (I had come to learn that the color is called "onion peel"), was smoking a cigarette in the parking lot. She did not seem to be in the mood for socializing, so I entered the building without speaking to her. As I walked into the triplex compound with fitness rooms, Pilates studio, and tennis, football, and basketball courts, I first saw the information desk right across to the entrance. Both receptionists were occupied, so I walked past them and entered the corridor on the left behind the desk. They had known me for a while, so they were no longer asking for my membership card. I passed the playroom to the left of the corridor, where the staff member Selda was playing with a girl with curly hair, around five, probably the daughter of one of the members. Selda noticed me immediately and quickly greeted me with her usual big smile. "Such a friendly spirit," I thought. The women's *mescit* (*masjid*, prayer room) was toward the end of the corridor, before the stairs. It barely fit six people. The door ajar, I could see the two people in the room. It was not quite *namaz vakti* (prayer time) yet, so it was appropriate to stop by to have a chat. Inside Hazine Abla was speaking with another woman whose face was familiar but whose name I could not remember. Hazine Abla was cheerful as always. They were speaking about the other woman's free appointment with the gym's nutritionist. She had her blood count from the public hospital with her. Arranging this lab work and the appointment with the nutritionist had taken so much time. I am always impressed with these women's skill in handling bureaucracy. The process sounded like so much work just to come up with a beneficial diet.

I left them after a few minutes and start climbing the stairs to the women-only section. One level up, there were two doors. One opened directly to the fitness room and is always locked during women's hours. I had seen it unlocked only once, when the vice principle Serkan was giving me a tour back in July, during men's hours.

During women's hours, entrance could be gained only from downstairs and those doors open directly to the changing room. The single entrance ensured discipline and control. Free-hour members were obliged to follow certain rules, such as queuing up and bringing training shoes that had not been worn outside (the bottoms of the shoes were regularly checked).

The changing room quickly got crowded as I took off my scarf and put it in the locker with my bag and boots. I found myself in the middle of a conversation about the swimming pool. Women at Hamza Yerlikaya had been waiting for the pool to open for two years. As I was changing, Hazine entered the locker room and immediately started taking the names of the women in order of arrival. The fitness room was not yet open, so the list would help the trainers usher the members through in the correct order. Women had already queued up, so Hazine's task was not too difficult. I did not have to get into the queue because, as everyone knew, I was there to do research. Although I didn't queue, I could still join the conversations because everyone was in earshot.

One of the women, who looked to be in her early thirties, had had her contraceptive coil removed before she came to the gym. Her husband was not in the city, so it seemed to be the best time to take care of this, she explained. Such topics were perfect for this type of homosocial space: an intimate topic but a shared or relatable experience. Everyone seemed to be eager to comment on it. Some of the comments were witty. A woman in her late forties elicited everyone's laughter with "Don't get too close to me. [If you don't have a coil today,] one can never predict what I will do to you [benim ne yapacağım belli olmaz], God forbid." "You might get pregnant" was what she was implying. Laughter at such (homo)erotic jokes was always stronger. I checked for disapproving faces but saw none. I was glad. Some of the comments were more serious and caring: "You should not have come to do sport right after the coil was removed. You will bleed more." To which the woman whose coil was removed responded, "My bleeding is not heavy; it should not be a problem," and "I can easily work out lightly, so that I won't be registered absent." Women would lose their free membership if they were absent two consecutive times or three times during an eight-week period.

In the middle of the conversations, the doors to the fitness room opened, and we flooded in. Five women at the top of Hazine's list moved to the treadmills. The free fitness hours were quite busy during cold days, so members had a maximum of ten minutes to run on a treadmill during these hours.

Space of Screening

Trainer Fatma was standing by her desk, screening women as we walked in. She must have been using the darkest black color available in the market to dye her short hair. Her facial features, bony jaw, and flat cheeks helped her maintain a serious authoritative look. One of her eyebrows was always raised as she talked to the members. She yelled at the crowd to stay on line and check their shoes. Her voice was as sharp as her looks. She seemed to enjoy keeping members disciplined. Following the gym policy, one of her duties was to police women's "progress."

Each member has her own personalized workout plan. The workout plans are not too different from one another. Each starts with a quick cardio and includes a combination of strength and cardio exercises. Members are measured regularly on a scale that prints out weight, height, and body-fat percentage. All of these statistics are written down on the chart with the fitness plan. Women can see their progress on the charts.[1]

The screening shapes women's relationship with one another as well. In the gyms and in the changing rooms, where most conversations take place, two members will usually initiate a conversation with the following two questions: "How long have you been coming here?" and "How many kilos have you lost?" After this initial interaction, the women converse about the classes they are enrolled in, which leads to the popular discussion of whether Pilates or step aerobics or fitness training is the most *verimli* (efficient) form of exercise. Efficiency is not simply about losing weight. It has multiple aspects. Can one stick to the exercise regime after the first few weeks? Is the weight loss hard to maintain? Does it affect appetite? "My sister-in-law did fitness for a few months. She lost several kilos. But then as soon as she stopped exercising, she regained all the weight, with a few extra."

In the early weeks of my fieldwork, I used to assume that these two opening questions reflected an obsession with weight loss. There is a feminist consciousness against aesthetic standards of beauty, and encountering such standards in the field after first reading about them in the literature conditions one's gaze, almost like the "tourist gaze" in John Urry's (1990) famous work.

The dominant public perspective on exercising women in Turkey is that women must be exercising to lose weight and to battle the curvy look they must despise. As soon as I tell people in Turkey that I am doing research on exercising women, they immediately start speaking about such women in terms of failure and futile effort. They tell me how these particular women, the sporty aunties, take back in all the calories they burn with postexercise tea parties featuring nice Turkish *poğaça* (dough pie), *börek* (layered pie), and cakes. According to this popular view, the women's main concern in exercising must be to lose weight, yet they are also incompetent in achieving this goal and prone to failure. Another assumption underlying here

1. I still keep my own chart from the fieldwork I did.

is that women's aesthetic concerns are immediately linked to the standards of beauty that centralize the heterosexual male gaze and male desire.

Isn't it too easy, however, to trivialize women's position by asserting that they both monitor their weight-loss trends and are reluctant to discipline themselves and push their limits? As the extended ethnographic fieldwork reveals, women have more complex ways of engaging with themselves and with the world. The masculinist perspectives and the androgenic gaze are among the many norms women navigate—and aren't necessarily the main or central ones, either.

Women are sometimes indeed reluctant to push their limits. Months pass, and neither the women's weight nor these two questions change. They do keep having conversations about easy weight-loss recipes and asking each other about their "progress."

During the course of my fieldwork, as I became more attuned, I came to understand the actual concern underlying those conversations, which was a shared disbelief about the beauty norms. Skinny bodies are everywhere: on billboards, on TV, in newspapers. Skinny, fit bodies are presented to women as the *ideal* in the culture of aesthetics. My interlocutors, however, questioned whether such bodies are beautiful in real life and if it is even possible to become that skinny without expensive treatments. Women speak about weight loss not because they are determined to lose weight. Rather, they seek confirmation that such a goal is neither ideal nor possible. Their relationship with the existing popular and normative discourses, including norms of aesthetics, are worked on, tested, renegotiated with, in homosocial spaces, where they are freed from the male gaze. This chapter provides a lens to view the ways women use homosociality in an intersubjective desiring self-formation. What is the role of female intersubjectivity in this process? How do women tailor their desires and desiring selves? What is the effect of homosociality in this process?

Homosociality I: Shared Concerns

Gül Hanım was a forty-one-year old professional businesswoman who had two children. She had a confident, educated, warm vibe about her. She was slimmer than most women her age in Turkey, although she could hardly be called skinny. Because of her busy work schedule, Gül Hanım still attended both mixed and women-only gyms that were within walking distance of her house. She and I talked about both types of gyms, and at one point she explained to me how she felt about women-only gyms:

GÜL: Because, when a man looks at you, he should only say, "What a nice woman!" However, a man sees you in the gym when you are making that effort. I don't think that it's pleasant; it has a negative effect. The whole messy mystery disappears.

SERTAÇ: What do you mean by "messy mystery"?

GÜL: For instance, when I dye my hair, I wouldn't want my husband to see me. It's just like that. I mean, he needs to see the finished product, not the whole effort when I am trying to burn calories and sweat and stink. He shouldn't know all that! Yes, I may have to go through it, but you don't need to see it. Women should be like flowers, smell nice. It's not nice for a woman to stink.

SERTAÇ: You mean like waxing legs.

GÜL: Yes, like waxing legs. Men should remain ignorant about a process that is ugly.[2]

The "mystery" Gül Hanım was referring to is an overlap between the Islamicate culture of *mahremiyet* (privacy, intimacy, discussed in chapter 5) that calls for hiding the *mahrem* (passive/female) side of the gender binary. The effort, the ugly part of achieving this beauty (the sweat, the smell, and the exhaustion), should remain hidden from whoever is considered to be the most distant—in this case, the male person.

In Gül Hanım's description, there is also a reference to the norm that female aesthetics are achieved through effort, whether by putting

2. Interview, Dec. 21, 2011.

on makeup, waxing, wearing heels, or sweating. It is also taken for granted that the result is meant for the woman's significant other, her heterosexual partner. I then asked, "How about the women working out near you?" To this, she responded, "Other women are not a problem since we share the same problems. We all try to lose weight and have smaller hips." She looked happy with her analysis, paused, thought for a few seconds, then added, "The women [working out] near you are your *dert ortağı* [confidants]; both of you are there for the same reason."

It is impetuous to suggest that women are *dert ortağı*, which literally means "fellow sufferers," as Gül Hanım proposed, and their shared concern is not suffering. Women's reasons for going to the gym vary, and even when weight loss or back ache repetitively pop up as topics of conversation, the way women approach such questions are too complex to lump them all under the category of "shared suffering."

One particular aspect of Gül Hanım's account is valid for almost all the women I met, however. It is true that the sort of privacy acquired through homosociality is comforting for women.

This comfort is mostly about the casual outfits women can wear at the gyms. The women in the gyms where I conducted my fieldwork were not as glamorous, as fit, or as fashionable in brand-name gym outfits as the women (and men) I saw in my London gym.[3] There were women like Feray Teyze, who wore a thermosuit to burn the body fat and calories faster but looked quite uncomfortable and not very feminine or attractive in it. Both in Hamza Yerlikaya Sports Center and in the Yeşilvadi gym alike, despite the fact that they attract women from two different socioeconomic classes, the women I met often wore the simplest and the most inexpensive tights and T-shirts. They looked plain and simple in contrast to their appearance in public,

3. Or compared to the women (and men) in the gyms I went to earlier in Toronto (2009–10) and Montreal (2007–9).

where they wore more fashionable clothes. Gül Hanım's reference to "being confidants" explains this casualness. Yet women also wanted to hide their "flaws" from their confidants. Feray Teyze, like a couple of other women of her age (older than forty-five), also wore a bonnet to cover her hair in the gym. Women did not keep the bonnet on for religious purposes, obviously, because religion does not dictate the wearing of a head scarf in the presence of other women. The bonnet was kept on to cover "bad hair": unstyled, gray, short, and not nice looking.

Removing the male gaze immediately establishes a sense of proximity among women. The proximity at stake is not homogenous, however.

Then how does homosociality operate if it does not bond women as confidants? This question is more related to how women actively use homosociality while they share the same space. Rather than using this homosocial space to transform their bodies into the ideals with which they are bombarded, women used it to find alternative, more realistic reference points. It is regarded and treated as a space where all the fakeness is removed: no heels, no makeup, no push-up bras, no tight outfits.

Homosociality II: Not the Ideal but the Possible

From the first week of my presence at Hamza Yerlikaya, I kept hearing women questioning those members of average weight, "Why do you come here?"—emphasizing *you* with their hands (not simply with their eyes) and gesturing toward the other woman's body. Sometimes the question was followed by further interrogation: "You do not have any reason to!" These conversations were sometimes posed as a compliment but often reflected discomfort at seeing a slimmer body at the gym. A slimmer body worked against a supportive relationship between the confidants.

I was interviewing Dürdane, a twenty-eight-year-old single dentist, at a coffee, tea, and *nargile* (*shisha*, waterpipe) shop in Fatih, and she mentioned how women do not seem to like skinny women at the gyms. I said, "It is almost as if the other women want to harass the slim women." Dürdane responded immediately with her big smile and wide-open eyes while hitting her hand on the table to confirm my discovery, "Of course they should not come! I do not want to see them there! These women totally break my enthusiasm [*şevkimi kırıyorlar*]." I was confused: "But you said that you also like Ebru Şallı. Doesn't she break your enthusiasm?" "Well," Dürdane answered, "[her standards] are up in the sky anyway [*o uçmuş zaten*]."[4]

In her exercise efforts, Dürdane was not aiming for the body of former fashion model Ebru Şallı, for two main reasons. First, as she put it, Şallı's beauty and fitness standards are unrealistically high and thus difficult to achieve. Women constantly question whether her beauty is *yapma*, "made" or "human-made" as opposed to natural, referring to probable plastic surgeries. More importantly, women question whether what looks beautiful on TV is beautiful in real life. Şallı must be "skin on bones [*bir deri bir kemik*] to look like that on TV," Dürdane explained to me. Unrealistic beauty standards were repeatedly mentioned in the gyms, locker rooms, and Pilates sessions. Disbelief in Şallı's ideal look became a topic of conversation with women especially after I visited and interviewed Şallı.

The media bombard women with images of the idealized bodies of models and soap opera stars as well as with continuous medical and nonmedical tips for health and beauty (see Chapter 5). Women-only gyms provide an ideal homosocial sphere to confirm, reject, or alter this information, turning this space into a borderscape. Women use homosociality to compare the *ideal* images with the *possible* ones, and the female gaze in that sphere enables a particular, desirable, and approachable self-imagination.

Many women, like Dürdane, go to the gym to find alternative and achievable options. They then compare the images presented to them through the media as "possible" and even "ideal," such as Şallı's abs, with the abs and tummies of the actual women they meet at the gym and in changing rooms.

4. Interview, Jan. 26, 2012.

These are the places where personal boundaries fade away and become porous and create a type of intimacy and privacy particular to that entry point. Thus, women carry publicly available perspectives about femininity, embodiment, health, exercise, and all the trends and tips related to them to this homosocial sphere and evaluate them privately, through the porous borders between one another, in an attempt to unveil the mystery about the desired look.

Homosociality III: Changing Rooms as Borderscapes

In feminist studies, women's homosocial spaces are discussed mostly in relation to liberation, with the argument that women open up space in order to free themselves from male dominance, especially in non-Western geographies (English 2004). Yet I suggest a more complicated picture here because although women are freed from male dominance in homosocial spaces, these spaces also offer a particular kind of normative bonding. The changing rooms can be better understood as a borderscape, first mentioned by Michel Foucault in his discussion of heterotopias that are relational and always under process. Heterotopias are spaces that function in nonhegemonic conditions. As the term suggests (*hetero* = an other, *topias* = place), heterotopias are where the physicality of the space triggers a temporal mental otherness. Foucault develops the concept from the notion of utopias: "Because they are utterly different from all the emplacements that they reflect or refer to, I shall call these places 'heterotopias,' as opposed to utopias; and I think that between utopias and these utterly different emplacements, these heterotopias, there must be a kind of mixed, intermediate experience, that would be the mirror" (1994, 178–79).

The image in the mirror, Foucault describes, is a "placeless place"; it is unreal but provides a tool to observe oneself. In this example, the image reflected in the mirror is utopia, but the mirror itself is heterotopia. The mirror, hence the heterotopia, is a tangible real object/space, whereas the image it reflects is virtual and intangible and unreal. This framework provides a conceptual space that contrasts with the spaces in everyday life. The formulation of heterotopia has been useful in theorizing space and modernization (Soja 1989; Sibley 2002; Bauman 2013), especially in works on museums (Hetherington 1995, 2011; Trodd 2003; Lord 2006) and the virtual (McNamee 2000; Morley 2003; Boellstorff 2015).

Gym changing rooms fit into Foucault's fifth principle of heterotopia: heterotopias "always presuppose a system of opening and closing that both isolates them and makes them penetrable" (Foucault 1986, 26). In the search for an intersubjective sphere of femininity, changing rooms appear to be the setting for the most dynamic interactions. They are borderscapes in Foucault's sense.

Borderscapes are entry points—transitionary, relational spaces (Foucault 1986)—that women pass through and where they form only temporary relationships with each other. In the same-sex space, women are isolated from mixed-gender public spaces, and in this isolation the boundaries between them become penetrable. This homosocial environment "is not freely accessible like a public place" (Foucault 1986, 26).

As entry points to the gyms, the changing rooms have a more complex position where several normative boundaries, including the ones established among female bodies, are troubled and blurred temporarily.

The interaction between women in the changing room is both verbal and nonverbal. Women encounter curious looks in the changing room. In a way, women are curious to see and become able to compare several things: a woman's appearance inside the gym, her appearance in the changing room, her appearance outside the gym, and her changing body (parts) over several weeks of working out. In other words, women evaluate each other with reference to a heterosexual aesthetic culture. In order to do this, they use the male gaze as a reference, which they inhabit through various media. Then they also compare the things they see with their own bodies, with the help of the multiple mirrors throughout the gym that reflect their own bodies and enable a comparison.

6. The trainer Fatma posing for the author in the Hamza Yerlikaya Sports Center and reflected in the mirrors in front of and near her, May 22, 2012.

7. The fitness room in Hamza Yerlikaya Sports Center, May 22, 2012. You can see the mirrors on the columns and on the walls, all reflecting the environment at multiple angles.

Homosociality IV: Female Gaze and Desire

The relationship between the gaze and desire is a long-established one, although the workings of this relationship has been the source of contention. The female gaze often appears in sociology, anthropology, cultural studies, and especially literature and media studies when women viewers or spectators are being analyzed (Gamman and Marshment 1989; Morales-Diaz 2002; Doane 2004; Schauer 2005; Larsson 2011; Salamandra 2012). Yet few works seem to have done justice to the significance of the female gaze as a form of communication among women, even despite the pronounced position of both gaze and the female gaze in contexts such as Turkey, the Middle East, and North Africa.

In one of the few attempts to locate the gaze (in general) in the debates on subjectivity, Cassandra Lorius (1996) evaluates the link between desire, the gaze, and the gendered body in the context of Egypt. She argues that it is equally important to look at media depictions of women as objects of desire (*shahwa*), depictions that are particularly denigrated by those who argue for a return to "Islamic values" (1996, 515).

The female gaze in the changing rooms brings out the complex processes of desiring in self-making. It signifies female intersubjectivity and manifests a specific kind of object of knowledge. The convoluted dynamics of gazing at women-only gyms are far more entangled than a simple performance between spectator and performer.

At the gyms, women check their own and each other's bodies from multiple angles and in various movements, as reflected in the dozens of mirrors affixed to the walls and columns. On a treadmill in Hamza Yerlikaya, for instance, just by looking at a mirror directly in front of her, a woman can see herself, her fellow users of the treadmills, the trainers as they walk around the gym, and anyone working out behind them and entering the gym from the front door. If she turns her head slightly to the right, then she can watch how her (and her fellow treadmill users') hips look during the workout. The multiplicity and vibrancy of the gazing relationship are enhanced by the mutuality. Screening each other's bodies is a central aspect of homosocial interactions at the gyms, and catching another woman's gaze in the mirror in the act of looking initiates conversations between women once they catch each other looking at the same person. These tangled female gazes play a central role in self-objectification.

The Female Gaze: Hide and Seek, Make and Be Made

Gaze and gazing have been so significant not only in Turkey but also in the broader region of the Middle East and North Africa that they often immediately intrigue foreigners when they first encounter them (see Chapter 5). Gaze has also been an object of fascination among authors and artists, some of whom capture the significance of gaze better than many ethnographic accounts. For instance, in her novel *The Gaze* (2012), Elif Shafak narrates the power of looking by telling the story of a dwarf and a fat lady who are lovers, and she carefully defines the power of looking as something that constructs bodies, desires, and selves. When the obese woman and the very short man flout the aesthetic norms imposed on their genders, they are the constant objects of staring looks. Gazing signifies bodies in the novel, a burden for some and a salvation for others.

The power of gaze and gazing is inflicted by any mechanism and institution of power. Therefore, it is, among other things, gendered. My interlocutors, like many women in Turkey, were aware of the power of both other women's gaze and their own. In a homosocial environment, this awareness puts women's bodies in the middle of a tension, where they both safely screen each other's bodies and simultaneously avoid exposure. The sort of exposure they avoid is more comprehensive than the exposure that requires the covering of private parts in that they also learn what their "flaws" are and whether they really need to hide or eliminate such "flaws" or simply ignore the norms about them.

Tuba, a skinny and tall nineteen-year-old woman, was telling me about her resentment when a couple of women at the gym pointed at her tummy.

TUBA: They told me a few times that I don't have to come [to the gym]. And just as I was feeling good about my looks, they make a comment about my tummy. Like they point out [my body] and say, "Except with that tummy."

SERTAÇ: What about your tummy?

TUBA: It is big for my body and loose [in shape]. . . . So now I always tuck my T-shirt in [so that women won't see it].[5]

Tuba also changed very carefully so as not to expose her tummy as a habit. She turned her back to the other women and pulled on one shirt while pulling off the other. Because of another woman's comment, she became aware of her "too big" tummy, and although she did not do any specific workout to change its shape, she learned to hide it from other women in order to avoid negative comments.

This self-consciousness didn't last long. About three months after the interview, she started ignoring the criticism.

Other women at the gyms were not very different from Tuba. Many of them lived nearby, and the idea of taking a shower in a public homosocial space was not very appealing, owing to both (hyper) hygiene and modesty principles they follow. At Hamza Yerlikaya, because many of the women lived within walking distance of the gym, they preferred to wear sweatpants and simple T-shirts (under their overcoats if they also wore a head scarf) during winter and to replace the sweaty shirts with clean ones after they exercised. If they needed to change all of their clothes, they never did it in the presence of other women. Everyone was aware of the prying female gaze. However, it was not very easy to change in privacy when there were no cubicles to do so, which was the case in Hamza Yerlikaya. The women's solution to this problem was either to find a corner or use the doors of two lockers as a temporary cubicle or change while their clothes were still on: putting on a skirt and then removing the sweatpants underneath or changing a bra while still wearing the T-shirt, and so on. The gyms

5. Interview, Jan. 8, 2012.

8. The changing corner in B-Fit Bulgurlu, 2012. The
blinds on the windows behind the room divider are shut.

converted from apartments have corners with curtains or separators
for privacy (figure 7).[6]

Another aspect of this tension is related to the fact that the curious female gaze is always mutual in the sense that it encapsulates both
the self and the other. One of the theories in this regard that comes

6. Changing in the showers is also an option, but owing to hygiene regulations
at Hamza Yerlikaya, members are obliged to put disposable blue galoshes on their feet
when entering the showers, which complicates the process and therefore is avoided.

to mind immediately is Maurice Merleau-Ponty's. His work is often used to signify the relation between the objective world and the experienced world through phenomenology. In order to see, one's body should be part of the visible. Further, he theorizes the relational gaze. He famously states, "When my gaze meets another gaze, I re-enact the alien existence in a sort of reflection" (1945, 410). Merleau-Ponty captures the mutuality and the dynamic aspect of the female gaze in referring to gaze as a reflexive relational object that bonds (female) bodies to one another.

The way the female gaze operates in the homosocial setting and in such close proximity also shares parallels with Merleau-Ponty's reflexive relational gaze. The female gaze becomes the reflexive tool for intersubjective relating, and it relates female bodies to each other at the gyms as well as in changing rooms. Therefore, when one woman, Züleyha, screened another woman, Nur, and commented on Nur's body ("Your body is quite clean of hair"), she in fact was not evaluating Nur's body solely on aesthetic standards established by heterosexual culture but was also comparing what she saw of her own body, gaining permission to do so from the intimate aspect of that homosocial sphere. Züleyha's comment on Nur's hair-free body (arms), therefore, was not necessarily about Nur but about Züleyha's own body.

In her ethnographically rich work on health and fitness culture in Japan, Laura Spielvogel looks at the tension between "the grounded practices of the club and the larger constructions of beauty, health and leisure" (2003, 6). Her work exemplifies the ways in which the culture of aesthetics and health operates in the larger society and the fitness culture disciplines bodies toward appropriating a certain body image. In a striking example, Spielvogel traces how Japanese women shape their legs by wrapping them with heavy rubber to sweat and make them slimmer. Spielvogel's example convincingly points to the local cultural aspects of the normative female body in that these women are concentrating on their legs because they are considered heavy by Japanese standards, though not by European standards. As Spielvogel cogently illustrates, Tokyo fitness centers provide an excellent area to utilize Foucauldian approaches to power, discipline, and the panopticon (2003, 61–86), yet his approach is hardly enough to understand the women-only gyms in Istanbul.

In the context of women-only gyms in Istanbul, the contribution of women's homosocial interactions toward the making of their selves and their desiring selves is crucial. Homosocial interactions take place both verbally and sensually (through the female gaze), often at the same time.

Esma: Between the Ideal and the Mediocre

So what happens when a woman refuses to follow the unspoken codes of hiding? I would never have asked this question if I had not noticed the interesting case of Esma, a forty-year-old single woman who became the subject not only of the female gaze in the changing rooms because of her appearance but also of conversations among those who were trying to figure out her fitness secret. She was a puzzling and tempting subject in this homosocial setting, and I was not aware that Sena and her gym buddy Tuba were talking about her when I asked them about their first day at the gym:

> TUBA: We had a shock on our first day there already: someone took a shower and took off her clothes!
>
> SERTAÇ: I don't understand. You mean, naked?
>
> TUBA: Well, with just a towel! Or in bra and briefs! [Laughter] . . . Everybody freezes when this woman leaves [the shower to go to the changing room]. Everyone turns her head toward her. They all whisper to each other, "Oh look, look!" [Tuba overacted how women raise their eyebrows and touch their friends with their elbows to point to the woman they are referring to.] . . .
>
> SERTAÇ: You mean women point at her? [They laughed and nodded their heads.]
>
> SENA: When a woman leaves [the shower and enters the changing room] looking like that, they all do that and stare. You know,

she leaves and dries her hair, and women line up and watch her drying her hair.[7]

Moments similar to the one Sena and Tuba described took place when I was in the changing rooms. Women did not watch Esma just as a spectacle. At those moments, the female gaze also became a tool for reflexivity. Looking at other women's bodies is often immediately followed by looking back at one's own.

Homosociality allows women to evaluate the actuality, the reality, of the "idealized" imagery available in the media. It enables an intimate encounter among women to clarify the new feminine bodily aspirations. Women-only gyms, their changing rooms, and even baby showers and tea parties operate as spheres to transcribe, appropriate, evaluate, and therefore actively translate the desires women are bombarded with. In their minds, as Züleyha once put it brilliantly, "women at the gym are more real than the women on the screen."[8] In this context, unlike the women seen on TV, Esma was not a media-imposed ideal. She was a real and achievable ideal.

Esma was aware of the female gaze directed at her and saw herself as one of the most accomplished attendants of the gym. Her resistance to the norm of hiding (her body) turned her into a medium, a reference point between the ideal and the possible, because she left less room for the "mystery" or the secret of her fitness. She explained to me how women wanted to become like her (*özeniyor*) and admired her (*beğeniyor*). She responded to these desires by informing them about what they saw as her "secrets":

> Women in here chat a lot. I see them, and their only worry is to lose weight. They say, "I haven't lost a bit," "I haven't lost a single kilo." And they *içiyorlar* [take and drink] all sorts of things to achieve that. I sometimes approach them and tell them they do it all wrong.

7. Field notes, Jan. 25, 2012.
8. Field notes, casual conversation, Feb. 17, 2012.

I warn them when they exercise wrong. I do this because I have prior knowledge and experience in sport. I used to do sport during the time I used to work. . . . I warn them and tell them how to exercise. They sometimes thank me and then say things like, "For how long have you been doing sport?" "I really admire you," "You are very passionate and never give up."[9]

Yet despite her willingness to inform women and her reluctance to hide her body, the other women talked about Esma as if she were someone who held a secret. Several women were amazed by her performance on the treadmill, where she was able to run faster, work out harder, and sweat more than most of them. Because she revealed more than enough of her body and performed too well to be true, I often caught women talking about the plastic water bottle she kept sipping from: "What does she have in it?" For about six months, she was using a transparent bottle (then I gave her a pink metal one) that revealed the color of her drink, which was yellow. Some believed the "secret" of her performance and fitness was in the plastic bottle, which, in their words, "she claims to be green tea" (highlighting the suspicion that it might well be a secret recipe rather than a simple green tea). Although the other women admired Esma, much as they admired famous women on TV, she was more approachable both in terms of her beauty standards (she was not skinny and did not follow any expensive recipes for her causal fit look) and in terms of being in close proximity at the gym and in the changing rooms. All of these factors made Esma the object of the female gaze. However, the female gaze operates to see the possible, and Esma's performance and fitness looked less possible, which put her in a difficult, puzzling, and perplexing position in the eyes of the other women.

Conclusion

An increasing number of ethnographic studies in the past decade have focused on women's exercise activities worldwide and have explored

9. Interview, Jan. 5, 2012.

themes as diverse as self-sculpting through discipline (Kohn 2008), self-asserting discourses (Mîndruṭ 2006), prenatal fitness and post-modern pregnancy (Nash 2012a, 2012b), and social capital and net-works (Crossley 2008). As a crucial methodological inquiry, a series of works have been published on ethnography and exercise (Bolin and Granskog 2003a, 2003b; Bolin 2009). Another related stream of research has focused on global exercise trends (Leshkowich 2008); the formation and proliferation of gym cultures in both Western cul-tures (Joseph Maguire 1993; Hedblom 2009; Boris and Parreñas 2010) and non-Western cultures, especially in Asia (Horne 2000; Edwards 2003; Spielvogel 2003; Ng 2005; Miller 2006; Rickman and Nauright 2007); the consumption and capitalism in fitness indus-tries (Edwards 2003; J. S. Maguire 2007); global gym brands in the making of standards of aesthetics (Savacool 2009); and the politi-cal critique of body size (Gremillion 2005; Grabe, Ward, and Hyde 2008). In this chapter, I explored ethnographic moments of homoso-ciality as a space where women refashion and reconstruct themselves intersubjectively. I focused on how individuals reimagine themselves in relation to others, how they have aspirations and hopes that go beyond changing their bodies and images, and how their exercise sig-nifies a resetting of horizons and a quest for self-making to navigate new aspirations.

Women-only gyms have the dual property of being both hetero-sexually private (concealing bodies and making them invisible to the male gaze) and homosocially public. In other words, women's bodies are freed from the penetrative power of the male gaze (chapter 5). The male cleaners, if there are any, are never allowed in during the women's workout hours. There are no CCTV monitors that can be screened by male security guards. The windows either have blinds or are covered with a film that blocks the view from outside. The foreign male gaze is obstructed, which brings comfort but not necessarily lib-eration or emancipation from male dominance.

Patriarchal ideologies, including the norms of aesthetics, do not stop objectifying women's bodies once men are removed from the picture. It is also important to remember that women engage in *spor meraki* not because doing so immediately confirms or wholly undoes any normative accounts of aesthetics. They do so because they are searching for the light between the cracks. The multiple and even sometimes contrasting patriarchal ideologies are studied, compared, challenged, learned, relearned, and unlearned in the homosocial public space—a space in which the aesthetics of fitness is expected to be central.

What dominates the changing-room atmosphere is a *search* for consensus on an alternative average—and achievable—body, beauty, and health. There are times when this search also means a search for affirmation. The conversations are always loaded with information, personal secrets, medical tips, and the trendy products that women have heard to be useful for weight loss, back pain, or smaller hips. In the first couple of weeks of my fieldwork, I found this highly panoptic comparative interaction disturbingly "result oriented," as if women were going to the gym only to lose weight and were calculating efficiency based on each other's changes. The interactions and conversations we had over almost a year revealed, however, not only that they wanted to cross-check the norms imposed on them via popular culture but also that they had established their own norms in these women-only spaces through processes of female intersubjectivity.

Time

7

Embodied Rhythms and Self-Time

It was a cold winter day in Istanbul. I was following Nazan, a house-wife in her early forties married to a car mechanic in the lower-class Istanbul suburb of Pendik. She had wrapped her neck tightly in a knitted scarf to protect her throat from the cold, her dark yet graying hair tied in a ponytail. I would have preferred to meet with her a bit earlier, but her morning routine did not allowed us do it, so we met at 10:30 by the corner of her house, near the park. We hugged and started walking to the center while telling each other what we did that morning. I complained about how I had to take multiple buses from Üsküdar to arrive in Pendik on time. She found my dreadful public-transportation story more interesting than hers. What she did that morning, in her words, was "not different than any other day." She then quickly summarized in a monotone and with a tired face how she woke up early to set up breakfast for her children, then for her husband. She rolled her eyes when she said that she even had a chance to complete some minor household cleaning after she said good-bye to her husband and tidied the breakfast table.

Our walk to the municipal training center took only thirteen minutes. The building looked like an old school or hospital—sim-ple, ugly, and concrete. It was cold, damp, and windy outside and slightly warmer inside. We went downstairs, where the step-aerobics class Nazan attended took place twice a week at 11:00 a.m. There was a separator just in front of the door to the exercise room so that women inside would not be seen even when the door was open. We were about fifteen minutes early to class, so it was not crowded yet. We took off our outdoor shoes—just as we did when entering houses, a custom of cleanliness observed in mosques and the majority of Turkish households—and put on clean sneakers.

The room was a basement with narrow windows, laminate floors, and one wall entirely covered with mirrors. Later on, I also noted how poorly ventilated this room was. The municipal training centers were not initially designed for exercise sessions. The room we were about to start working out in was converted from a classroom used to teach adults language skills, crafts, or skills for employment. Before joining trainer Filiz's step-aerobics class, Nazan had experimented with a couple of the other classes offered there. She enjoyed the fun in step-aerobics classes.

We found a spot somewhere in the middle of the room and spread out the mats we had picked from the pile. I talked to Filiz until the class began—it was she who had first introduced me to Nazan—while Nazan was socializing with other members coming in.

And the Drumming Begins

When the clock hit 11:00 a.m., there were twenty-six women in the room, including me and the trainer. Filiz took attendance and marked six women absent. Twenty-four Istanbulite women, including twenty-one housewives and three retired career women, all between the ages of thirty and sixty-three, would soon begin exercising in their tights and T-shirts as they faced the room's sole mirrored wall. Filiz started directing her trainees in a sharp, strong voice, reminding me of a military commander.[1]

> Breathe in, out!
> Right, hop!
> Breathe out! Tem-po!
> Hop, two! Arms up!

1. For an example of this military-commander style of leading an exercise session, see the video I recorded in another class by Filiz at http://youtu.be/6XcjIj5 _Nqw (Sehlikoglu 2013b).

Breathe in!! Breathe out!
The trainer claps her hands as she watches the class.
Yes, breathe out!
Arms up! Right! Left!
*The drumming of footsteps is heard as the music slows down
    before the next song.*[2]

The temperature inside was getting hotter and hotter, while outside the temperature was below freezing. As we all warmed up, the loud music reverberated against my ear drums. Filiz continued to direct her class in her booming voice.

Hop two, three, four! Tem-po!
Breathe in! Now! Breathe out!
Arms down! Yes! Now left!

Filiz was working hard to synchronize the set of body movements to the rhythm of the music. She often referred to her workouts as choreography and liked to spice them up with belly-dance moves, which brought a coquettish smile to her trainees' faces.

Augmenting the loud music and synchronized movements with her commanding voice, Filiz was compelling her trainees' bodies to unite in a shared rhythmic energy.

One, two, three, four!
Right! Left! Tem-po!

Filiz was emboldened by the surge of energy in the room. She rose like a conductor before a chorus of rhythmic zeal. The drumming of footsteps, the heat, the sweat, the flushed cheeks—all united into one ball of energy compressed in this very space, at this very moment.

Everything outside that time and space seemed to move slowly and serenely in comparison with the upbeat embodied rhythms we were experiencing there together. Every other routine had a slower pace. We became as one flesh in the pulsing energy that vibrated

2. Field notes, Feb. 29, 2012.

through the walls and columns of the room. Our facial muscles were shaking along with the other muscles in our bodies, leaving us with fatigued but contented expressions. The embodied rhythm was carrying us away with it.

We were experiencing an affective refuge from the habitual routines in this new temporal zone.

Women's Routine Time Regimes

Women's daily routines outside of the temporal zone created in the exercise sessions are determined by their social roles. While most of the women attending the free exercise sessions at women-only gyms are housewives, some university students and career women also attend. More than three-quarters of the women attending gyms are married, and more than half have children, meaning that their duties at home often dominate and organize their days into fixed routines. Women's time regimes are thus organized tightly around their gender roles and family life and are marked by clocks, calendars, timetables, and fixed work, school, and gym hours.

Nazan's morning routine is a good example of the routine followed by a majority of the women I met. I wrote in my field notes: "She wakes up at 6:00 a.m., prepares breakfast for her children, and makes sure they are fed and ready to leave by 7:30. After the children leave, she clears the table, puts on a fresh pot of tea, and wakes her husband at 8:00. Her husband then leaves for work around 9:00. She then tidies the table once more, does the dishes and some small prep work for dinner, such as soaking dried beans or chickpeas, and finally leaves home after 10:00 a.m. to attend trainer Filiz's 11:00 a.m. step-aerobics class."[3]

This, as I quickly learned during my time in Istanbul, is the daily routine of many housewives with young or adolescent children or both.

Mevhibe was a married woman in her late thirties with two young children in elementary school. She lived close to Gaziosmanpaşa, a

---

3. Field notes, Feb. 29, 2012.

suburban neighborhood of Istanbul inhabited by first- and second-generation migrants to the city. On the day of my second interview with her, we met at the gym where she works out. She was wearing a pale-blue blouse and a navy skirt. She had tied an orange-blue head scarf loosely around her face and neck, looking comfortable and dry despite the humidity in the air. Before we started the interview, she explained to me at great length how she prided herself on the colorful outfits she wore during exercise and on the diverse friendships she had. Although she cherished how vibrant her social life was, especially compared to her peers (i.e., other housewives), her answer to my question about her daily routine was typical: "I wake up at 6:30 a.m. and prepare breakfast for the kids. I walk them to school and come home at 8:30. I either leave the tea on or sometimes prepare a new pot of tea before I wake up Serkan [her husband]. We have breakfast together. He leaves before 9:30, and after that I usually go grocery shopping or hand-pick stones from the grains that I will cook for the dinner."[4]

Gülru was thirty-five years old, married, with three children. Few women are as privileged as Gülru, who used to employ a Turkish maid to come to her home to clean and cook twice a week. Gülru did not have a live-in maid, as several of her wealthy neighbors did. Considering the size of the holding company and the hospitals her husband ran, her reluctance to hire a maid-in-residence was a statement against the opulent lifestyle of her peers and neighbors. Although Gülru's was a wealthy household, her daily routine was strikingly similar to that of the other housewives with children whom I talked to:

She starts the day with the morning prayer at dawn and prepares breakfast. She wakes her children and husband up halfway through the breakfast preparation, thereby giving them enough time to sleep in and to sit a while at the breakfast table, where she has set out tea and eggs ready and warm. She then rushes her children out to the school shuttle, the *servis*, walks her husband to work, and comes

4. Follow-up interview, Apr. 28, 2012.

back to the kitchen to clear the table. She does not eat breakfast with them but prefers instead to exercise on an empty stomach while it is still early in the day. On dry days, she sets off for her exercise routine at around 9:00 a.m. by driving to the Bosphorus and walking along the waterfront for five kilometers [around three miles]. On rainy days, she goes to the gym in the gated community where she lives."[5]

Gülru and Mevhibe's daytime activities vary, but their morning and evening routines are virtually identical to that of other Istanbulite housewives. In the afternoon and evening, they all plan dinner, prepare the table, and, if they have school-age children, as Mevhibe and Gülru do, make sure to be back home before their children return from school. The husbands typically are home after the children. On regular schooldays, these housewives have a light snack (often baked goods in a low-income household) ready for the children when they arrive home. If their father will arrive home late, the children don't wait up but instead have their dinner alone as soon as their mother has prepared the table and filled their plates. Women pass the time between breakfast and evening in other variable ways—that is, so long as they have seen to the cleaning and prepared dinner to be ready on time.

Embodied Rhythms and Joy

Just as social roles impose a particular type of temporal regime, the gyms and fitness classes have their own temporal regimes bolstered by rhythms—rhythms that are embodied. In the gym, the women let the loud, percussive sounds possess their bodies and spirits.[6] In exercise classes, body movements are repeated in sets in an accelerating rhythm to the beat of a blaring soundscape. Loud music, mirrors, and sweat are compulsory. These *embodied rhythms* remind me of the

5. Fieldnotes, Apr. 28 and 29, 2012.

6. Another exercise session, this one in Hamza Yerlikaya across the Bosphorus Sea, can be seen at http://youtu.be/DHvfvMB94JY (Sehlikoglu 2013c).

philosopher and sociologist Henri Lefebvre's requisite: "In order for there to be rhythm, there must be repetition in a movement" (2004, 78). Embodied rhythms are composed of temporal repetitions, but they are also more than that. They are about the temporal (re)structuring of corporeal actions and those actions' entrainment to "an external timekeeper, such as the beat of a drum or the movements of another person" (Bunt 2004, 56). They are composed of flow, sound, and silence. Lefebvre's contribution to our understanding of the rhythm of everyday routines centers on his analysis of the relative relation between time and space: all rhythms and routines are knotted in a particular time and place.

Following Lefebvre, we can conceptualize these embodied rhythms as involving regulated time (the hours and minutes of a schedule) in a delimited space (women-only gyms). In other words, women's exercise contains both temporal and spatial elements, which are then choreographed in a new rhythm. The exercise thus embodies an "order in the movement," as Paul Fraisse repeats from Platonian description of rhythm (1981, 217). Lefebvre says, "Everywhere there is interaction between a place, a time and an expenditure of energy, there is rhythm" (2004, 26). The time spent in the gym encapsulates all of these elements. The rhythm that emerges during exercise is embodied, which simultaneously reorganizes the embodied relationship women have with their lives. The energy expended at the gym is released as an *inexplicable joy* that women talk about, share, and perform together.

In one of the few attempts in the literature to discuss rhythm in anthropological theory, Haili You states that "without the perception of a proper tempo, there is no rhythm" (1994, 362). The drumlike tempo of the music and the movements in exercise generates an alternative embodied rhythm in the lives of Istanbulite women. The joy such a shift brings to their lives is not easy for them to describe. In interviews, I always asked them what it is about sports that they liked. As with Züleyha, many women found the joy they experienced difficult to explain, often resorting to the words *keyifli*, "joyous," and *eğlenceli*, "fun."

SENA: It's fun.

SERTAÇ: How is it fun?

SENA: Well . . . it's just fun.[7]

Although several of the women addressed the joy without explaining it, as "just" fun, some tried harder to explain it. Hilâl Teyze, a fifty-seven-year-old, upper-middle-class, religious woman, lived in the United States for several years, looking after her grandchildren. She thought that people in Turkey are unhappy because they do not exercise regularly.

HILÂL TEYZE: You don't see flabbiness among people over there. They exercise and are always fit. You see them standing erect, not with poor posture,[8] because when you engage in sports, your body needs air, and your chest needs to be opened. Here, people look down, bent over. I was out for a walk the other day, and I looked at people's faces, then I smiled at them. Everyone looked very grumpy to me. . . . Look around yourself. You will see that Turkish people do not smile.

SERTAÇ: Because they don't exercise?

HILÂL TEYZE: Exercising makes people happy, and it changes your body to make you happy.[9]

This *inexplicable joy* is unleashed at least in part by the release of hormones during exercise, a fact my interlocutors often never failed to mention. Simultaneously, it also arises from taking a pause in daily routines spatially and temporally—from engaging in homosocial interactions, following commands or instructions, and repeating and accelerating movement.

The most crucial aspect of this inception of joy is how the women let the rhythm take over their bodies in a collective activity. Losing

7. Interview, Jan. 25, 2012.

8. Given Hilâl Teyze's class status, it is likely that she frequented middle-class neighborhoods in the United States—hence, her observation of fit American bodies rather than obese ones.

9. Interview, Mar. 26, 2012.

oneself in synchronized movements performed with a group report-edly has an ecstatic effect. In her work on collective joy in communi-tas, Edith Turner (2012) connects music and sport. The combination of movement (sport) and music creates a zone and a flow, which then together form an invisible bond among the group members. Turn-er's examples are similar to the drumming embodied rhythms that Istanbulite women experience, and she explains how such moments bind the individuals through joy: "By intimately sharing precise time, owing to the transformative power of rhythm, we *can* merge, and we find we are not separate" (2012, 48, emphasis in original).

Studies in psychology also help us to understand the joy in such collective activities with embodied rhythms. Jonathan Haidt, Pat-rick Seder, and Selin Kesebir (2008), for instance, study happiness by developing what they call "the hive hypothesis" in human psychology. The hive hypothesis aims to understand group cohesion and shared emotive forces in groups. Haidt, Seder, and Kesebir argue that a par-ticular type of joy is felt in a large group performing synchronized movements, including those done in exercise. They refer to this feel-ing as "the ecstatic joy of self-loss" (S133).[10] In a similar vein, Wil-liam McNeill (1995) has examined the connection between individual muscular movement rhythms and group solidarity as an experience that alters other experiences and emotionally connects the participants to each other. Although exercise is not always shared or performed synchronously in a group, it is always rhythmic, repetitive, energizing, and embodied.

Throughout my field research, women insisted repeatedly that exercise made them "feel good" in multiple ways. Socializing, becom-ing fitter, and caring for the self and the body were mentioned as major motivations for exercising. When women talked about exercise

10. An extensive literature in leisure and sports studies supports the assertion of the positive influence of exercise on happiness (Jiang et al. 2011; Rasmussen and Laumann 2014), mood (Maroulakis and Zervas 1993; Berger and Motl 2000; Crocker et al. 2004), and mental well-being (Teychenne, Ball, and Salmon 2008; Cerin et al. 2009).

making them feel good, they often stressed how enrollment in fitness, Pilates, or aerobics classes introduced a new pattern to their daily routines. Although there are studies suggesting the importance and effect of music on mood during exercise, little attention has been paid to the embodied and everyday rhythms of exercise or whether and how exercise itself may shift daily rhythms and individual experiences of time.

Women referred to the shift from the regular time and space of their daily routines to the alternate rhythmic pattern of exercise time and space as both relaxing and liberating. They described how it helped them forget the outside world and their personal lives. In the next section, I try to understand women's enjoyment of exercise in relation to the rhythmic shift that comes with exercise and that allows them to experience an alternative pace, a different tempo.

Altchronic Practices

Municipally run gyms in Istanbul offer both Pilates and step aerobics as studio sessions, and their fitness rooms are supplied with treadmills, elliptical cross-trainers, exercise bikes, and various weight machines for working out different muscle groups. The exercise done in fitness rooms is different from that done in studio sessions. An average fitness-room session usually lasts sixty to ninety minutes. Each member is offered a training program, slightly tailored based on body shape and composed of a range of exercises for weight loss, tummy flattening, back pain, and cardio health. Importantly for the discussion here, each individualized program is implemented in accordance with certain time-regulatory dimensions—the duration of each set, the number of sets, the total duration of the exercise. Certain exercises are repetitive in nature, with discrete movements done in sets of twenty or more repetitions. In an individualized program, the member can check her training program, which includes time designations, to decide how many sets she needs to do. The member is taught stretching techniques and is told to follow them carefully when switching from one exercise to another. She is also told to take short pauses between each set. Züleyha, twenty-four years old, had never tried a studio session but instead preferred the fitness-room memberships because she could have an individualized program. She told me her routine: "It lasts for two hours. I start with the treadmill—I really love the treadmill. I always think that the treadmill must be the most effective way to lose weight. Then I move on to cycling. I try to allocate fifteen minutes for each phase. I stick to the training program and follow the recommendations of our trainers at the gym."[11]

Züleyha was responsible for the little store her father and uncle ran. The family earned little from the store, and she was not paid for her work there. The way her family treated her and her free labor at the store always upset her close friends. She sat behind the counter throughout the day and, except for the housework she did to help her mother, she was physically inactive. Exercising thus brought a new *tempo* to Züleyha's otherwise sedentary daily life. Despite the intervention of this new tempo, Züleyha described herself as someone who is "stuck in a rut" because she had left school several years earlier. She wanted to progress, which for her meant getting married and having children (she is now married with a baby girl). At the gym, she often joked about it and asked the other women whether they knew any candidates for her. To Züleyha, *spor merakı* and her gym routine broke up her monotonous life. Her gym routine also seemed to give her hope to move *forward* toward her goal of having a family: "My initial aim when I decided to do sports was to lose weight. I wanted to become a beautiful girl. But now my primary goal is health related."

The now prioritized health-related improvement was not about any immediate improvement in her health, and she didn't have any medical problems. Rather, Züleyha was stating the fact that since she had started to exercise, she *felt* healthier and more energetic. At one stage during the interview, she said, "At the gym, I get rid of all the stress, forget all my troubles. . . . I realize that the exercise itself makes me very happy." She then switched back to the subject of weight loss and continued to explain to me how good it felt to lose weight and

11. Interview, Dec. 4, 2011.

become more beautiful. As the conversation deepened, she reflected: "Sports makes me feel alive. It gives me a [sense of] *yaşam sevinci* [joy of life]. I become very happy when I am involved in it."

Giulia Liberatore (2016, 2017) discusses marriage as an aspiration through which her Somalian British interlocutors debate and experiment with multiple moral registers. For Züleyha, marriage offered a way to break away from the life imposed on her by her family. But breaking away required an inner strength as well as a social (network) and physical capital (beauty). Exercising at the gyms seemed like a good place to start this process of breaking away. In her search for this break, she also discovered the joy of forming her own time–space and her own embodied rhythms. The joy hooked her in and enabled her to keep on working out. Finding a "candidate" for marriage took much longer than she anticipated, but the joy Züleyha discovered in exercise helped her to keep going, and she continued with it even after marrying and having her first baby.

When we look carefully at the exercising of Istanbulite women in gyms, we see that their practice illustrates all the components of Lefebvre's analysis of rhythm, the "interaction between a place, a time and an expenditure of energy" (2004, 26). Regulated by gym hours and delimited by homosocial space, the practice of exercising possesses the characteristic temporal and spatial dimensions of rhythm, with an expenditure of energy released as inexplicable joy.

Through exercise, Istanbulite women regain control of their *own* time and movements insofar as it allows them to restructure their daily habits. This control, experienced as a form of freedom and a move away from former socially imposed routines that I call *time regimes* (after M. Young 1988), resynchronizes the body to a newly patterned temporality. These altchronic practices interrupt routine temporalities and form new, idiosyncratic ones suited to the new self.

The patterned remaking of space and time that characterizes embodied rhythms is an important element of Istanbulite women's everyday altchronic practices. They recalibrate their biological and social timescales by altering the mundane, repetitive time regimes imposed on them by their familial and gender responsibilities. In recalibrating their bodily movements to patterned intervals and rhythms, these women experience and share together an inexplicable joy and a new *self-time*.

I use the term *altchronic* to refer to temporalities that do not fit shared, traditional time regimes. Women in Turkey are subjected to a particular type of *time regime*, a term I borrow from the sociologist Michael Young (1988), which refers to a shared, communal, objective sense of time. Forging new temporalities opens up cracks in existing time regimes that are often culturally specific, revealing how our understanding of time is embedded in the gendered and acculturated self. Indeed, because time regimes are also gendered, Istanbulite women's given familial time regimes are communal and relational as opposed to independent and solitary. The given social time regime at stake is similar to the concept of *nomos* (Castoriadis 1991). Cornelius Castoriadis uses the Greek term *nomos* to refer to the rules, customs, and institutions created and maintained within society. He defines autonomy (*autonomos*) as the ability to set one's own rules, which he associates with freedom: "If we want to be free, we have to make our own *nomos*" (1991, 162). By bringing Young's and Castoriadis's analyses together, then, we can say that the establishment of or entrainment to an alternative time regime will bring about autonomy.

My interlocutors brought about their own autonomy through altchronic practices. These alternative time-regime practices restructured their daily social schedules and allowed them to open up an emancipated, individualized, alternative social time regime structured within a women-only space. Their experience is comparable to what Asef Bayat (2007) describes in relation to fun and temporality. Turning the concept of "fun" into an object of sociological analysis, Bayat suggests that we understand fun as the human capacity for imagining new possibilities and alternative freedoms in lived and shared moments of daily life. He describes how Egyptian youth use fun to free themselves temporarily from normative obligations, the disciplined constraints of daily life, and organized power. Istanbulite women attempt to create their own *autonomos* in a similar way. By turning toward their embodied selves and experimenting with alternative social and gendered time regimes in their otherwise hyperpatterned everyday lives, they fashion an autonomous state through access to their own agency.

Time for the Self inside a Vortex

Women can have both negative and positive motives for the autonomy they seek by means of altchronic practices. Women who use exercise to cure an emotionally or physically damaged self may simultaneously do it purely for enjoyment. Using exercise as a project for the self is all the more significant for those who describe a turning point triggered by an important life event. This was the case with the young woman Nur.

Nur was one of the first women from the gym with whom I became friends. We first met at the gym in mid-July 2011, two weeks before Ramazan.[12] It was Şaban, the second month of Üç Aylar, the three holy months, and four women were talking about how difficult it would be to fast during the long, hot, humid days of summer. Nur joined the conversation with her big smile and cheerful tone. "God will help [you]; don't worry. I have been fasting since the beginning of Üç Aylar."[13] The women responded with a chorus of "Maşallah," looking at Nur in wide-eyed surprise. One, a dark-haired tall and slender woman, censured her. "You are torturing yourself! You should not have come to exercise while fasting. It is *günah* [forbidden]!" Although the other women did not put it as bluntly as she, they were curious as to how Nur could be so energetic while fasting and exercising. Nur laughed and shook her head. "It is not forbidden, *canım* [my dear or my soul]." The conversation then moved on to how to eat well before and after fasting. Using strategies I picked up during the first few weeks of my fieldwork, I stepped into the dialog by sharing tips on eating green lentils for *sahur*, the predawn meal before a day of fasting. Lentils help with endurance by maintaining balanced

---

12. "Ramazan" is the Turkish version of "Ramadan," the name for the holy month during which Muslims fast from dawn to sunset. Fasting includes abstaining from both eating and drinking, including water.

13. Field notes, July 18, 2011.

blood-sugar levels throughout the day, I said. Although the women were typically captivated by any information about foods that help cravings, digestive teas, and magical products that are supposed to burn body fat (but have in fact been proven ineffective), this time their interest was marked by disbelief. They knew that the reality is that it does not matter how one manages fasting; it is always extremely difficult. Rather than speculating on healthy fasting tricks, Nur just confidently smiled and shone, softly proving us all wrong, evidence that one can be energetic despite fasting, the hot weather, and long days.

Nur's irresistible energy made it easier for us to develop rapport. She was my age and quickly became interested in providing the data I needed for my research. I could also sense that my living abroad was appealing to her, as was the charm that my academic project was about women like herself. We talked every week at the gym when she came for her sessions. Quickly realizing that her help would make it easier for me to connect with other women at the gym, she began introducing me and my research to her gym friends.

When it was time to set up our first interview, she arranged it as she did with her other female friends—away from her three children's hectic interference and her in-laws' surveillance. She said we should pick a place other than her home or the gym so that she could spoil herself (*kendini şımartmak*). We decided to meet in one of the big franchise patisseries of Istanbul in Sultangazi at eleven o'clock in the morning. It was a cold, sunny December day in Istanbul. She was wearing a tight brown blouse and a pair of pants with extra-wide legs popular among women who wear head scarves. We chose a table inside at the back, insulated from the cold and smoke.

Our meeting began with reminiscences about the first time we met, as though we were talking about a nostalgic moment. Her answer to my question about *how* she started to exercise brought her back to the temporal setting for the decision. Nur, much like Hilâl Teyze, started to exercise after resolving to pay more attention to herself. This moment of autonomy was triggered by a particular incident that had taken place a couple of years earlier: "After that, I told myself that I would never get upset about anything. Nothing could stop me. I would lose my kilos through exercise. And it's not just the kilos. I am not getting any younger. Exercise is not just for losing weight. Aging brings arthritis, bone loss, and so forth. I see this in my mother. I don't want to face these things. Even if I inherit them, I can at least minimize them."[14]

Nur decided that her battle against the potential effects of time on her female body, anticipated by its effects on her mother's body, was one pressing thing in life she could not put off.

As we talked further about her interest in exercise, her family life, her in-laws, her taste in outfits and leisure-time activities, she referenced again and again the same period five years earlier. Although her initial signals about this period discouraged me from inquiring further about it, she made it clear that her answers would have been different had we conversed five years earlier. "I was a different person back then," she kept saying.

The conversation got cozier and more familiar. When Nur mentioned her transformation for the third time, I got up the nerve to be more direct. "You keep mentioning the same period in your life. It's as though something in your life changed dramatically." She looked straight into my eyes with an expression that said either "you caught me" or "finally you ask." I had the feeling it was both. Although she was not comfortable enough to share with me the particulars of her tragedy, she was willing to share its influence on her life.

The patchy clues she shared revealed an incident involving her spouse and his family that left her feeling lonely in the world. In the aftermath, she "decided to be strong," in her words, and made a series of life decisions that included exercising, distance learning, and financial independence. Two sources of inspiration encouraged her to make the decision to change her life: her elder sister advised her to "let others cry instead of letting them make you cry," and she read the life of the prophet Noah. Nur described in detail a scene from the flood in

14. Interview, Dec. 5, 2011.

which Noah tells his wife not to look back, or she will be destroyed. In the version Nur read, Noah's wife disobeys him, looks back, and dies instantly.[15] Once Nur read this, she decided that she would never look back again or let her past influence her future; otherwise, she would never get out of "this *girdap*"—literally, "this vortex," a Turkish metaphor used to describe catastrophic events that make one feel pessimistic and depressed. That same year she lost her elder sister. I couldn't tell if it was the same sister who had advised her to become stronger and did not feel I should ask.

> When I saw my sister in that coffin, I told myself that death was very close and that never again would I postpone my life for anyone else. You know how people always say that they have children and all sorts of things and priorities to deal with in their lives. No, none of that is true. Nothing should come before me. A simple example is when they ask me how I find time for everything, or they ask me when I clean my house. Sometimes I don't sweep my house for two days, and then on the third day, if you come to my house, you see that everything is shining. None of these things are more important than me. Who cares about the house if my well-being is at stake?

The combination of the incident with her in-laws and the loss of her sister culminated, it seems, in Nur revisiting her life and altering her relationship with herself and the world. To strengthen herself against forces she experienced as a vortex threatening to swallow her up, she developed a set of goals: she would get her degree, improve her looks, regain her physical strength, and achieve a measure of independence. During our conversation, she told me, perhaps too many

15. The version Nur read is an amalgam of the Qur'anic story of Noah and the Old Testament story of Lot. In the Qur'anic story, Noah's unbelieving wife perishes in the flood alongside their unbelieving son (whose name is "Kenan" in Turkish, "Yam" in Arabic) because they would not join Noah on the ark. In the Old Testament story of Lot, his disobedient wife takes one last look at the doomed city of Sodom and turns into a pillar of salt instantly.

times, how she did everything "for my*self* [kendim *için*]." "I realized that I should be stronger, more confident." In training for a degree, she finished her primary and secondary education and began studying for a certificate in accounting in case she ever needed a job. She mentioned her *bilgi açlığı* (thirst for knowledge) multiple times during the interview. Switching from the theme of exercise to education, she emphasized how her thirst for knowledge was a summons to a new self, triggering new self-knowledge.

With the decision to rebuild herself physically, emotionally, and intellectually, Nur began exercising. It made her feel physically and emotionally stronger. Now she wanted to spend some of her time only for herself. "Exercise is something I do only for me [Kendim için yaptığım bir şey spor]." Exercise for Nur was not simply something to hold onto in the middle of a life crisis; it opened up the possibility of a temporal break from her daily routine and repetitive lifestyle. In devoting more time to her education and leisure, she simultaneously decreased her family time, which she felt to be dictated by her in-laws, relatives, and neighbors. Family time was always filled with the duties of motherhood and housekeeping. Nur's "me time" was not only an alternative to family time in the here and now of exercising at the gym but also an investment in a more secure and independent future when she could work as an accountant. Nur reorganized her time both in the present and for the future. As a conscious form of refusal to a scheduled life that was presented to her as her fate, she created her own temporal connection to life. Exercise was a mechanism through which she could pull herself out of the vortex, from which she could emerge transformed into a confident, strong, and independent Istanbulite woman.

About six months after our interview, Nur moved to Tekirdağ with her family, a small city by western Istanbul. We continued to call and email one other. Even in this city without an exercise program for women, she made friends and formed an exercise circle. She said, "Of course I will continue [to exercise]! Don't you know me at all?" A few years later she started her university degree as well.

Conclusion

It is through these moments of inexplicable joy, high energy, and orchestrated embodied rhythms that women alter their routines and synchronize their lives to the beats of an imagined global world and its trends. The embodied rhythm, with its music and its globalized form of exercise, takes women away and temporarily alters their connections with the world, recharging their newly formed awareness of self. These patterned temporal moments, ephemeral and corporeal, represent instances where Istanbulite women's emerging selves take shape and become visible. It is in these moments that women become the cosmopolitan world citizens they aspire to be. These rhythms are not simply in or of the moment; they also point to what is coming next as women aspire to new lifestyles and attune themselves to new desires and needs. Haili You claims that "the essence of rhythm is not merely the perceived order (or pattern) of repetition (recurrence) of something; it is the demand, preparation and anticipation for something to come" (1994, 363). With the end of an earlier event, a new event may begin. It is the anticipation of this new event that proves to be crucial for the women I interviewed. The rhythmic movements of exercise that drive the mover forward in anticipation of the rhythm continue to open up the possibility for there to be cognitive and emotional anticipation as well. Women's embodied rhythmic experience brings to the fore that which they desire to become—not just slim or pretty women but women who move with energy, live with passion, and belong to a broader world. Without abandoning their family-centered time regimes, they expand on what they already have.

As demonstrated in this chapter, the relationship between the changing self and the world can be analyzed through the lens of temporal patterns or rhythms that are felt through the body during exercise. Everyday time regimes are reformed through the altchronic rhythms of exercising, thereby connecting women with their desire to engage with the world. At this level, my analysis of temporality is grounded in the physicality of embodied rhythms. Exercise breaks through everyday routines to inaugurate an alternative rhythmic, temporal space. By examining exercise as an embodied experience with temporal patterns, beats, and rhythms, we have seen the entangled aspect of enjoyment—how women experience exercise as desirable and how it can alter each one's relationship with her lifestyle and her society.

Throughout my fieldwork, it became clear to me that women's relationships with their bodies change throughout the course of their lives—although their commitment to recalibrate their daily rhythms remains. As we shall see in the next chapter, regaining control of the temporal patterns in one's life extends beyond the reorganization of leisure time and into the gendered and sexed demands of pregnancy and menopause.

8

Gendered Temporalities

"You have a particular physical appearance at the moment now, don't you? If I told you that you would gain twenty kilos [forty-five pounds], your face would become swollen, your veins would become visible, your tummy would have stretch marks, and your skin would sag, wouldn't you want to get back to your former body? Naturally you would."[1]

This was how Dr. Aytuğ Kolankaya, the gynecologist and medical celebrity described in chapter 3, responded to my observation of the fact that a large number of gym goers, women between twenty and forty years of age, begin exercising after giving birth. Dr. Kolankaya is talking about something with which we all are familiar: particular aesthetic norms, reinforced through neoliberal marketing of fitness and healthy living, marking women's regaining of their prenatal bodies as a form of "success" (Bordo 1993; Markula 1995; Dworkin and Wachs 2004).

The way individuals experience time is often embodied in the most literal sense in how time leaves marks on their bodies. So, then, the question is, How do women relate with the gendered aspect of their temporal bodies?

As became apparent in the interviews, several of the aesthetic features Dr. Kolankaya described have sentimental value to women. The changes and degeneration women's pregnant bodies undergo have multiple meanings and values in women's imagination. In other words,

1. Interview, Mar. 12, 2012.

the gendered aesthetic norms may not fully reflect women's perceptions of their childbearing bodies. There are certain marks that time has left on women's bodies that they want to remove, whereas there are other marks that they feel affectionate toward. The answer to the question of whether and how certain traces of life are to be erased is not always a straightforward one. Owing to the multiple and conflicting ways that sexed bodies are socially constructed, women have a complex relationship with their natal and postnatal bodies, so that driving postnatal bodies to exercise might or might not be about aesthetics.

This chapter takes as its starting point the assertion that the biological constraints and cycles of a woman's life, including fertility and menstrual cycles, impose specific temporal forces on her body. The phenomenology of the body as lived throughout the different stages of a woman's life is experienced in personal transitions and discrete bodily changes. The many ways that women experience and narrate these changes are informed by larger normative themes, including the sanctity of motherhood, on the one hand, and the neoliberal commodification of maternal bodies, on the other. As discussed in earlier chapters, women do not embrace or resist the normative mechanisms, mostly because these mechanisms are not singular but multiple. Women instead navigate through them, selectively "playing along" with or avoiding confrontations with some of the expectations while resisting others.

This chapter, descriptive in nature, delves into women's narratives of pregnancy, a major biological life event. Through their narratives, I aim to calibrate anthropological knowledge on the temporal demands of femininity to the question of the body and agency. These narratives record women's constantly changing relationship with their biological, corporeal, embodied time and the ways they pilot the direction of such change. Women intervene in these changes in endless conversation with the larger systems that come to bear upon them.

Prenatal Bodies?

In her classic study of embodiment and social status in the lives of elite Yemeni women, Gabriele Vom Bruck examines the social aspects of pregnancy and temporality. She notes that the anticipation of an unmarried woman's future as wife and mother results in a particular social treatment of her as having a "differential gender attribution." This specific gender attribution serves to distinguish unmarried women both from unmarried men and from "married women who conceal the potent symbols of sexuality and femininity" (1997, 178). In her study, Vom Bruck expands Sherry B. Ortner's (1981) analysis on how institutions of marriage and kinship determine women's position in a society and helps us to understand how those institutions also determine the multiple forms of navigation that women of different status and subject position have to perform.

In the contexts of Yemen and Turkey, unmarried women are traditionally perceived as potential mothers. This perception in Turkey marks women's relationship with their social bodies as prenatal bodies. Such anticipation inevitably has consequences in the present as well as in the future. During the interviews, even women with no possibility of pregnancy in the near future explained how they regulate their exercise regimes to ensure a healthy pregnancy and easy delivery.

In a context where motherhood is considered sacred (Bora 2001; Dedeoglu 2010; Bayraktar 2011) and where it is thought that a woman's sole duty is motherhood (J. White 2003), the significance of pregnancy is made socially visible before it actually begins. A number of my unmarried interlocutors who were not in any romantic relationship were constantly reminded by their close relatives and friends of their potential as mothers. This social anticipation of motherhood and pregnancy influences the way women imagine the temporality of their bodies.

Turkish women begin learning about the ideal of motherhood at an early age, often through daily conversations. There are also ritualized investments in marriage and pregnancy. One such investment is in the *çeyiz* (trousseau), which mothers of brides-to-be begin to prepare when their daughters reach puberty (Sandikci and Iljan 2004; K. Hart 2007). This was the case for Mübeccel, a young woman in her early twenties attending evening lectures to complete her BA. She told me how many nice vests her mother knitted for her and put into her *çeyiz*. Some of them were "knitted large so that I can wear them when I get pregnant."[2] Mübeccel found her mother's investment in "some unknown future," in her words, quite amusing. She blushed slightly when she said that becoming a mother is an experience she did not want to miss.

> SERTAÇ: Do you think you will become a mother eventually then?
> MÜBECCEL: Of course. God willing [İnşallah].

This socially potent notion of investing in pregnancy and motherhood as an unknown but desired future is reflected in several women's exercise in contemporary Istanbul. We can see this in the case of another woman from a socially and economically different background than Mübeccel's. Zeliha, a thirty-year-old single professional woman with a PhD from a university in the United States, came from an educated upper-middle-class family. For the interview, we met in a restaurant. As she described to me how she worked out at the gym just below her office, going into some detail about the movements, I realized that she was doing all this as an investment in her potential future pregnancy. Exercise presented a way for Zeliha to mitigate any complications that might occur because of her age.

> ZELIHA: I sometimes do the movements I have learned elsewhere. But I mostly work on my abs: upper abs and lower abs.
> SERTAÇ: Why do you work specifically on abs?
> ZELIHA: The reason is that my mother [a medical doctor] always tells me to work on my abs because they become saggy after pregnancy. It may help to work out the abs before that.
> SERTAÇ: So your concerns are about aesthetics?
> ZELIHA: Not really. I mean, that's part of it, of course. But if you have strong abs, it eases the delivery. Then the recovery is

2. Interview, Dec. 30, 2011.

easier. Plus, thanks to the exercise, I now have a firm tummy. It's "mother's advice," but I find it medically valuable as well.[3]

Although the pain associated with delivery is less talked about in public, it is of great concern to expectant mothers and unmarried women. Women often discuss the extended hours of their painful deliveries with their friends and relatives, comparing their stories of pain. Women's pregnant bodies are a subject of both private and public conversations. One year after my interviews, a national political debate on cesarean sections took place, initiated by then prime minister Recep Tayyip Erdoğan and the Ministry of Family and Social Policies. In July 2013, Erdoğan's address on the ministry's launch of a new project, Aile Olmak (Becoming a Family), argued forcefully that family planning, abortion, and cesarean sections pose a threat to the Turkish family. Following his speech, a series of public debates resulted in new restrictions aimed at lowering the percentage of cesarean sections performed in Turkey, which ranked then at 46 percent of total births, among the highest in OECD countries (OECD 2013). In many Turkish hospitals, cesarean sections were offered to the patient as a pain-free delivery option rather than as an emergency-only procedure.

During my fieldwork, I met women who had opted for a cesarean because they were afraid of the pain and were now afraid of further complications during the birth of their second or third child because of the earlier cesarean. I also met women who exercised and practiced Pilates so as to lessen the pain of vaginal birth. Seda, an upper-class woman in her early thirties, was in the United States while pregnant with her second son. This meant that she did not have the option of choosing a hospital or gynecologist willing to perform a cesarean section if and when she wanted one. She then invested in regular exercise.

I would take my baby and go to a park. I was in the US back then, during the last one and a half months [of my pregnancy]. I would

---

3. Interview, Feb. 17, 2012. Eight months after this interview, Zeliha got married, and sixteen months later she had a baby. She is now a mother of two.

follow a circular path around the park while my son was playing there. You know, the playgrounds are surrounded with fences there. It allowed me to walk around the park from a distance where I could watch him. And since I was in the US, I was going to have a normal [vaginal] birth, and I was scared of it. I was trying to work out my [pelvic] muscles.[4]

Practicing Pilates during pregnancy is an emerging trend among women with concerns like Seda's and Zeliha's. The Pilates guru Ebru Şallı, described in chapter 3, is one of the leading figures in this movement. In 2003, her first pregnancy when she was thirty-five drove her to Pilates.

> I was first introduced to Pilates when I was expecting my first child. Pilates was not common in Turkey back then, but it was slowly starting. At that time, I would go to a sports center where there was one coach to teach Pilates. I was a member of the sports center. I found Pilates to be an enjoyable option. I watched the training and asked if pregnant women might do this as well. They then directed me to another Pilates session specifically for pregnant women. That was how I first got involved in Pilates. I loved and enjoyed it so much that I started doing research and learning more about it. . . . Of course, my delivery was naturally a very easy one since I had been doing exercise and Pilates during pregnancy.[5]

Pilates during pregnancy became a trend in Turkey after Şallı published a self-help book entitled *Hamilelikte sağlıklı ve güzel kalma* (Staying Healthy and Beautiful during Pregnancy, Şallı 2005). The book was first published in 2005, and its fourth edition was still on the shelves in 2017. Its cover depicts Şallı in black and white from her

4. Interview, Dec. 1, 2011. Women are able to request a cesarean section in Turkey, and it is quite common to do so. According to statistics from 2011, the rate of caesarean sections among the total number of births in Turkey was 46.2 percent, in contrast with a rate of 31.4 percent in the United States (OECD 2013).

5. Interview, Mar. 14, 2012.

knees up, wearing dark skinny pants pulled down under her pregnant belly and a white tank top lifted above it. The blurb on the cover says that the book "includes valuable tips and advice for women during the pre-pregnancy, pregnancy, and postnatal periods."

Şallı also put out a DVD, *Ebru Şallı ile hamilelikte Pilates* (Pilates during Pregnancy with Ebru Şallı, 2010), which was one of the best-selling DVDs in media stores in Turkey when I was conducting field-work. Şallı filmed the video when she was pregnant with her second child. "The Ministry of Health watched the DVD and really liked it. They are now showing my DVDs in state hospitals from 8:00 a.m. to 5:00 p.m. . . . In Zeynep Kamil Hospital, they are now using my DVDs as training for expectant mothers."

Şallı also pointed out that previously "many found it [doing such exercise while pregnant] unacceptable, thinking that body movements are dangerous during pregnancy." Although Şallı is right to point out that she was the first to introduce to the Turkish public the idea of exercising for natal and postnatal physical health, the notion of invest-ing in pregnancy already existed in Turkish culture. The publication of Şallı's book and DVD coincided with a period when the relationship between women and their bodies was changing both in Turkey and in the wider world. This change was also visible to me when I compared women's attitudes about exercising during pregnancy.

In 2008, the trainer Aslı at the women-only gym Cemal Kamacı told me that women generally stop coming to the gym during their pregnancy because they think working out may damage the baby's health.[6] What I witnessed during my second fieldwork three years later, however, was women investing in their bodies by attending pregnancy-related exercise classes geared to having an easier delivery. The demand and interest in exercise during pregnancy are related to two important concerns: minimizing the effects of pregnancy on the body by preventing too much weight gain or the development of swollen legs and facilitating an easier delivery. The latter is important

6. Field notes, Aug. 2008.

not only because birth can be a painful process but also, as we shall see in women's own accounts, because birth by cesarean section, very common in Turkey, is much more invasive and requires a longer recovery period.

Meziyet, my host in Yeşilvadi for some four months, repeatedly mentioned how much she loved being pregnant and treasured her relationship with her children. She also mentioned several times how she "seriously considered" having a fourth child (which she did later). Each time she spoke of her desire to have a fourth child, she also talked about the difficult deliveries she had had with each of her children. On one of these occasions, she showed me her pregnancy photos. She subsequently shared two of these photos on Facebook with the following caption: "Me, 9 months, 15 days pregnant. Age: 21. Weight: 76 kg [168 pounds]. Get pregnant if you dare. I am saying this to myself."[7] One of the photos she shared on Facebook showed her swinging from a tree branch as a way of vaunting her physical strength despite her extended pregnancy. As a woman who saw motherhood as a core part of her subjectivity, she "loved" being pregnant and proudly shared photos of herself looking overweight and pregnant.

Postnatal Conversations

Zerrin was twenty-eight years old when we met in 2011. Married to an engineer and the mother of two children (she now has three), Zerrin's passion for sports and fitness was well known among her friends. One of them, Firuze, had directed me to Zerrin, whom she had met in child-rearing seminars given by a conservative charity. Both women had small children and were pregnant around the same time. Their acquaintance turned into friendship when Firuze was helping me with my fieldwork. Zerrin quickly lost weight following her second pregnancy, and the change in her body attracted women's positive attention. Her case was passed around as a success story and marked her as "*sporcu* Zerrin" (sporty/sportswoman Zerrin).

---

7. Posted Feb. 24, 2012; referenced with permission.

Insisting that I should meet Zerrin, Firuze invited her to the next event she was hosting, a garden party at her parents' house in early October 2011. Zerrin, thrilled to increase her recognition as a *sporcu* woman internationally,[8] gave me her cell phone number after the party and agreed to participate in my research.

On the day of our interview, I went to Zerrin's house with Firuze, whom Zerrin had invited to come along. Zerrin's house was located in a gated community in Bulgurlu, on the Asian side of Istanbul. She welcomed us in a gray knee-high dress and high-heeled shoes but without a head scarf because she was at home with women. Her hair was nicely done, and she was wearing coral lipstick, which brightened the contented expression on her face. Zerrin and Firuze were accompanied by their young daughters during the interview, ages two and four. As I would find out, meeting housewives with small children in their homes would mean multiple interruptions. Zerrin was being a generous host, serving us two sets of plates, one for the savory nibbles and another for the desserts, as well as tea in Turkish tea glasses. Despite her multitasking skills, it was difficult for her to manage it all: deal with the children, excel at her hosting duties, and answer my questions. When one of the girls spilled tea on the carpet, Zerrin was visibly uncomfortable about interrupting the interview further. She was, however, determined to share her story, so she started telling me what prompted her to begin exercising. It was after her first pregnancy.

Zerrin wanted to express her strong disappointment with her post-pregnant body and how much she had disliked its new shape: "I hated my look so much. I was punishing myself by buying extra-large clothes. I felt so fat, so down, such a mess, and unattractive all the time that I bought several large-size skirts. I didn't even want to try them on in the store. I didn't want to look at myself in the mirror."[9]

Zerrin's depression continued for some two years after the birth of her first child, subsiding only after she found the physical and

8. As stated earlier, *sporcu* can mean both "sports(wo)man" and "athletic (wo)man" or "sportsperson" in Turkish. The word is also gender neutral.

9. Interview, Nov. 28, 2011.

emotional strength to begin losing weight through diet and exercise. When she finally reached her pre-pregnancy size, she promised herself that she would not let herself gain the same amount of weight in her future pregnancies. She kept her promise. During the write-up of my research, she gave birth to her third child and after only two months began uploading postpregnancy photos of her "size eight" (US size) body on Instagram and Twitter.[10] She appears in one of the photos wearing makeup and high heels and flashing a broad, confident smile.

Zerrin was one of the first women I interviewed in 2011. Admittedly, no one else was as specific and as detailed as she was in her dislike of her postnatal shape. She described her postnatal depression as caused by a sense of failure regarding her weight gain, so she perceived her weight loss as a success.

Several months after my interview with Zerrin, I arranged a focus-group interview with four women who were able to converse openly and amicably about their pregnant and postnatal bodies: Zerrin, Firuze, Serra, and Meziyet. Although difficult, selecting the right people for the group proved to be the easiest part of the arrangement.[11] Every challenge or joy these four women shared was shaped around their common status as mothers of young children. Once I had the correct interview lineup, the next step was to choose a comfortable location that would allow me to talk with them for an uninterrupted stretch of three to four hours. The problem was that each of the four women might have to bring her two or three children, some of them infants, along with her. I was lucky that Serra generously invited everyone to her home for breakfast and her home had a playground for the children.

This was to be the first time after delivering her second baby that Firuze would be participating in a social event. She was excited to be going out after such a long time and dressed up for the occasion.

---

10. Zerrin's Instagram and Twitter accounts are open only to approved friends.

11. Pulling together the right mix of women for the focus group took more than a month because it was a challenge to find women who would have an enjoyable time together.

She was wearing a long, black, size-eight skirt with a high waist that showed off her flat tummy. On top, she tucked in an ivory silk blouse that highlighted her curves. In this combination of skirt and blouse, she was delighted to have received just the response she was looking for: "How did you get back to such a thin waistline?"

We began talking while helping ourselves to Serra's selection of charcuteries, cheeses, and healthy pastries accompanied by Turkish tea in *ajda* glasses, a larger version of the regular tulip-shaped Turkish tea glass. Everyone was excited to talk about the research subject, and, Firuze, sitting there with her young baby and her thin postnatal belly, served as the natural conversation starter. The others called her "successful" not because she had regained her former shape but because she was able to minimize the visibility of her postpartum body shape by choosing the right outfits that highlighted her breasts and covered her waist tightly. There was a consensus among the women that their bodies never looked the same after childbirth. All these physical changes—enlarged tummies, stretch marks, weight gain, wider hips—were less upsetting during pregnancy but became more worrisome after childbirth.

> SERRA: I never felt ugly during my pregnancies, but I did feel ugly right after them. I always feel bad about myself. It's almost as though during your pregnancy you have an excuse to look that way—you're carrying a baby inside. But then after the delivery, you tell yourself, "Why do I look ugly?"
>
> FIRUZE: Bedriye once told me that she felt uncomfortable looking like she was still pregnant after the birth. She used to have a belly this big. [She demonstrated with her two hands, as if touching her imaginary seven-months-pregnant belly.]
>
> SERRA: Oh, thank God I no longer have a belly![12]

---

12. Focus group, Mar. 6, 2012. Serra was thirty-one years old and a mother of three (she now has four); Firuze was thirty-two years old and a mother of two (she now has three).

Serra's, Firuze's, and Bedriye's narratives of feeling comfortable about their pregnant bodies during pregnancy are in line with studies conducted in Taiwan (Huang, Wang, and Dai 2010), the United Kingdom (Patel et al. 2005), and Australia (Clark et al. 2009a) documenting the temporary release from aesthetic standards women experience while developing a pride in their pregnant bodies.

Firuze then shared her shock upon realizing that her body did not look the same after her second baby.

> FIRUZE: After my first baby, I stood up and realized that I didn't have a tummy at all! It was because the baby developed more inside, and I weighed around fifty-three kilos [117 pounds] when I got pregnant. I didn't have a belly popping out until the fifth month. But it wasn't like that with my boy [her second baby]. I left the hospital with a big tummy as though I were four months pregnant. I was so panicked.
>
> SERRA: But you know what, it was because he was your second. They always say that. Even Gülhan told me that.[13] She said, "Look, they say it is always different after the third, and we shall wait and see." And I remember responding to her, "Oh, for goodness sake, people are just making things up!"

This conversation is a good illustration of the changing perception of pregnancy and women's bodies in Turkey. Serra and Firuze compared their own experience with that of Gülhan, a mutual friend approximately ten years older. Women of Gülhan's age tell younger women that the body changes irreversibly after the third child. Although Serra cited Gülhan's advice, she then refuted it with her own experience: "Oh, for goodness sake, people are just making [these] things up!"

Paula Nicolson, Rebekah Fox, and Kristin Heffernan (2010) conducted an interesting study comparing the perspectives of British

---

13. Gülhan, also one of my interviewees, was Serra and Firuze's mutual friend. At the time of the interview, she was a mother of three and expecting her fourth child.

middle-class white women from three different generations about their pregnant and postnatal bodies. According to their findings, women from all three generations had concerns about their postnatal body size, but the concerns differed. The youngest generation of women, pregnant during the 2000s, were more concerned about regaining their pre-pregnancy size. According to Nicolson, Fox, and Heffernan, this overriding concern was related to the "changing ideals of 'beauty' and body size over time and/or media exposure of the 'celebrity mum' which may put unrealistic demands on women to appear glamorous during pregnancy and quickly achieve their pre-pregnancy shape" (2010, 583). Both Firuze and Serra were known for the "glamour" of their postpregnancy shape. Although I do not suggest (and have not witnessed) any aspiration among my interlocutors to mimic celebrity mothers, Nicholson, Fox, and Heffernan's research does parallel Istanbulite women's changing perspectives of their postnatal bodies. Examining the social aspects of pregnancy sheds light on female "body time" and on how pregnancy shapes female temporalities.[14]

Despite the great number of studies written about social and political control over reproduction and reproductive technologies as well as the anthropological interest in the rituals of marriage and childbirth, the making of pregnant and postpregnant bodies has until recently escaped attention. This lack of attention has resulted in a social science lacuna on pregnancy as a separate category of analysis (Ivry 2010; Han 2013). In her work on pregnancy among middle-class American women, the feminist anthropologist Sallie Han (2013) suggests

14. The changing relationship between women and their pregnant and postnatal bodies has been studied across disciplines in relation to aesthetics (see, e.g., Nicolson, Fox, and Heffernan 2010); public and private health-related surveillance (Crossley 2007; Fox, Heffernan, and Nicolson 2009); the maternal body and identity (Haynes 2008); dissatisfaction and depression related to matters of aesthetics (Skouteris et al. 2005; Haedt and Keel 2007; Clark et al. 2009b); and exercise during pregnancy (Wallace et al. 1986; Wang and Apgar 1998; Downs, DiNallo, and Kirner 2008). Iris Marion Young (1984) explains the subjectivity of a pregnant body through multiple levels of alienation from the body.

that the everyday social practices that surround and form ordinary, uncomplicated American pregnancies cluster into two main areas: (1) literacy events involving the reading of pregnancy books, the maintenance of fertility-cycle charts, and the interpretation of home pregnancy tests and ultrasounds; and (2) consumption activities such as nursery decoration, baby showers, and gift registries. Han argues that these social practices of literacy and consumption in fact discipline and police pregnant bodies, rendering them docile bodies that follow social recommendations for an ordinary pregnancy. In her work, Han opens up the concept of "ordinariness" as a locus of inquiry, suggesting that these mundane social practices of making records and following routines also produce meanings about pregnant bodies as ordinary. Her focus on ordinariness is a way to turn both the practices and their artifacts—ordinary pregnant bodies—into the primary objects of analysis.

According to Tsipy Ivry (2010), pregnancy has a transformative effect on a woman's life in Israel and Japan. Her work reveals how pregnancy's transformative capacity is both medical and social and how gendered meanings inscribed upon pregnant bodies are not fixed. This suggests that women's relationships with these meanings may be fluid as well.

Conclusion

This chapter located pregnancy as a pivotal point in the gendered temporality of Istanbulite women and suggests that the effects of this point in time on women's bodies span both before and after pregnancy. Pregnancy lies at the intersection of two different temporal norms, one that centralizes motherhood by sanctifying it and one that glorifies prenatal young and fit female bodies. Pregnancy manifests the complex dynamics of and constraints on the female body. Because these constraints are in constant conversation with the way women experience embodied time, women's agentive responses to the conflicting temporal demands of femininity are also always shifting.

Because time is experienced differently in, on, and by different bodies, it is important to avoid theories of time that unintentionally privilege the accounts of certain temporalities over others—for example, the temporalities of able, heterosexual males. Even when scholars recognize gender in their analysis of the ways time is experienced by bodies, androgenic biases continue to dominate. The scholarly perspective often projects the concerns of a male-centered gaze onto women's experiences of embodied time, with the expectation of finding homogenized aesthetic ideologies. As we have seen in the case of Istanbulite women, the consideration of which physical traces of time are to be erased and which are to be cherished as a source of pride differs across distinctions of class, age, and number of children. Most women in their thirties begin their exercise stories with reference to their pregnancies, exhibiting, as Zerrin did, a set of diverse and conflicting sentiments about their pregnant bodies.

If, as Mark Flinn and Allen Bluedorn (2002) argue, human life is constrained by bioschedules, the corporeal lifetime constraints imposed on women's lives are most certainly related to biological schedules that include childbirth. Women's *spor merakı* has become a socially sanctioned way of managing these biological constraints. My respondents interpreted their narratives of leisure and exercise through the bioscheduled temporal lens of childbirth.

9

Emanet Corporalities

"Our bodies are God's *emanet* to us. It is a duty to be healthy."[1] These were the words Gülizar used when I asked her about her *spor merakı* after a Pilates session. Many of my interlocutors expressed similar sentiments with different words: that exercise is about the temporality of the body. When used in reference to body and exercise, *emanet*—translatable as "trust," "charge," or "responsibility"— denotes women's corporeal obligation to keep the body physically undamaged. As I have delved into *emanet* ethnographically, the shift in Istanbulite women's understanding of corporeal time started standing out. The body, once perceived as something finite, was now part of the infinite cosmological temporality of God. This shift in women's understandings and reflections of corporeal time simultaneously allows them to approach exercise not only as a way to stave off the eventual decline of a finite aging body but also as a means to preserve corporeal wholeness.

Old Ideas in New Bottles

On a spring day in Istanbul, Meral and I were sitting in Eski Kafa, a *nargile kafe* (*shisha* or waterpipe café) in Fatih at the center of Istanbul. With its modern-meets-old-world atmosphere, homemade dishes, and free snacks of monkey nuts, unshelled sunflower seeds, and Turkish tea, Eski Kafa is one among the many new *nargile kafe*s that have

1. Casual conversation with Gülizar, Feb. 11, 2012.

sprung up in Istanbul since the 1990s. Part of a new trend, these cafés serve as leisurely meeting venues for Islamic youth. This one, owned and run by a fairly well-known Islamic intellectual, attracts many like-minded intellectuals and academics, who gather to discuss politics, literature, philosophy, Sufism, and the never obsolete Islamic subjects of modernity, tradition, and westernization. The café's name, "Eski Kafa," clearly chosen as praise for a more traditional worldview, translates as "Old Mentality," a phrase most often used figuratively in the sense of "outdated."

As I sat studying the shop and its clientele, I spotted two women I recognized—Sibel Eraslan, a religious female intellectual and Islamist activist, and Hümeyra, a young woman I had met just a few months earlier, who would later become a columnist for a daily newspaper. They were on their way out but had a minute or two to speak with me. Hümeyra kindly introduced me to Eraslan, explaining that I was working on Istanbulite women's *spor merakı*. In this limited time, Eraslan perhaps felt the need to bring perspective to my research topic and commented on how problematic it was for Muslim women to "get caught up in the madness of the beauty and consumption culture." I asked her if she would be willing to talk to me more, to which she kindly responded, "İnşallah," God willing. An indefinite "İnşallah" almost always means a polite no, and we all knew that. I thanked her anyway, hugged Hümeyra, and went back to smoking *shisha* with Meral.

Eraslan's words stuck with me; she was plainly expressing certain ideas that have been in circulation for a while. Indeed, I was quite familiar with this particular kind of Islamic critique that considers capitalist and consumerist values to be Western, modern, and un-Islamic. This particular Islamic perspective argues that consumerist culture draws Muslims slowly away from their Islamic values, and it therefore calls for Muslims to be aware of and on the lookout for such hazards (Aktaş 1988; Dilipak 1988; Ramazanoğlu 2000; Şişman 2005, 2006; Barbarosoğlu 2006). According to this perspective, the transformation of women's bodies is the most symbolic and alarming signifier of the domination of non-Islamic values because it embodies the presence of those values in the *mahrem* zone, the private realm. Indeed, the need for public awareness of the potential influence of consumerist culture was one of the pillars of the Islamic Revivalist discourse in Turkey throughout the 1990s. It remains a subject of debate in certain Islamic intellectual circles, where it is argued that rather than fully embracing modern values and practices, Muslims need to critically engage with them in the light of Qur'anic principles.

This particular Islamic view perceives the growing number of exercising women in Istanbul to be the result of an expanding aesthetic and consumer culture that idealizes slim bodies. Parallel accounts can be traced in sociology and anthropology: commercialized exercise disciplines by producing docile bodies that conform to heterosexual aesthetic norms propagated through the media (Markula and Pringle 2006). This view is in line with the dominant proclivity in social science analysis to link exercise and fitness to body image and thus to apprehend them as an extension of aesthetic culture (Bordo 1990; Marzano-Parisoli 2001; Miller 2006). In this understanding, *spor merakı* is taken to be a fashion in fitness and beauty but not in health and well-being. Women's beauty is considered something requiring work so as to render the female body desirable for the (male) public gaze. The evidence, however, suggests that diverse groups may have very differing relationships with exercise (Grant 2001; Poole 2001; Dionigi 2002; Courneya et al. 2003; Paulson 2005).

In the Islamic view, reforming physical female bodies with reference to the normative male gaze runs counter to the true purpose for which these bodies were created. Another religious female intellectual, Nazife Şişman,[2] develops these critiques in detail in her influential book *Emanetten mülke: Kadın, beden, siyaset* (From Trust to

---

2. I do not refer to Şişman as a feminist because she rejects being identified as such. It is important to highlight, however, that she writes almost exclusively on women's issues. She is one of many female religious intellectuals who object to being referred to as "feminist" because their arguments do not stem from (Western) feminist motivations but are based in Islamic ethics.

Property: Woman, Body, Politics, 2006). Şişman criticizes changes in Turkish women's status brought about by a globalized modernization project that promotes westernization and secularization. The modernization project Şişman examines is not the secular Kemalist project of the twentieth century but rather the way a globalized modernity has entered Turkey through capitalist means. Her critiques of the change in women's status are not about women's participation in the public sphere or their access to equal rights. Rather, Şişman argues that modernization has resulted in women's bodies being perceived as *mülk* (property) as opposed to *emanet* (a trust): "Once the *self* regards the body as a project with which to actualize itself, it is then trapped in the vicious circle of the 'young, beautiful body' image, plastic surgeries, and the culture of consumption" (2006, 39, emphasis added).[3]

Şişman's account has Sufi and spiritual elements as well, warning the reader that the materiality of the body should never dominate our understanding of self. Moreover, most of the time, caring for the physical body is not the same thing as and even works against caring for the self.

According to Şişman, as soon as women begin caring for the aesthetics of their physical bodies, they do so in order to try to fit in with particular cultural norms. Those norms force women to pay more attention to the aesthetics of the body and less to the values in spirituality—more to the package, less to the content, as often put more crudely. In Şişman's view, this excess attention to the body reflects a change in women's perspective on the body's relationship to God and the afterlife. In other words, Şişman does more than simply echo Islamic critiques from a woman's perspective. She also links women's changing relationships with their bodies to their changing understanding of embodied time in a larger cosmology of temporality.

3. In the original Turkish: "Benliğin kendini gerçekleştirmek üzere bedenini bir proje gibi değerlendirilmesi, 'genç, güzel beden' imajının sarmalında, estetik cerrahinin ve tüketim kültürünün esareti altına girmeye yol acmaktadır."

Whose Bodies Are These We Hold?
The Divine Call for Exercise

Two questions arise in relation to the Islamic perspective on the body as *emanet* and the critique of the new exercise culture. Do women exercise simply to change their physical bodies in relation to a socially received image of beauty? Where do women locate their bodies in relation to cosmological time? *Emanet* can be translated as "custody" or "entrustment" and is thus understood as a thing given or taken for safeguarding and care. In her monograph on organ transplants in Egypt, *Our Bodies Belong to God* (2012), Sherine Hamdy discusses the original Arabic word for "trust," *amana*, in terms of the body being conceived as a trust given by God to each person for safekeeping (162, 187, 202), but only for a short time during life in this world. Once the body is conceived as *emanet*, it then follows that such a trust must be kept healthy, well preserved, and in the best possible condition until such time as it is returned to God after death. The concept of *emanet* thus embodies a cosmological understanding of the temporality of life and its impermanence. Because the individual is in possession of her body only temporarily, she needs to imagine a cosmology in which her body does not represent the whole of her true self, but merely its physical portion.

Fatma Bayram, an Islamic preacher who is not only an exercising woman but also an influential figure in upper- and upper-middle-class Islamic circles in Istanbul, defined taking care of the body as an Islamic duty.

> As with any other opportunity given by God, a Muslim is required to benefit from her body while it is at its best. I believe that the crucial point here is this: we will have to give an account of our bodies as well [i.e., on the Day of Judgment, after death and resurrection]. Thus, the body does not belong to me. According to the Islamic perspective, the body is also an *emanet*. We will be required to give an account of whether or not we used it correctly. Therefore, a Muslim should think reflectively and ask themselves, "How can I

utilize [the body] while it is at its best?" This is one of the duties of a Muslim.[4]

Women's engagement in and enthusiasm for exercise, their *spor merakı*, provide an answer to Fatma Bayram's question. Mehlika, a pious, head-scarf-wearing woman in her early thirties who studied at an Imam Hatip school from age twelve to eighteen,[5] was now pursuing an MA in social sciences. Havva Abla, a secular, fifty-one-year-old housewife and a high-school graduate, did not wear a head scarf. Despite the differences in their level of religiosity and religious knowledge, both Havva and Mehlika voiced similar ideas about their bodies, health, and exercise. Their views are reflective of a larger Islamic cosmology that imagines humans as temporary owners of their bodies.

I was introduced to Mehlika during a breakfast at Meziyet's house in late 2011. Like Meziyet, Mehlika was also attending the gym in Yeşilvadi. She had been involved in sports since the age of fourteen and had a black belt in taekwondo, although she could never compete owing to application regulations concerning the head scarf.[6] She also worked as a fitness trainer for a year. As an educated woman who comes from a religious background, Mehlika thought reflectively on contemporary issues relating to religion. During our interview, she developed a critical perspective on the rising consumption culture and women's obsession with fashion. "When we adapt Muslim lifestyle to the concepts we borrow from the West, it gets problematic," she

4. Interview, Feb. 15, 2012.

5. Imam Hatip schools, established in the early twentieth century as secondary educational institutions designed to educate government-employed imams, offer language training in Arabic and courses on Islamic teachings. For some religious families in Turkey, Imam Hatip schools are a place where their children can gain proper knowledge of Islam, obtain a gender-segregated education, and, if they are girls, wear the head scarf. For a more extensive analysis of Imam Hatip schools, see Ozgur 2012.

6. Prior to 2012, to apply as a national sportswoman in Turkey, an applicant was required to provide a photo that revealed her neck and hair, which those who wore a head scarf could not do. This requirement is no longer enforced.

stated. I asked her whether she saw fitness as an extension of this idea. "To begin with," she replied, "sports really exist in *sünnet-i seniyye* [the good deeds of the Prophet Muhammad, an example to Muslims]. It has been seriously recommended by our prophet, peace be upon him. And, if I am not mistaken, he has a *hadis-i şerif* [a saying of the prophet] that says 'Those who engage in sports find well-being [Spor yapan sıhhat bulut].' Therefore, we are advised to take good care of our bodies."[7]

I was a bit puzzled by the last part of her answer where she was citing a *hadis-i şerif.* I expected her to know that even the word *sport* is a modern import and did not exist as a term or concept fourteen hundred years ago in the Saudi Arabian Peninsula. She was trying to remember another phrase, "Oruç tutan sıhhat bulur," which means "Those who fast find well-being," and although this phrase is not a *hadis-i şerif* either, it is often written as *mahya* (lit-up letters between the minarets of mosques). So I asked for further clarification.

SERTAÇ: To engage in sports? But *spor* is a new concept, isn't it?

MEHLIKA: Well, maybe not the same word, but in terms of looking after the body. I mean, it was something that could be interpreted as such. I am not translating but am trying to convey a meaning here [Mealen söylemiyorum, manen söylüyorum]. Now, first, our bodies are *emanet* [entrusted] to us from God. And that's why sports are important. It is not necessary to explain. You know, yoga is actually a religious ritual. Every religious act we do has meaning and is good for our body.

SERTAÇ: By "religious," you aren't referring to Islam, then?

MEHLIKA: No, but you create *rabıta* [a Sufi term indicating the creation of a spiritual connection]. They distribute pictures of *sahaja.*[8] You look at them, and you reflect and think about it.

7. Interview, Feb. 15, 2012.

8. Mehlika was referring here to the practice of distributing pictures of Shri Mataji Nirmala Devi during Sahaja Yoga practice as a meditation device. Sahaja Yoga is practiced in Istanbul.

> So, in a way, things we do for the well-being of our body have
> meaning. Why do we use this [body], and for what?

Because Mehlika believed herself to be in possession of her body
only for a temporary period of time, she found it normal for religion
to recommend exercise to Muslims. She viewed exercise as a means of
protecting the health and well-being of the body for all time. Therefore, exercising is a form of spiritual activity with the aim of safeguarding the body as, in a sense, a treasure of God. She clarified her point:

> Let's think this example through. Imagine two people paying 2,000
> Turkish lira [$600] for their own enjoyment. One buys an expensive
> camera for her hobby [with that money]; the other spends the same
> amount on a bag, a shoulder bag. The value these two objects pro-
> duce differs completely. With the camera, you produce beauty, you
> produce art. But with the expensive shoulder bag, the only thing
> you produce is status that makes you feel superior to others. I see
> sports as something that brings health, brings quality, to one's life.
> It improves mental health. That's how I see it.

According to Mehlika, exercise is one of the most important ways
to preserve the body in its "best condition," a concept that encapsulates the corporeal conservation project of maintaining both one's
physical and mental health. This explains why she believed that it is
natural for Islam to recommend that Muslims exercise. Mehlika's
belief in Islam and God demanded that she balance all the elements
of God's creation—body, soul, and physical world. Health occurs as a
result of the balance between these three elements. Importantly, taking good care of the body and one's health in this sense proposes a
specific temporality, conceptualized as an investment in the afterlife.
In other words, the temporal nature of the corporeal existence of the
body—its temporary nature—suggests that exercise is rendered as a
spiritually meaningful act, as Mehlika expressed it.

Havva Abla was at the time in her early fifties with two adult
children. Because she found gyms to be overcrowded and smelly, she
preferred to exercise in public parks, which she did every weekday for

approximately one and a half hours. She recounted that she used to attend two morning exercise sessions (an hour each) while living in Fatih. "On top of these [two hours], I had to walk for half an hour to reach the exercise area and another half an hour to return home." Quite surprised by her stamina, I responded, "Three hours! Isn't that too much?" "I like it, and my vertigo is completely gone now," she explained. Havva Abla was a size six (US size), petite, and had several times been mistaken for a teenager when she exercised in the park. She looked perhaps even more petite when surrounded by women of her age, who often wore a size fourteen or higher. She tied her dark hair back in a ponytail and never wore bright or pale colors; I always saw her wearing brown, gray, dark green, or black, her athletic body hidden under modest clothing. Yet in terms of performance, endurance, and flexibility, she was almost as good as the trainers.

Unlike Mehlika, Havva Abla never received formal religious education. She cannot read the Qur'an, does not pray, and is secular in her political ideas. What she shared with Mehlika, however, was her view of the meaning and purpose of exercise in life. "Since God knows us best, He tells us to exercise. This way, we stay healthy and protect our bodies, which are *emanet* to us."[9]

Reconnecting the Body with Nature

Despite their contrasting religious backgrounds and political views, both Mehlika and Havva Abla imagine religion as an ordinary aspect of their exercise lives and argue that Islam should entreat believers to exercise. This understanding of exercise as a requisite of well-being, exhibited across Havva Abla, Mehlika, and Fatma Bayram's narratives despite their demographic differences, is rooted in the idea of the temporality of corporeal existence, whereby body, life, earth, and everything in it are owned by God for eternity and given temporarily in trust to humans. When bodies are located within this temporal cosmology, exercise is God's command.

9. Field notes, Nov. 30, 2011.

The Islamic roots of the term *emanet*—again, meaning "trust" or "charge"—comes from surah Al-Ahzab 33:72 of the Qur'an: "Indeed, we offered the trust to the heavens and the earth and the mountains, and they declined to bear it and feared it; but man [undertook to] bear it. Indeed, he was unjust and ignorant." The content of *emanet* has been a matter of spiritual debate among scholars of Islam but is generally considered to refer to Muslims' religious duties (Ghazali 1985; Hökelekli 1988; Al Qurtubi 2003). When *emanet* is discussed by scholars of Islam in relation to the body, it refers to Muslim duties owed to the organs and limbs, which must be kept away from sinful acts and be returned to God without spiritual blemish or damage.

This idea of preserving the body and returning it to its ultimate owner has traditionally been articulated with respect to an inner, non-corporeal purity of spirit and absence of sin. In contrast, the way women describe *emanet* today reflects a shift in the concept's definition and usage. Although it still refers to the religious duty of safeguarding the body, it no longer suggests avoidance of sin. Well-being in the sense in which Istanbulite women understand it cannot be protected through inaction or idleness. In women's understanding, the *emanet* nature of the body as trust demands active participation in exercise and diet. This new notion, not unique to Istanbulite women, constitutes a significant shift away from traditional admonitions to guard one's body parts from certain actions to ensure that they do not commit sins. The new interpretation of Islamic values entreats Muslims to actively look after and care for the body. Indeed, numerous scholars within sport studies have documented Muslim social acceptance of sport as a highly recommended and Islam-appropriate activity (De Knop et al. 1996; Kay 2006; Tober and Budiani 2007; Amara 2008).

As discussed in chapter 4, women's *spor merakı* in Istanbul is related to women's ability to transcend the fast-paced rhythms and unnatural concrete ecosystem in the city by means of their living flesh. The bodies of the city's residents are the corporeal reflection of the fact that their *fıtrî* (innate/natural) connection to the earth has been broken. Women's struggle to reconnect with their own bodies and the *emanet* given to them by God is part of a protracted human effort to restore this imbalance between the body and the natural environment. Havva Abla succinctly explained this larger human struggle against the unnatural: "My daughter [addressing me], nothing we do or eat is natural anymore. They talk about this on TV all the time. Everything is *kanserojen* [carcinogenic]. Even the milk and water we drink are not natural. We need to make an effort to protect our body, our health."[10]

From the perspective of many women, their bodies are being invaded by the artificial, unhealthy, and unnatural ingredients in their food. As Hilâl Teyze once said to me and as *fıtrat* (creation/nature) dictates, their bodies should be more *tabii* (natural, earthly) and connected to nature, not torn from the earth (*topraktan kopmamış*).[11] Women perceive aesthetic and health-related issues as symptoms of a larger underlying problem—an unnatural lifestyle. This was especially apparent when during a conversation over dinner Hilâl Teyze talked about the effects on her body of too much salt in her diet.

> HILÂL TEYZE: Some evenings I lay my hands on my kidney [putting her hand on her left abdomen] and say, "Oh, my kidney, I have failed to look after you. I promise to take better care of you from now on. But please rejuvenate yourself now." [Laughed.]
>
> SERTAÇ: And how will it rejuvenate itself?
>
> HILÂL TEYZE: I am trying to consume less salt [sodium]. Salt damages the kidneys.

Women perceive the sources of their feeling of disconnection from the earth as their urban lifestyle, new technologies, and industrially produced foods, all of which alter their physical bodies. The urban material environment in which the bodies of city residents exist limits movement and muscle work. Those who were born and raised in Istanbul grew up when the city still had crop lands and more soil to walk on. Modern technologies, urbanization, and conveniences restrain bodies from their natural state in motion. Paved streets are

10. Field notes, Mar. 14, 2012.
11. Field notes, Jan. 12, 2012.

flatter and less varied than rocky field paths, making for less whole-body muscle work. Urban lifestyles leave less and less room for physical movement, resulting in health problems (Katzmarzyk and Mason 2009; Wells 2010; Kalra and Unnikrishnan 2012). One of these problems, a main cause of modern-day weight gain, is insulin resistance (Watve and Yajnik 2007).

Havva Abla and Hilâl Teyze's conceptualization of the assaults on their bodies segues with the medical discourse on the "behavioral switch hypothesis," which posits that insulin resistance is a socioecological adaptation mediating the transition from a muscle-dependent (active) lifestyle to a brain-dependent (sedentary) lifestyle.

It is during exercise that women are able to experience a harmony with all of creation and a sense that they are preserving the *emanet* of their bodies, given to them by God for safekeeping. Exercise in this sense is not merely a passing fad sparked by a desire for instant and earthly gratification. It is a temporal solution to the unnaturalness of modern material culture: the way bodies interact with technological devices, physical surroundings, and urban environments in the contemporary world.

In light of my conversations, Sibel Eraslan's disdain for exercising women who "get caught up in the madness of beauty and consumption culture" warrants reappraisal. Similar Islamic critiques imagine women's changing relationship with their bodies as a move away from *emanet* and as a kind of voluntary submission to the consumerist culture of beauty. But as we have seen in this chapter, women do not view their bodies exclusively in terms of the contemporary culture of aesthetics. My field notes are filled, line upon line, with women's accounts of their fluctuating relationship to exercise and discipline, their unremitting contestation with the culture of aesthetics, and their suspicions about the fit and trim bodies presented to them as both ideal and possible. These field notes suggest that women's many and varied understandings of the temporal aspects of their bodies are too complex to stuff into a preconceived analysis of docile, agentless bodies. My interlocutors' perspectives seem to suggest a more nuanced relationship with their bodies, with their own agency, and with time.

Conclusion

Shifting time and temporality also shift the perception of reality—if not the reality itself. In his famous novel *Time Regulation Institute* (2014), Ahmet Hamdi Tanpınar tells us creatively how realities are formed through temporal divisions. He presents us with a struggle between two different social lives, Eastern and Western, through the struggles between two different times and temporalities. In Maureen Freely and Alexander Dawe's beautiful translation, Tanpınar points out how the Islamic regulation of time also creates an Islamic life, a sense of reality, a sense of self, and a sense of relationship between the self and the world: "Everyone knows that in former times our lives revolved around the clock. . . . The clock dictated all manner of worship: the five daily prayers, as well as meals during the holy month of Ramadan, the evening *iftar* and morning *sahur*. A clock offered the most reliable path to God, and our forefathers regulated their lives with this in mind" (21).

Istanbulite women invest in their agentive desires by creating their own temporalities in which their new self-imaginations can be practiced and performed. Women's redefinition of *emanet* reveals two themes. First, ordinary Muslims' ability to locate current Islamic concepts within their changing lifestyles is much more creative and agentive than assumed in the literature discussed in the introduction to this book. Second, although the temporality of corporeal existence is salient in women's discourses, their engagement with the temporality of their bodies remains less explored within social science discourses. By reconceptualizing and redefining *emanet*, women are able to locate their temporal bodies as part of a larger cosmology, which in turn complicates their relationship with normative aesthetics.

A crucial point here is that women imagine their bodies as being something that belongs to God, who is also understood in their cosmology to be the creator of the universe. This perspective imposes the need for harmony in God's creation—in other words, between nature and humans—which is interpreted through the concept of *emanet* as bodily health. In this cosmological mapping, exercise is conceived as a way of reinstalling the harmony lost in the urban lifestyle, which reduces the physical movements of the body and thereby causes health problems. In this way, women imagine their involvement in exercise as a necessary means of maintaining the newly defined cosmological temporality of their corporeal existence.

Spor merakı recalibrates the way women understand and experience the relation between time and the body. The way Istanbulite women experience, desire, and redefine *spor merakı* enables them to gain their own sense of temporality. In the process, *spor merakı* opens up a path for change far beyond the physical. What changes is also the way they see their temporal connection to the world and their lives. The change at stake relates to women's physical bodies as they are experienced through movement and to women's own embodied ability to keep pace with the city and the world.

Coda

Tracing Desire

So what does it mean to study desire ethnographically? How can one approach something like desire, which can constantly escape from control mechanisms and from discourses, methods, and genres? What sort of investments are required to witness the moments when women's desiring selves escape from normative realms?

Part of conducting an ethnography of desire lies in good old friendships, establishing ties with the people you have met beyond some intellectual project where you *see* them merely as "informants" or "subjects"—admittedly, I find the latter term irritating. Becoming the person with whom women feel comfortable enough to talk about moments of joy, moments that are otherwise judged, is at the center of the ethnographic aspect of this study. Another element of this study is about recognizing how easily realms of desire can escape from analytical focus. These women's desiring selves are not formed through a collective identity or political formation. They do not either immediately or visibly challenge or resist normative perspectives. They do, however, pierce through them, create cracks, diverge from them, fool them, as longitudinal ethnography has revealed more clearly. There is, however, another dimension in understanding the scholarly value of such research. Tania Modleski (2007) urges feminist scholars to take women's popular entertainment seriously. As the research I have done for this project has grown, I have developed a stronger concern with investigating the "feminine perspective" (Boddy 1989, passim) and with celebrating femininity (Braidotti 1991) as a corrective to earlier masculinist normative approaches. Women's attempt to form desiring subjectivities is worthy of deeper analysis, whether those desires are initiated by masculinist systems or not.

On the Banality of Women's Desire

Paradoxically, the same perspective that centralizes masculinist normative approaches also regards women's *spor meraki* as a somewhat witless fad. Yet I concur with Lauren Berlant and Michael Warner's assertion that "[an activity's] very banality calls us to understand the technologies that produce its ordinariness" (1998, 549). In order to further understand and perhaps trouble the technologies Berlant mentions, I propose a "celebration of femininity," to use Rosi Braidotti's term (1991, 134). I believe the gendered, hierarchical perceptions of enjoyment result in depriving women's homosocial enjoyments and leisure of a contingent analysis, in trivializing them, and in allotting to them only a voyeuristic interest.

I agree with Kathleen Stewart (2008), who brilliantly theorizes that everyday life and the everyday require a "weak" theory as opposed to a "strong" one—a task that is challenging yet necessary and quite unfinished. Ordinariness enables a particular subjecthood that not only is a product of an affective aspect of life but also has the capacity to affect daily life. Stewart suggests that "a world of shared banalities can be a basis of sociality" (2007, 27). It is in this ordinary web of trajectories that my interlocutors have come to shape their interconnected desiring subjectivities.

The ethnographic call to focus on banality and the seemingly mundane aspects of everyday life is in fact related to a broader obstacle in social studies that often limits our ability to capture the ordinariness, complexities, ephemeral and fading temporalities, contradictions, and intricacies of people's everyday lives. These aspects are what I have attempted to unfold throughout this book. Istanbulite women connect with larger social structures through their bodies, their femininities, their womanhood, their subjectivities—all of which also become part of their desiring subjectivities and thus connect women from various backgrounds. Although they might attach different meanings to exercise and are involved in it in different settings and in different outfits, both a lower-class Sunni woman from Kayseri in her late fifties and an upper-class Kemalist woman from Izmir in her early twenties think of *spor merakı* as an object of desire. They use *spor merakı* in the formation of their desiring selves. As a result, women from different political spectrums share parallel experiences in the way they imagine their selves in relation to the world.

A core challenge in this study has been to produce an ethnography with multiple voices and perspectives representing both the interlocutory process of fieldwork and the process of collaboration with my interlocutors. In order to find ways for women to speak for themselves, I have repeatedly consulted interview and field data and have shared the emergent results and analysis with my interlocutors to get their feedback on the representations of them. Academic work is accustomed to making itself vulnerable to the critique of other academics; making it vulnerable to the critique of nonacademic interlocutors can be even more rewarding.

On "the Transforming Ethnographer"

Toward the end of my fieldwork, I went to the Hamza Yerlikaya Sports Center. One of the most senior attendees of the gym, Sacide Hanım, who was always trying to keep skinny women away from the gym, noticed my weight loss. She asked, "How many kilos have you lost?" Sacide Hanım's question attracted the attention of two relatively younger women working out within earshot, so they joined in her inquiry: "Yes, how many?" Feeling a bit embarrassed about the multiple stares over my body, I just wanted to escape from that moment and so blurted, "I don't know." My response was not convincing. Our weights are regularly checked for free at the gym and written down on the individualized charts. I had the written printouts of my weight, my height, my body-mass index, and even my body-fat percentage. Sacide Hanım pressed with disbelief, "You must know the number." Getting nervous, I lied: "Maybe three or four kilos [seven or nine pounds]." Sacide Hanım would not believe me; she had the memory of my body. In fact, the majority of the regulars would have an idea of what their fellow gym members looked like when they first met. So Sacide Hanım said, "No, you must have lost more," and started pointing out the visible changes she was observing on my body. Then she asked me about what else I had been doing to lose weight. Did I diet? "No, but I stopped eating bread," I said. "Oh, Karatay diet.[1] I can never do that." She was happy to expose what she saw to be the secret behind my transition.

Sacide Hanım's reflection was not an isolated incident. It kept happening in the last few weeks of my fieldwork. The most illustrative time was during one of the farewell gatherings I organized before my departure. I visited the gyms one last time and went to the parks I frequented to tell everyone that it would be my last week there. The very last visit was with my upper-class interlocutors, with whom I organized a farewell party in the restaurant at the Yeşilvadi Community Center on May 23, 2012.

As usual, I arrived early at the community center, and I picked a spot in the restaurant garden, close to the playground in case any of my friends brought their children and preferred to watch them play while having breakfast. I was wearing my camel-colored silk scarf wrapped around my head, wide-legged trousers made with fine denim, and a matching blouse. In about ten minutes, Serra showed up. As we were waiting for the others to arrive, Serra and I spent some time catching up. We knew we would very soon have to say good-bye to each other, so there was a hint of sadness in the air. We talked about whether she could visit me in London, given her housework and childcare responsibilities and various other duties. "It has been very difficult just to come here today," she said. She then detailed everything she had to arrange that day so that she could make it on time for our gathering. It was a long and complicated list. She had three children and was managing a large house. "You could easily become a manager

1. A protein- and fat-based diet developed by a medical doctor Canan Karatay. She is known as the doctor against bread, rice, pasta, and pastries.

of a small company with this experience," I said, sharing my honest opinion. Then, somewhat abruptly, she stopped and turned to me: "Sertaç, my girl, you have become seriously womanly [Sertaç, kızım sen resmen kadınsılaştın]." She did not sound as if she were trying to compliment me. Rather, she stated this with a serious tone in her voice, solemn face, and raised eyebrows, as if it were a sudden discovery to her. I erupted in laughter and asked, "What does 'becoming womanly' mean?" She replied, "You have changed so much! We have done a good job on you."[2] Maybe the intersubjective exchanges my interlocutors and I had for the duration of my fieldwork had changed me. Or perhaps I hadn't changed at all. Perhaps it was they who had become more familiar with my already existing but somewhat different femininity.

At that stage, I had been exercising since July 2011 and had lost ten kilos (twenty-two pounds) and had generally become much fitter. Yet the change that was obvious to Serra and others was not purely physical, it seemed. According to Serra, "becoming womanly" entailed "change . . . not in your face, your height, or your body, but [in] your pose, your smile, even your voice!"[3]

After that moment, I started thinking more closely about the change in my relationship with both myself and my interlocutors over the past year. I reflected on how my use of verbal and body language in daily life had been altered. Part of that transformation was inevitable, even necessary and voluntary. In the early weeks of my fieldwork, not everyone was comfortable with me. I was perceived as an (over) educated woman from abroad, which caused several of my interlocutors to be formal, to try to sound smart, to use a formal tone, all of which erected an invisible barrier between us.[4]

2. Field notes, May 23, 2012.

3. I loved the way she said this in Turkish: "Canım yani değiştin resmen. Öyle yüzün, boyun, posun değişmedi ama duruşun, gülüşün hatta sesin kadınsılaştı!"

4. A significant number of works approach ethnography as performance. As an example, see Madison 2011. Please see the introduction to this book as well.

There are always barriers between the ethnographer and her field site, her interlocutors. These barriers include cultural, racial, linguistic, and other social biases; culture shock (on the ethnographer's part); the sense of a presumed hierarchy between people; and, above all, the definition of "self" and "other." The rapport can be established in multiple ways, but both parties need to work on it. Simply being an "insider" in a colloquial anthropological sense—that is, someone who grew up in Istanbul—would not make this ethnography easy if *the field* did not open itself up for me. And *the field* is never only about the region, the country, or the city where ethnographic fieldwork is conducted but also about the aspects of the lives of the individuals in that field—their realities, socialities, and everyday concerns. The kind of connection I sought with each and every interlocutor in the field would come from being able to enjoy life in the way she does, to connect to her perspective, to share her experiences, to try to undergo her frustrations, and to feel her aspirations. I reflected on and worked on toning down the vocabulary and body language that seemed to put women off. The more I worked on myself, the more comfortable they became with me, and the more "womanly" I seemed to become.

Serra's comments about me point out the transformative capacities of an interrelated combination of factors, including the self, one's willingness to change, interactions among women, Istanbul, a collective dynamism unleashed through movements and magnetically drawing women to each other, and a series of shared aesthetic references. The women I met were interested in transformation in all its forms: transformation of me and transformation of themselves. It is this transformation—one that I, too, experienced—that I have been exploring and unraveling in the context of this broader study of *spor merakı*. I had physically and subjectively become part of my study when these women's gaze was directed at me (chapter 6).

Letting the transformation women have been desiring for themselves take over the ethnographer was almost a more extensive form of "stepping off the porch." The sterile distance between the ethnographer and her interlocutors was forming an obstacle in the anthropological research. The more I toned down what marked me as foreign, overeducated, or less womanly, the better I connected with the women and the more easily we could speak about and share enjoyments and desires.

The better I connected with the women, the more this fieldwork became a rite of passage for me.

I have always been uneasy with certain scholarly approaches that tend (if not openly suggest) to treat the field like a lab to test a theory, as if each theory were somehow a free-floating concept and not a product of social systems, structures, interactive processes, and power mechanisms. In this treatment, all theories eventually work toward abstraction if not distance themselves from the field. There is a rising demand for and interest in this kind of philosophical anthropology, but, even aside from its limits and ideological and political tendencies, this is not what I have been aiming for. Now looking back, I could not have done an anthropological work on subjectivity without turning myself into an object of inquiry—for my own work and for my interlocutors.

The longer we are able to study women's *spor merakı*, however, the better we will understand how it generates a transformation in women's lives and in the broader systems that limit, control, and organize their lives. Desire is agentive, it is unexpected, and even when it is unconfrontational, it is still capable of creating fundamental, if not radical, change. The movements in which women are involved trouble the boundaries and territories they interact with and deterritorialize several borders surrounding them (Skalli 2006; see also chapters 5 and 7). Women mediate these boundaries dynamically through improvisation and negotiation with various actors, including media figures (chapter 3).

The results and insights generated in this research have revealed more than the expressions of the broader predicament of Istanbulite women's crafting of their own selves, temporalities, and spaces against the systemic operations that are imposed on them. It has revealed how forceful these women have had to be, but their forcefulness is that of a tree that is able to pierce through stone wall, making the cracks it opened bigger every day.

The Imaginaries of Desire, Imaginaries of Muslims

On one of my flights between Istanbul and London, I came across a gripping piece of art in the inflight Turkish Airlines magazine: *Impossible Dream* by the Gaza-born Palestinian artist Laila Shawa. The picture portrays ten women in colorful burqas, each holding a cone piled high with many scoops of ice cream that they are unable to eat because of their face veils. Their closed, presumably dreaming—as the title implies—almond-shaped eyes outlined in dark kohl and their fisted hands cupping the cones are the only parts of them uncovered. By the time I saw this artwork, I had already presented parts of my research at several conferences. Despite detailed ethnographic descriptions of my chosen subject—exercising Istanbulite women—one variety of awkward question kept being lobbed back at me at the end of my talks. The type of question would be awkward in the sense that no matter what the focus of the talk was (agency and desire, embodied rhythms or the female gaze in changing rooms), it would ask me to elaborate on Islam: how pious the women are; how many different types of *hijabi*s I have seen; how exactly they tie their head scarf while exercising; and whether the chosen style might be an indication of their level of religiosity. If I made my point about desiring self-making very clear, then I would be asked whether female gym attendees are exclusively secular (because religious women attend mosques, not gyms). I kept hitting on an obvious mental barrier in my academic audience, and Shawa's painting induced in me one of those rare eureka moments a researcher experiences in her work. This marvelous painting portrays the single most salient obstacle to thinking about women's desire.

Desire and women who happen to be Muslims are simply incompatible in our Eurocentric minds—or *impossible*, as the artist puts it. In the dominant cultural discourse, desire is temporary, melting away like the ice cream the women hold. Islam, in contrast, is (viewed as) an enduring regulatory and nonliberatory religion that disavows women's temporary desires, requiring piety and modesty in their place. Islam, it has been theorized, builds barriers in women's lives; unless women resist it, Islam will block women's access to desire, joy, and pleasure.

Women's desiring subjectivities, as manifested in complex, inter-linked, and dynamic ways that are explored ethnographically in this book, reveal a nuanced embroidery, however. The academic and cultural narratives on Muslim women that extensively focus on the conundrums of piety, chastity, obedience, resistance, oppression, or liberation are too narrow to represent the experience of women—who happen to be Muslim. Although earlier research on Muslim women extensively focused on the barriers they faced and their struggles, there has never been the opposite, and in fact there has been a recurring dis-missal of researching how these women share moments of joy, pursue desires, create humor, and connect with one another in the fabric of daily life. This study attempts to fill in this lacuna in the research by portraying a more nuanced picture of the everyday experiences and stories of Istanbulite women who momentarily dissolve the border between the self and the other in the pursuit of *spor merakı*, thereby shifting the dominant narrative surrounding Muslim women into a story of self-making through everyday practices involving hybridity, liminality, and fluidity.

Glossary

❧

References

❧

Index

Glossary

açık. Open or available, also used in a pejorative sense for those who do not wear a head scarf (see *kapalı*)

abla. Elder sister

beğenmek (*beğeniyor*). To like or appreciate

bilgi açlığı. Thirst or hunger for knowledge

canım. My dear or my soul

çeyiz. Trousseau

dert ortağı. Confidant or "fellow sufferer"

dışarıda. Out in public

emanet. Trust or charge or responsibility

gecekondu. Shantytown but literally meaning "built overnight"

girdap. Vortex

harem(*lik*): The domestic sphere in a household that is accessible to all females and male relatives; a place where men who are not members of the family are not traditionally allowed

hemşehrilik. Colocalism or colociality

içmek (*içiyorlar*). To take, drink, and/or smoke

İnşallah (Arabic: Inshallah): "God willing" or "If God wills it"

İstanbullu/Istanbuli. Istanbulite; "Istanbuli," the Arabic version used with a cosmopolitan Ottoman reference to signify those who have been living in the city for several generations

kapalı. Literally "closed/covered," used for a woman who covers her head with a scarf

kendim için. For myself

kendini şımartmak. Spoil oneself

kentli. Urban

köylülük. Literally "villagerness" but used by the urban elites to refer to rural migrants who have failed to integrate into the city life

markasız. Without a brand name, referring to those products produced with the lowest-cost labor and material by unregistered companies and used in conjunction with the term *marka* for even the least-expensive consumer product that has any brand name

Maşallah (Arabic: Mashallah). "With the wish of God (it happened)"

mescit (Arabic: *masjid*). Prayer room

metrobüs. Public transport vehicle in Istanbul that connects the most-crowded neighborhoods

nazar. Literally "gaze, but meaning "strong gaze" and often incorrectly translated as the "evil eye," referring to the strong gaze that is believed to bring misfortune to the person seen or gazed upon and that is a result of the seer's or gazer's heightened feelings of love, jealousy, desire, and so on

özenmek (*özeniyor*). To admire or emulate

rahat. Comfortable

spor merakı. Interest or curiosity in sports

sporcu teyzeler. Sporty aunt/aunties

Üç Aylar. The three holy months in the Islamic calendar, Recep, Şaban, and Ramazan, with Ramazan the holiest of three

yalı. An Ottoman-era house by the shore of the Bosphorus

yaşam sevinci. Joy of living

yeşil sermaye. Green capital, a phrase used by the media in the 1990s to refer to the newly rising Islamic middle class because the color green is believed to be the color of Islam

Note to Glossary

Several words in Turkish have Arabic origins, especially religious terms. In the book, I use the words my interlocutors used, explaining their meaning and giving their more widely known Arabic versions if needed. For instance, staying faithful to my interlocutors, I used the word *head scarf,* a direct translation of the Turkish word *başörtüsü,* although I explain in the text that *hijab* is instead widely used in the literature. Or instead of the Arabic term *masjid,* I use the Turkish word *mescit* but explain its meaning in English and provide the Arabic equivalent.

Turkish Letters and Sounds

A/a: /a/, as *a* in f*a*ther
B/b: /b/, as *b* in *b*oy
C/c: /d͡ʒ/, as *j* in *j*oy
Ç/ç: /t͡ʃ/, as *ch* in *ch*air
D/d: /d/, as *d* in *d*oor
E/e: /ɛ/, as *ea* in d*ea*d
F/f: /f/, as *f* in *f*ield
G/g: /g/, as *g* in *g*oin*g*
Ğ/ğ: /:/, a silent letter that extends the previous vowel
H/h: /h/, as *h* in *h*ospital
I/ı: /ɯ/, as *e* in op*e*n
İ/i: /i/, as *ee* in m*ee*t
J/j: /ʒ/, as *s* in era*s*ure
K/k: /k/, as *k* in *k*ennel
L/l: /ɬ/, as *l* in *l*ittle
M/m: /m/, as *m* in *m*iddle
N/n: /n/, as *n* in *n*ever
O/o: /o/, as *o* in c*o*ld
Ö/ö: /ø/, as *ur* in n*ur*se, with lips rounded
P/p: /p/, as *p* in *p*roblem
R/r: /r/, as *r* in *r*ough
S/s: /s/, as *s* in *s*ingle
Ş/ş: /ʃ/, as *sh* in *sh*ow
U/u: /u/, as *oo* in sh*oo*t
T/t: /t/, as *t* in *t*ick
Ü/ü: /y/, as *u* in p*u*re
V/v: /v/, as *v* in *v*anish
Y/y: /j/, as *y* in *y*ou
Z/z: /z/, as *z* in *z*ebra

References

Abu-Lughod, Lila. 1986. *Veiled Sentiments: Honor and Poetry in a Bedouin Society*. Berkeley: Univ. of California Press.

———. 2002. "Egyptian Melodrama: Technology of the Modern Subject." In *Media worlds: Anthropology on New Terrain*, edited by Faye D. Ginsburg, Lila AbuLughod and Brian Larkin, 115–33. Berkeley: Univ. of California Press.

Abu Zahra, Nadia M. 1970. "On the Modesty of Women in Arab Muslim Villages: A Reply." *American Anthropologist* 72, no. 5: 1079–92.

Ad-Dab'bagh, Yasser. 2008. "The Transformative Effect of Seeking the Eternal: A Sampling of the Perspectives of Two Great Muslim Intellectuals—Ibn-Ḣazm and Al-Ghazāli." *Psychoanalytic Inquiry* 28, no. 5: 550–59.

Afsaruddin, Asma. 1999. Introduction to *Hermeneutics and Honor: Negotiating Female Public Space in Islamic/ate Societies*, edited by Asma Afsaruddin, 1–28. Cambridge, MA: Center for Middle Eastern Studies, Harvard Univ.

Agathangelou, Anna M. 2004. *The Global Political Economy of Sex: Desire, Violence, and Insecurity in Mediterranean Nation States*. London: Palgrave Macmillan.

Ahıska, Meltem. 2003. "Occidentalism: The Historical Fantasy of the Modern." *South Atlantic Quarterly* 102, no. 2: 351–79.

Akınerdem, Feyza, and Nükhet Sirman. 2017. "Melodram ve oyun: *Tehlikeli Oyunlar* ve *Poyraz Karayel*'de bir temsiliyet rejimi sorunsalı." *Monograf Edebiyat Eleştirisi Dergisi* 7, no. 1: 212–45.

Akşit, Elif Ekin. 2005. *Kızların sessizliği: Kız enstitülerinin uzun tarihi*. Istanbul: İletişim Yayınları.

Aksoy, Asu. 2014. "Istanbul'un neoliberalizmle Imtihani." In *Yeni Istanbul çalışmaları: Sınırlar, mücadeleler, açılımlar*, edited by Cenk Özbay and Ayfer Bartu Candan, 26–46. Istanbul: Metis.

Aktaş, Cihan. 1988. *Sistem içinde kadın*. Istanbul: Beyan Yayınları.

Alemdaroğlu, Ayça. 2005. "Politics of the Body and Eugenic Discourse in Early Republican Turkey." *Body & Society* 11, no. 3: 61–76.

Allouche, Sabiha. 2019. "Love, Lebanese Style: Toward an Either/And Analytic Framework of Kinship." *Journal of Middle East Women's Studies* 15, no. 2: 157–78.

Alloula, Malek. 1986. *The Colonial Harem*. Minneapolis: Univ. of Minnesota Press.

Altan-Olcay, Özlem. 2009. "Gendered Projects of National Identity Formation: The Case of Turkey." *National Identities* 11, no. 2: 165–86.

Altınay, Rustem Ertug. 2013a. "From a Daughter of the Republic to a Femme Fatale: The Life and Times of Turkey's First Professional Fashion Model, Lale Belkıs." *Women's Studies Quarterly* 41, no. 1: 113–30.

———. 2013b. "Sule Yüksel Senler: An Early Style Icon of Urban Islamic Fashion in Turkey." In *Islamic Fashion and Anti-fashion: New Perspectives from Europe and North America*, edited by Emma Tarlo, 107–22. London: Bloomsbury.

Amara, Mahfoud. 2008. "An Introduction to the Study of Sport in the Muslim World." In *Sport and Society: A Student Introduction*, edited by Barrie Houlihan, 532–53. London: Sage.

Amman, Tayfun. 2005. *Kadın ve spor*. Istanbul: Morpa Kültür Yayınları.

Andrews, Gavin J., Mark I. Sudwell, and Andrew C. Sparkes. 2005. "Towards a Geography of Fitness: An Ethnographic Case Study of the Gym in British Bodybuilding Culture." *Social Science & Medicine* 60, no. 4: 877–91.

Antoun, Richard T. 1968. "On the Modesty of Women in Arab Muslim Villages: A Study in the Accommodation of Traditions." *American Anthropologist* 70, no. 4: 671–97.

Appadurai, Arjun. 1996. *Modernity at Large: Cultural Dimensions of Globalization*. Minneapolis: Univ. of Minnesota Press.

Arat, Yesim. 1998. "Feminists, Islamists, and Political Change in Turkey." *Political Psychology* 19, no. 1: 117–31.

Arat, Zehra F. 1998. "Educating the Daughters of the Republic." In *Deconstructing Images of "the Turkish Woman*, edited by Zehra F. Arat, 157–80. New York: St. Martin's.

Arıpınar, Erdoğan, Cem Atabeyoğlu, and Tuncer Cebecioğlu. 2000. *Olimpiyat oyunlarında Türk kızları*. Edited by Türkiye Milli Olimpiyat Komitesi. Istanbul: Olimpiyat Komitesi Yayınları.

Aslan Ayar, Pelin. 2014. "Türk tiyatrosunda kadin temsili üzerine feminist eleştiri denemesi: Beş farkli oyun hep ayni kadin (Representation of Women in Turkish Theatre: Five Plays, One Woman)." *Electronic Turkish Studies* 9, no. 9: 235–46.

Atalay, Ayşe. 2007a. "Osmanlı ve genç Türkiye Cumhuriyeti Döneminde sporda Batılılaşma Hareketleri." *Spor Yönetimi ve Bilgi Teknolojileri Dergisi* 2, no. 2: 30–35.

———. 2007b. "Türkiye'de Osmanlı döneminde ve uluslaşma sürecinde kadın ve spor." *Spor Yönetimi ve Bilgi Teknolojileri Dergisi* 2:24–29.

Babayan, Kathryn, and Afsaneh Najmabadi, eds. 2008a. *Islamicate Sexualities: Translations across Temporal Geographies of Desire*. Cambridge, MA: Center for Middle Eastern Studies, Harvard Univ.

———. 2008b. Preface to *Islamicate Sexualities: Translations across Temporal Geographies of Desire*, edited by Kathryn Babayn and Afsaneh Najmabadi, vii–xiv. Cambridge, MA: Center for Middle Eastern Studies, Harvard Univ.

Bali, Rıfat N. 2004. *Devlet'in Yahudileri ve "öteki" Yahudi*. Istanbul: İletişim.

———. 2012. *Tarz-ı Hayat'tan life style'a: Yeni seçkinler, yeni mekânlar, yeni yaşamlar*. Istanbul: İletişim.

Barbarosoğlu, Fatma Karabıyık. 2006. *İmaj ve takva*. Istanbul: Timaş Yayınları.

Baronyan, Hagop. 2014. *İstanbul mahallelerinde bir gezinti*. Translated by Paris Hilda Teller Babek. Istanbul: Can Yayınları.

Baş, Murat, Azmi Şafak Ersun, and Gökhan Kıvanç. 2006. "The Evaluation of Food Hygiene Knowledge, Attitudes, and Practices of Food Handlers in Food Businesses in Turkey." *Food Control* 17, no. 4: 317–22.

Bauman, Zygmunt. 2013. *Liquid Modernity*. New York: Wiley.

Bayat, Asef. 2007. "Islamism and the Politics of Fun." *Public Culture* 19, no. 3: 137–60.

Baydar, Gülsüm. 2002. "Tenuous Boundaries: Women, Domesticity, and Nationhood in 1930s Turkey." *Journal of Architecture* 7, no. 3: 229–44.

Bayraktar, Sevi. 2011. *Makbul anneler, müstakbel vatandaşlar: Neoliberal beden politikalarında annelik*. Istanbul: Ayizi Kitap.

Belghiti, Rachid. 2013. "Dance and the Colonial Body: Re-choreographing Postcolonial Theories of the Body." Ph.D. diss., Faculté des arts et des sciences, Université de Montréal.

Benjamin, Jessica. 1986. "A Desire of One's Own: Psychoanalytic Feminism and Intersubjective Space." In *Feminist Studies/Critical Studies*, edited by Teresa de Lauretis, 78–101. Bloomington: Indiana Univ. Press.

Benn, Tansin, Gertrud Pfister, and Haifaa Jawad, eds. 2010. *Muslim Women and Sport.* London: Routledge.

Berger, Bonnie G., and Robert W. Motl. 2000. "Exercise and Mood: A Selective Review and Synthesis of Research Employing the Profile of Mood States." *Journal of Applied Sport Psychology* 12, no. 1: 69–92.

Berlant, Lauren Gail. 1998. "Intimacy: A Special Issue." *Critical Inquiry* 24, no. 2: 281–88.

Berlant, Lauren Gail, and Michael Warner. 1998. "Sex in Public." *Critical Inquiry* 24, no. 2: 547–66.

Besnier, Niko, and Susan Brownell. 2012. "Sport, Modernity, and the Body." *Annual Review of Anthropology* 41:443–59.

Bezmez, Dikmen. 2008. "The Politics of Urban Waterfront Regeneration: The Case of Haliç (the Golden Horn), Istanbul." *International Journal of Urban and Regional Research* 32, no. 4: 815–40.

Boddy, Janice. 1989. *Wombs and Alien Spirits: Women, Men, and the Zar Cult in Northern Sudan.* Madison: Univ. of Wisconsin Press.

Boellstorff, Tom. 2015. *Coming of Age in* Second Life: *An Anthropologist Explores the Virtually Human.* Princeton, NJ: Princeton Univ. Press.

Bolin, Anne. 2009. "Embodied Ethnography: Seeing, Feeling, and Knowledge among Bodybuilders." In *Global Culture*, edited by Frank A. Salamone, 19–30. New Castle, UK: Cambridge Scholars.

Bolin, Anne, and Jane Granskog, eds. 2003a. *Athletic Intruders: Ethnographic Research on Women, Culture, and Exercise.* Albany: State Univ. of New York Press.

———. 2003b. "Reflexive Ethnography, Women, and Sporting Activities." In *Athletic Intruders: Ethnographic Research on Women, Culture, and Exercise*, edited by Anne Bolin and Jane Granskog, 7–26. Albany: State Univ. of New York Press.

Booth, Marilyn. 2010a. *Harem Histories: Envisioning Places and Living Spaces.* Durham, NC: Duke Univ. Press.

———. Introduction to *Harem Histories: Envisioning Places and Living Spaces*, 1–22. Durham, NC: Duke Univ. Press.

Bootsman, Nicole, David F. Blackburn, and Jeff Taylor. 2014. "The Oz Craze: The Effect of Pop Culture Media on Health Care." *Canadian Pharmacists Journal/Revue des Pharmaciens du Canada* 147, no. 2: 80–82.

Bora, Aksu. 2001. "Türk modernleşme Sürecinde Annelik Kimliğinin Dönüşümü." In *Yerli bir feminizme doğru*, edited by Necla Akgökçe and Aynur İlyasoğlu, 77–105. Istanbul: Sel Yayıncılık.

Bordo, Susan. 1990. "Reading the Slender Body." In *Body/Politics: Women and the Discourses of Science*, edited by Mary Jacobus, Evelyn Fox Keller, and Sally Shuttleworth, 83–112. New York: Routledge.

———. 1993. *Unbearable Weight: Feminism, Culture, and the Body*. Berkeley: Univ. of California Press.

Boris, Eileen, and Rhacel Salazar Parreñas, eds. 2010. *Intimate Labors: Cultures, Technologies, and the Politics of Care*. Stanford, CA: Stanford Univ. Press.

Bourdieu, Pierre. 1984. *Distinction: A Social Critique of the Judgement of Taste*. Cambridge, MA: Harvard Univ. Press.

Braidotti, Rosi. 1991. *Patterns of Dissonance: A Study of Women in Contemporary Philosophy*. London: Polity Press.

———. 2013. *Nomadic Subjects: Embodiment and Sexual Difference in Contemporary Feminist Theory*. New York: Columbia Univ. Press.

Brav, Aaron. [1908] 1992. "The Evil Eye among the Hebrews." In *The Evil Eye: A Casebook*, edited by Alan Dundes, 44–54. Madison: Univ. of Wisconsin Press.

Brown, Jo. 2011. "The Athenian Harem: Orientalism and the Historiography of Athenian Women in the Nineteenth Century." *New Voices in Classical Reception Studies* 6:1–12.

Buccianti, Alexandra. 2010. "Dubbed Turkish Soap Operas Conquering the Arab World: Social Liberation or Cultural Alienation?" *Arab Media & Society* 10:1–11.

Bunt, Leslie. 2004. *Music Therapy: An Art beyond Words*. London: Routledge.

Burul, Yeşim. 2007. *Entertainment at Home in Turkey: A Rough Guide*. Istanbul: Popular Culture Institute.

Butler, Judith. 1987. *Subjects of Desire: Hegelian Reflections in Twentieth-Century France*. New York: Columbia Univ. Press.

Buyukbese, Mehmet Akif, and Betul Bakar. 2012. "Diabetes Where Continents Meet: Turkey." *European Journal of Medical Genetics* 9, no. 3: 214–15.

Canpolat, Seda. 2015. "Scopic Dilemmas: Gazing the Muslim Woman in Fadia Faqir's *My Name Is Salma* and Leila Aboulela's *Minaret*." *Contemporary Women's Writing* 10, no. 2: 216–35.

Castoriadis, Cornelius. 1991. *Philosophy, Politics, Autonomy: Essays in Political Philosophy*. Edited by David Ames Curtis. New York: Oxford Univ. Press.

Cavill, Nick, Sonja Kahlmeier, and Francesca Racioppi, eds. 2006. *Physical Activity and Health in Europe: Evidence for Action*. Geneva: World Health Organization.

Çayır, Aliye, Nazlı Atak, and Serdal Kenan Köse. 2011. "Beslenme ve diyet kliniğine başvuranlarda obezite durumu ve etkili faktörlerin belirlenmesi." *Ankara Üniversitesi Tıp Fakültesi Mecmuası* 64, no. 1: 13–19.

Cerin, Ester, Eva Leslie, Takemi Sugiyama, and Neville Owen. 2009. "Associations of Multiple Physical Activity Domains with Mental Well-Being." *Mental Health and Physical Activity* 2, no. 2: 55–64.

Chavez, Christina. 2008. "Conceptualizing from the Inside: Advantages, Complications, and Demands on Insider Positionality." *Qualitative Report* 13, no. 3: 474–94.

Çınar, Alev. 2005. *Modernity, Secularism, and Islam in Turkey: Bodies, Places, and Time*. Minneapolis: Univ. of Minnesota Press.

Clark, Abigail, Helen Skouteris, Eleanor H. Wertheim, Susan J. Paxton, and Jeannette Milgrom. 2009a. "My Baby Body: A Qualitative Insight into Women's Body-Related Experiences and Mood during Pregnancy and the Postpartum." *Journal of Reproductive and Infant Psychology* 27, no. 4: 330–45.

———. 2009b. "The Relationship between Depression and Body Dissatisfaction across Pregnancy and the Postpartum: A Prospective Study." *Journal of Health Psychology* 14, no. 1: 27–35.

Clifford, James. 1983. "On Ethnographic Authority." *Representations*, no. 2: 118–46.

Coss, Richard G. 1974. "Reflections on the Evil Eye." *Human Behavior* 3, no. 10: 16–22.

Courneya, Kerry S., Christine M. Friedenreich, Rami A. Sela, H. Arthur Quinney, Ryan Rhodes, and Michael Handman. 2003. "The Group Psychotherapy and Home-Based Physical Exercise (Group-Hope) Trial in Cancer Survivors: Physical Fitness and Quality of Life Outcomes." *Psycho-Oncology* 12, no. 4: 357–74.

Crăciun, Magdalena. 2013. *Material Culture and Authenticity: Fake Branded Fashion in Europe*. London: Bloomsbury.

Crocker, Peter R. E., Kent C. Kowalski, Sharleen D. Hoar, and Meghan H. McDonough. 2004. "Emotion in Sport across Adulthood." In *Developmental Sport and Exercise Psychology: A Lifespan Perspective*, edited by M. R. Weiss, 333–55. Morgantown, WV: Fitness Information Technology.

Crossley, Michele L. 2007. "Childbirth, Complications, and the Illusion of Choice: A Case Study." *Feminism & Psychology* 17, no. 4: 543–63.

Crossley, Nick. 2008. "(Net) Working Out: Social Capital in a Private Health Club." *British Journal of Sociology* 59, no. 3: 475–500.

Dağtas, Mahiye Seçil. 2009. "Bodily Transgression: Conflicting Spaces and Gendered Boundaries of Modernity and Islam in Contemporary Turkey." *Anthropology of the Middle East* 4, no. 2: 1–13.

Dedeoglu, Ayla Ozhan. 2010. "Discourses of Motherhood and Consumption Practices of Turkish Mothers." *Business and Economics Research Journal* 1, no. 3: 1–15.

Deeb, Lara. 2006. *An Enchanted Modern: Gender and Public Piety in Shiʿi Lebanon*. Princeton, NJ: Princeton Univ. Press.

———. 2015. "Thinking Piety and the Everyday Together: A Response to Fadil and Fernando." *HAU: Journal of Ethnographic Theory* 5, no. 2: 93–96.

Defrance, Jacques. 1995. "The Anthropological Sociology of Pierre Bourdieu: Genesis, Concepts, Relevance." *Sociology of Sport Journal* 12, no. 2: 121–31.

Delice, Serkan. 2017. "'We Cannot Have Love without Lovers': Sexuality and Self-Fashioning in Early Modern Ottoman Istanbul." Paper presented at the "Desiring and Deorienting the Middle East" series, Pembroke, Cambridge, June 2, 2017.

De Knop, Paul, Marc Theeboom, Helena Wittock, and Kristine De Martelaer. 1996. "Implications of Islam on Muslim Girls' Sport Participation in Western Europe: Literature Review and Policy Recommendations for Sport Promotion." *Sport, Education, and Society* 1, no. 2: 147–64.

Devlet İstatistik Enstitütüsü (State Institute for Statistics). n.d. At http://tuik.gov.tr/Kitap.do?metod=KitapDetay&KT_ID=0&KITAP_ID=158.

Di-Capua, Yoav. 2004. "Sports, Society, and Revolution: Egypt in the Early 1950's." In *Rethinking Nasserism: Revolution and Historical Memory in Modern Egypt*, edited by Elie Podeh and Onn Vinclair, 144–62. Gainesville: Univ. Press of Florida.

———. 2006. "Sports and the Female Body in Arab States." In *Encyclopedia of Women in Islamic Cultures*, edited by Suad Joseph and Afsaneh Najmabadi, 439–40. Leiden: Brill.

Dilipak, Abdurrahman. 1988. *Bir başka açıdan kadın*. Istanbul: Risale Basın-Yayın.

Dionigi, Rylee A. 2002. "Resistance and Empowerment through Leisure: The Meaning of Competitive Sport Participation to Older Adults." *Loisir et société/Society and Leisure* 25, no. 2: 303–28.

Doane, Mary Anne. 2004. "Film and the Masquerade: Theorising the Female Spectator." In *Hollywood: Critical Concepts in Media and Cultural Studies*, edited by Thomas Schatz, 95–110. London: Routledge.

Downs, Danielle Symons, Jennifer M. DiNallo, and Tiffany L. Kirner. 2008. "Determinants of Pregnancy and Postpartum Depression: Prospective Influences of Depressive Symptoms, Body Image Satisfaction, and Exercise Behavior." *Annals of Behavioral Medicine* 36, no. 1: 54–63

Duncan, Margaret Carlisle. 1994. "The Politics of Women's Body Images and Practices: Foucault, the Panopticon, and *Shape* Magazine." *Journal of Sport & Social Issues* 18, no. 1: 48–65.

Durakbaşa, Ayşe. 1988. "Cumhuriyet döneminde kadın kimliğinin oluşumu." *Tarih Toplum* 51:37–48.

Durakbasa, Ayse, and Aynur Ilyasoglu. 2001. "Formation of Gender Identities in Republican Turkey and Women's Narratives as Transmitters of 'Herstory' of Modernization." *Journal of Social History* 35, no. 1: 195–203.

Durkheim, Émile. 1915. *The Elementary Forms of the Religious Life*. Translated by Joseph Ward Swain. New York: Allen & Unwin.

Dworkin, Shari L., and Faye Linda Wachs. 2004. "'Getting Your Body Back': Postindustrial Fit Motherhood in *Shape Fit Pregnancy* Magazine." *Gender & Society* 18, no. 5: 610–24.

Edwards, Elise. 2003. "Bodies in Motion: Contemplating Work, Leisure, and Late Capitalism in Japanese Fitness Clubs." *Anthropological Quarterly* 76, no. 1: 165–76.

Ekinci, Oktay. 1994. *Istanbul'u sarsan on yıl*. Istanbul: Anahtar Kitaplar.

English, Leona M. 2004. "Feminist Identities: Negotiations in the Third Space." *Feminist Theology* 13, no. 1: 97–125.

Erder, Sema. 1999. "Where Do You Hail From?" In *Istanbul between the Global and the Local*, edited by Çağlar Keyder, 161–73. New York: Rowman and Littlefield.

Fadil, Nadia, and Mayanthi Fernando. 2015a. "Rediscovering the 'Everyday' Muslim: Notes on an Anthropological Divide." *HAU: Journal of Ethnographic Theory* 5, no. 2: 59–88.

———. 2015b. "What Is Anthropology's Object of Study? A Counter-response to Deeb and Schielke." *HAU: Journal of Ethnographic Theory* 5, no. 2: 97–100.

Faier, Lieba. 2009. *Intimate Encounters: Filipina Women and the Remaking of Rural Japan*. Berkeley: Univ. of California Press.

Farooq, Samaya. 2010. "'Muslim Women,' Islam, and Sport: 'Race,' Culture, and Identity in Post-colonial Britain." PhD diss., Univ. of Warwick.

Fasting, K., G. Pfister, S. Scranton, and A. Bunuel. 1997. "Cross-Cultural Research on Women and Sport." *Women in Sport and Physical Activity Journal* 6:85–108.

Fişek, Kurthan. 1980. *Devlet politikası ve toplumsal yapıyla ilişkileri açısından spor yönetimi: Dünyada—Türkiye'de*. Ankara: Ankara Üniversitesi Siyasal Bilgiler Fakültesi Yayınları.

———. 1985. *100 Soruda Türkiye spor tarihi*. Istanbul: Gerçek Yayınevi.

Flinn, Mark V., and Allen C. Bluedorn. 2002. "The Evolution of Times." *Current Anthropology* 43:117–19.

Foucault, Michel. 1986. "Of Other Spaces." Translated by Jay Miskowiec. *Diacritics* 16:22–27.

———. 1994. *Aesthetics, Method, and Epistemology*. Translated by Robert Hurley and others. Edited by James D. Faubion and Paul Rabinow. Essential Works of Foucault, 1954–1984, vol. 2. New York: New Press.

Fox, Rebekah, Kristin Heffernan, and Paula Nicolson. 2009. "'I Don't Think It Was Such an Issue Back Then': Changing Experiences of Pregnancy across Two Generations of Women in South-East England." *Gender, Place, and Culture* 16, no. 5: 553–68.

Fraisse, Paul. 1981. "Multisensory Aspects of Rhythm." In *Intersensory Perception and Sensory Integration*, edited by Richard D. Walk and Herbert L. Pick Jr., 217–48. New York: Plenum Press.

Gamman, Lorraine, and Margaret Marshment, eds. 1989. *The Female Gaze: Women as Viewers of Popular Culture*. Seattle: Real Comet Press.

Ghazali, Imam. 1985. *Ihya' ulum-ud-din*. Chicago: Kazi.

Gilligan, Carol. 1982. *In a Different Voice: Psychological Theory and Women's Development*. Cambridge, MA: Harvard Univ. Press.

Gilligan, Carol, Nona P. Lyons, and Trudy J. Hanmer, eds. 1990. *Making Connections: The Relational Worlds of Adolescent Girls at Emma Willard School*. Cambridge, MA: Harvard Univ. Press.

Glynos, Jason, and Yannis Stavrakakis. 2008. "Lacan and Political Subjectivity: Fantasy and Enjoyment in Psychoanalysis and Political Theory." *Subjectivity* 24, no. 1: 256–74.

Gökarıksel, Banu. 2009. "Beyond the Officially Sacred: Religion, Secularism, and the Body in the Production of Subjectivity." *Social & Cultural Geography* 10, no. 6: 657–74.

Göle, Nilüfer. 1996. *The Forbidden Modern: Civilization and Veiling*. Ann Arbor: Univ. of Michigan Press.

Goody, Jack. 1961. "Religion and Ritual: The Definitional Problem." *British Journal of Sociology* 12, no. 2: 142–64.

Grabe, Shelly, L. Monique Ward, and Janet Shibley Hyde. 2008. "The Role of the Media in Body Image Concerns among Women: A Meta-analysis of Experimental and Correlational Studies." *Psychological Bulletin* 134, no. 3: 460–76.

Grant, Bevan C. 2001. "'You're Never Too Old': Beliefs about Physical Activity and Playing Sport in Later Life." *Ageing and Society* 21, no. 6: 777–98.

Gregg, Melissa, and Gregory J. Seigworth. 2010. "An Inventory of Shimmers." In *The Affect Theory Reader*, edited by Melissa Gregg and Gregory J. Seigworth, 1–25. Durham, NC: Duke Univ. Press.

Gremillion, Helen. 2005. "The Cultural Politics of Body Size." *Annual Review of Anthropology* 34:13–32.

Grosz, Elizabeth A. 1994. *Volatile Bodies: Toward a Corporeal Feminism*. Bloomington: Indiana Univ. Press.

Gülalp, Haldun. 2001. "Globalization and Political Islam: The Social Bases of Turkey's Welfare Party." *International Journal of Middle East Studies* 33, no. 3: 433–48.

Güven, Özbay. 1999. *Türklerde spor kültürü*. Ankara: Ataturk Kultur DIL Ve Tarih Yuks.

Haag, Laurie L. 1993. "Oprah Winfrey: The Construction of Intimacy in the Talk Show Setting." *Journal of Popular Culture* 26, no. 4: 115–22.

Haedt, Alissa, and Pamela Keel. 2007. "Maternal Attachment, Depression, and Body Dissatisfaction in Pregnant Women." *Journal of Reproductive and Infant Psychology* 25, no. 4: 285–95.

Haidt, Jonathan, J. Patrick Seder, and Selin Kesebir. 2008. "Hive Psychology, Happiness, and Public Policy." *Journal of Legal Studies* 37, no. S2: S133–56.

Hafez, Sherine. 2011. *An Islam of Her Own: Reconsidering Religion and Secularism in Women's Islamic Movements.* New York: New York Univ. Press.

Hamdy, Sherine. 2012. *Our Bodies Belong to God: Organ Transplants, Islam, and the Struggle for Human Dignity in Egypt.* Berkeley: Univ. of California Press.

Han, Sallie. 2013. *Pregnancy in Practice: Expectation and Experience in the Contemporary US.* New York: Berghahn Books.

Harani, Yavuz. 2001. "Türk kadının sporla ımtihanı." *Hürriyet*, Jan. 13. At webarsiv.hurriyet.com.tr/2001/01/13/282581.asp.

Hargreaves, Jennifer. 2000. *Heroines of Sport: The Politics of Difference and Identity.* Road Hove, UK: Psychology Press.

Hart, Angie. 2017. "Missing Masculinity? Prostitutes' Clients in Alicante, Spain." In *Dislocating Masculinity: Comparative Ethnographies*, edited by Andrea Cornwall and Nancy Lindisfame, 46–62. London: Routledge.

Hart, Kimberly. 2007. "Love by Arrangement: The Ambiguity of 'Spousal Choice' in a Turkish Village." *Journal of the Royal Anthropological Institute* 13, no. 2: 345–62.

Haynes, Kathryn. 2008. "(Re)figuring Accounting and Maternal Bodies: The Gendered Embodiment of Accounting Professionals." *Accounting, Organizations, and Society* 33, no. 4: 328–48.

Hedblom, Christina. 2009. *"The Body Is Made to Move": Gym and Fitness Culture in Sweden.* Stockholm: Stockholm Universitet.

Hegel, G. W. F. [1807] 2010. *Phenomenology of Spirit.* Edited by Terry Pinkard. Bamberg, Germany: Joseph Anton Goebhardt.

Heryanto, Ariel. 2011. "Upgraded Piety and Pleasure: The New Middle Class and Islam in Indonesian Popular Culture." In *Islam and Popular Culture in Indonesia and Malaysia*, edited by Andrew N. Weintraub, 60–82. London: Routledge.

Hetherington, Kevin. 1995. "The Utopics of Social Ordering—Stonehenge as a Museum without Walls." *Sociological Review* 43, no. 1, suppl.: 153–76.

———. 2011. "Foucault, the Museum, and the Diagram." *Sociological Review* 59, no. 3: 457–75.

Hirschkind, Charles. 2006. *The Ethical Soundscape: Cassette Sermons and Islamic Counterpublics.* New York: Columbia Univ. Press.

Hökelekli, Hayati. 1988. "Fıtrat." In TDV İslam Araştırmaları Merkezi, *İslam ansiklopedisi,* 13:47–48. Istanbul: Türkiye Diyanet Vakfı.

Hoodfar, Homa, ed. 2015. *Women's Sport as Politics in Muslim Contexts.* London: Women Living under Muslim Laws.

Horne, John. 2000. "Understanding Sport and Body Culture in Japan." *Body & Society* 6, no. 2: 73–86.

Hoşer, Firdevs. 2000. *Spor ve kadın özel 2000 ajandası.* Istanbul: Kadın Eserleri Kütüphanesi.

Huang, Tzu-Ting, Hsin-Shih Wang, and Fong-Tai Dai. 2010. "Effect of Prepregnancy Body Size on Postpartum Weight Retention." *Midwifery* 26, no. 2: 222–31.

Hughes, Bettany. 2017. *Istanbul: A Tale of Three Cities.* London: Weinfeld & Nicolson.

Huq, Maimuna. 2008. "Reading the Qur'an in Bangladesh: The Politics of 'Belief' among Islamist Women." *Modern Asian Studies* 42, nos. 2–3: 457–88.

———. 2009. "Talking Jihad and Piety: Reformist Exertions among Islamist Women in Bangladesh." *Journal of the Royal Anthropological Institute* 15, no. S1: S163–82.

İnceoğlu, İrem. 2015. "Beyaz Perdede Kadın Anlatısı: Mavi Dalga filminin Feminist İncelemesi." *Fe Journal: Feminist Critique/Fe Dergi: Feminist Elestiri* 7, no. 2: 87–94.

İnel, Berke, and Burcak Inel. 2002. "Discovering the Missing Heroines: The Role of Women Painters in Early Modernist Art in Turkey." *Middle Eastern Studies* 38, no. 2: 205–12.

İşcan, Fehmi. 1988. *Türklerde spor.* Ankara: Milli Eğitim Basımevi.

Işık, Mehmet, and Şakir Eşitti. 2015. "Türk Sineması'nda sıra dışı bir kadın karakter olarak Aliye Rona (Aliye Rona as an Unusual Female Character in Turkish Cinema)." *Kadin/Woman 2000* 16, no. 1: 119–41.

İslamoğlu, Mustafa. 1999. "Hangisi daha büyük?" At http://www.mustafa islamoglu.com/yazar_146_8_hangisi-daha-buyuk-.html.

———. 2000. "Abartılmış sevinç gösterisi değil, tersinden ifade edilmiş bir toplumsal protesto." At http://www.mustafaislamoglu.com/yazar _253_8_abartilmis-sevinc-gosterisi-degil-tersinden-ifade-edilmis-bir -toplumsal-protesto.html.

———. 2003. "Sizin Züleyhanız kim?" At http://www.mustafaislamoglu .com/HD548_sizin-zuleyhaniz-kim-.html.

———. 2005. "Kalpleri oyunda oynaşta olanlar." At http://www.mustafa islamoglu.com/yazar_451_35_-kalpleri-oyunda-oynasta-olanlar-.html.

Ivry, Tsipy. 2010. *Embodying Culture: Pregnancy in Japan and Israel.* New Brunswick, NJ: Rutgers Univ. Press.

Jacob, Wilson Chacko. 2011. *Working Out Egypt: Effendi Masculinity and Subject Formation in Colonial Modernity, 1870–1940.* Durham, NC: Duke Univ. Press.

Jiang, Jiang, Qin Ming, Ke Yan-nan, and Ying Xiao-ping. 2011. "Leisure Activities and Subjective Sense of Happiness." *Tourism Tribune* 9:016.

Johnson, Clarence Richard. 1924. "The Evil Eye and Other Superstitions in Turkey." *Journal of Applied Sociology* 9:259–68.

Jones, Carla. 2010. "Materializing Piety: Gendered Anxieties about Faithful Consumption in Contemporary Urban Indonesia." *American Ethnologist* 37, no. 4: 617–37.

Joseph, Suad. 2005. "Learning Desire: Relational Pedagogies and the Desiring Female Subject in Lebanon." *Journal of Middle East Women's Studies* 1, no. 1: 79–109.

———. 2012. "Thinking Intentionality: Arab Women's Subjectivity and Its Discontents." *Journal of Middle East Women's Studies* 8, no. 2: 1–25.

Kadıoğlu, Ayşe. 2010. "The Pathologies of Turkish Republican Laicism." *Philosophy & Social Criticism* 36, nos. 3–4: 489–504.

Kalender, Seher. 2013. "Uğur Tanyeli–Engin Gerçek, İstanbul'da mekân mahremiyetinin ihlali ve teşhiri: Gerilimli bir tarihçe ve 41 fotoğraf." *FSM İlmî Araştırmalar İnsan ve Toplum Bilimleri Dergisi* 2:397–402.

Kalra, Sanjay, and Ambika Gopalkrishnan Unnikrishnan. 2012. "Obesity in India: The Weight of the Nation." *Journal of Medical Nutrition and Nutraceuticals* 1, no. 1: 37–41.

Kandiyoti, Deniz. 1987. "Emancipated but Unliberated? Reflections on the Turkish Case." *Feminist Studies* 13, no. 2: 317–38.

———. 1988. "Slave Girls, Temptresses, and Comrades: Images of Women in the Turkish Novel." *Gender Issues* 8, no. 1: 35–50.

————. 1989. Women and the Turkish State: Political Actors or Symbolic Pawns. In *Woman–Nation–State*, edited by Deniz Kandiyoti, 126–49. London: Palgrave Macmillan.

————. 1997. "Cariyeler, fettan kadınlar ve uoldaşlar: Türk romanında kadın imgeleri." In *Cariyeler, bacılar, yurttaşlar: Kimlikler ve toplumsal dönüşümler*, 133–47. Istanbul: Metis Yayınları.

Karaman, Hayrettin. 2000. *Günlük hayatımızda helaller ve haramlar.* Istanbul: İz Yayıncılık.

————. 2003. "Siyasî ve sosyal hayatımızın bazı meseleleri." In *İslam'ın ışığında günün meseleleri*, 3:345–46. Istanbul: İz Yayıncılık.

————. 2005. "Böyle bir cami." At http://www.hayrettinkaraman.net/yazi /laikduzen/4/0107.htm.

Katzmarzyk, Peter T., and Caitlin Mason. 2009. "The Physical Activity Transition." *Journal of Physical Activity & Health* 6, no. 3: 269–80.

Kay, Tess. 2006. "Daughters of Islam Family Influences on Muslim Young Women's Participation in Sport." *International Review for the Sociology of Sport* 41, nos. 3–4: 357–73.

Kepecioğlu, Fuat. 1946. *Türklerde spor.* Istanbul: İkinci Türk Tarihi Kongresi.

Kevles, Daniel J. 1995. *In the Name of Eugenics: Genetics and the Uses of Human Heredity.* Cambridge, MA: Harvard Univ. Press.

Keyder, Çağlar. 1987. *State and Class in Turkey: A Study in Capitalist Development.* London: Verso.

————, ed. 1999a. *Istanbul: Between the Global and the Local.* New York: Rowman and Littlefield.

————. 1999b. "The Setting." In *Istanbul: Between the Global and the Local*, edited by Çağlar Keyder, 3–28. New York: Rowman and Littlefield.

Keyder, Çağlar, and Ayşe Öncü. 1994. "Globalization of a Third-World Metropolis: Istanbul in the 1980s." *Review* 17, no. 3: 383–421.

Khalili, Laleh. 2016. "The Politics of Pleasure: Promenading on the Corniche and Beachgoing." *Environment and Planning D: Society and Space* 34, no. 4: 583–600.

Kıvılcım, Gönül. 2009. *Yaşayan tanıklarla Karaköy.* Istanbul: Heyamola Yayınları.

Koca, Canan, and Ilknur Hacısoftaoğlu. 2009. "Struggling for Empowerment: Sport Participation of Women and Girls in Turkey." In *Muslim Women and Sport*, edited by Tansin Benn, Gertud Pfister, and Haifaa Jawad, 154–66. London: Routledge.

Kohn, Tamara. 2008. "Creatively Sculpting the Self through the Discipline of Martial Arts Training." In *Exploring Regimes of Discipline: The Dynamics of Restraint*, edited by Noel Dyck, 99–112. New York: Berghahn.

Kraidy, Marwan M., and Omar Al-Ghazzi. 2013. "Neo-Ottoman Cool: Turkish Popular Culture in the Arab Public Sphere." *Popular Communication* 11, no. 1: 17–29.

Kramer, Lawrence. 2003. *Franz Schubert: Sexuality, Subjectivity, Song*. Cambridge: Cambridge Univ. Press.

Kreil, Aymon. 2016a. "The Price of Love: Valentine's Day in Egypt and Its Enemies." *Arab Studies Journal* 24, no. 2: 128–47.

———. 2016b. "Territories of Desire: A Geography of Competing Intimacies in Cairo." *Journal of Middle East Women's Studies* 12, no. 2: 166–80.

Kristeva, Julia. 1980. *Desire in Language: A Semiotic Approach to Literature and Art*. New York: Columbia Univ. Press.

Kruse, Corinna. 2010. "Producing Absolute Truth: CSI Science as Wishful Thinking." *American Anthropologist* 112, no. 1: 79–91.

Kurt-Karakus, Perihan Binnur. 2012. "Determination of Heavy Metals in Indoor Dust from Istanbul, Turkey: Estimation of the Health Risk." *Environment International* 50:47–55.

Kuyucu, Tuna, and Özlem Ünsal. 2010. "'Urban Transformation' as State-Led Property Transfer: An Analysis of Two Cases of Urban Renewal in Istanbul." *Urban Studies* 47, no. 7: 1479–99.

Lacan, Jacques. 1981. *The Four Fundamental Concepts of Psychoanalysis*. Translated by Alan Sheridan. Edited by Jacques-Alain Miller. New York: Norton.

———. 1988. *The Seminar of Jacques Lacan, Book II: The Ego in Freud's Theory and in the Technique of Psychoanalysis*. Translated by Sylvana Tomaselli. Edited by Jacques-Alain Miller. Cambridge: Cambridge Univ. Press.

Lad, Jateen. 2010. "Panoptic Bodies: Black Eunuchs as Guardians of the Topkapı Harem." In *Harem Histories: Envisioning Places and Living Spaces*, edited by Marilyn Booth, 136–76. Durham, NC: Duke Univ. Press.

Larsson, Mariah. 2011. "'I Know What I Saw': The Female Gaze and the Male Object of Desire." In *Interdisciplinary Approaches to Twilight: Studies in Fiction, Media, and a Contemporary Cultural Experience*, edited by Mariah Larsson and Ann Steiner, 63–80. Lund: Nordic Academic Press.

Lazaridis, Gabriella. 1995. "Sexuality and Its Cultural Construction in Rural Greece." *Journal of Gender Studies* 4, no. 3: 281–95.

Lefebvre, Henri. 2004. *Rhythmanalysis: Space, Time, and Everyday Life.* Translated by Gerald Moore and Stuart Elden. London: Continuum.

Le Guin, Ursula K. 2004. *The Wave in the Mind: Talks and Essays on the Writer, the Reader, and the Imagination.* Boston: Shambhala.

Le Renard, Amélie. 2011. *Femmes et espaces publics en Arabie Saoudite.* Paris: Dalloz.

———. 2014. *A Society of Young Women: Opportunities of Place, Power, and Reform in Saudi Arabia.* Stanford, CA: Stanford Univ. Press.

Leshkowich, Ann Marie. 2008. "Working Out Culture: Gender, Body, and Commodification in a Ho Chi Minh City Health Club." *Urban Anthropology and Studies of Cultural Systems and World Economic Development* 37, no. 1: 49–87.

Lewis, Reina, and Sara Mills. 2003. Introduction to *Feminist Postcolonial Theory: A Reader,* edited by Reina Lewis and Sara Mills, 1–23. New York: Routledge.

Liberatore, Giulia. 2016. "Imagining an Ideal Husband: Marriage as a Site of Aspiration among Pious Somali Women in London." *Anthropological Quarterly* 89, no. 3: 781–812.

———. 2017. *Somali, Muslim, British: Striving in Securitized Britain.* London: Bloomsbury.

Long, Nicholas J., and Henrietta L. Moore. 2012. "Sociality Revisited: Setting a New Agenda." *Cambridge Anthropology* 30, no. 1: 40–47.

Lord, Beth. 2006. "Foucault's Museum: Difference, Representation, and Genealogy." *Museum and Society* 4, no. 1: 1–14.

Lorius, Cassandra. 1996. "Desire and the Gaze: Spectacular Bodies in Cairene Elite Weddings." *Women's Studies International Forum* 19, no. 5: 513–23.

Luhrmann, Tania M. 2006. "Subjectivity." *Anthropological Theory* 6:345–59.

Lüküslü, Demet, and Şakir Dinçşahin. 2013. "Shaping Bodies Shaping Minds: Selim Sırrı Tarcan and the Origins of Modern Physical Education in Turkey." *International Journal of the History of Sport* 30, no. 3: 195–209.

Madison, D. Soyini. 2011. *Critical Ethnography: Method, Ethics, and Performance.* Los Angeles: Sage.

Maguire, Jennifer Smith. 2007. *Fit for Consumption: Sociology and the Business of Fitness.* London: Routledge.

Maguire, Joseph. 1993. "Bodies, Sportscultures, and Societies: A Critical Review of Some Theories in the Sociology of the Body." *International Review for the Sociology of Sport* 28, no. 1: 33–52.

Mahmood, Saba. 2001. "Feminist Theory, Embodiment, and the Docile Agent: Some Reflections on the Egyptian Islamic Revival." *Cultural Anthropology* 16, no. 2: 202–36.

———. 2005. *Politics of Piety: The Islamic Revival and the Feminist Subject.* Princeton, NJ: Princeton Univ. Press.

———. 2011. *Politics of Piety: The Islamic Revival and the Feminist Subject.* Paperback reissue with a new preface. Princeton, NJ: Princeton Univ. Press.

Mankekar, Purnima. 1999. *Screening Culture, Viewing Politics: An Ethnography of Television, Womanhood, and Nation in Postcolonial India.* Durham, NC: Duke Univ. Press.

———. 2012. "Television and Embodiment: A Speculative Essay." *South Asian History and Culture* 3, no. 4: 603–13.

Markula, Pirkko. 1995. "Firm but Shapely, Fit but Sexy, Strong but Thin: The Postmodern Aerobicizing Female Bodies." *Sociology of Sport Journal* 12, no. 4: 424–53.

Markula, Pirkko, and Richard Pringle. 2006. *Foucault, Sport, and Exercise: Power, Knowledge, and Transforming the Self.* London: Routledge.

Maroulakis, Emmanuel, and Yannis Zervas. 1993. "Effects of Aerobic Exercise on Mood of Adult Women." *Perceptual and Motor Skills* 76, no. 3: 795–801.

Marzano-Parisoli, Maria Michela. 2001. "The Contemporary Construction of a Perfect Body Image: Bodybuilding, Exercise Addiction, and Eating Disorders." *Quest* 53, no. 2: 216–30.

McNamee, Sara. 2000. "Foucault's Heterotopia and Children's Everyday Lives." *Childhood* 7, no. 4: 479–92.

McNay, Lois. 1992. *Foucault and Feminism: Power, Gender, and the Self.* Cambridge: Polity Press.

———. 2000. *Gender and Agency: Reconfiguring the Subject in Feminist and Social Theory.* Cambridge: Polity Press.

———. 2003. "Agency, Anticipation, and Indeterminacy in feminist Theory." *Feminist Theory* 4, no. 2: 139–48.

———. 2008. "The Trouble with Recognition: Subjectivity, Suffering, and Agency." *Sociological Theory* 26, no. 3: 271–96.

McNeill, William H. 1995. *Keeping Together in Time: Dance and Drill in Human History*. Cambridge, MA: Harvard Univ. Press.

Merleau-Ponty, Marcel. 1945. *Phenomenology of Perception*. Translated by C. Smith. London: Routledge.

Mernissi, Fatima. 1975. *Beyond the Veil: Male–Female Dynamics in Modern Muslim Society*. Cambridge, MA: Schenkman.

Messner, Michael. 1990. "Boyhood, Organized Sports, and the Construction of Masculinities." *Journal of Contemporary Ethnography* 18, no. 4: 416–44.

Mesutoğlu, Neşe. 2014. *Yazarların İstanbul'u*. 2nd ed. Istanbul: Pozitif.

Miller, Laura. 2006. *Beauty Up: Exploring Contemporary Japanese Body Aesthetics*. Berkeley: Univ. of California Press.

Mîndruţ, Petruţa. 2006. "Aerobics and Self-Asserting Discourses: Mapping the Gendered Body in Post-socialist Romania." *Anthropology of East Europe Review* 24, no. 2: 13–24.

"The Ministry of Sports, which Acts to Prevent the Failure of the Olympics from Recurring, Is Preparing to Gradually Increase the Number of Sports Equipment in the Parks." Zaytung, Aug. 2, 2012. At https://www.zaytung.com/haberdetay.asp?newsid=186518.

Mitchell, Timothy. [1988] 1991. *Colonising Egypt*. Berkeley: Univ. of California Press.

Mittermaier, Amira. 2012. "Dreams from Elsewhere: Muslim Subjectivities beyond the Trope of Self-Cultivation." *Journal of the Royal Anthropological Institute* 18, no. 2: 247–65.

Modleski, Tania. 2007. *Loving with a Vengeance: Mass Produced Fantasies for Women*. London: Routledge.

Moore, Henrietta L. 1988. *Feminism and Anthropology*. Cambridge: Polity Press.

———. 1994. *A Passion for Difference: Essays in Anthropology and Gender*. Cambridge: Polity Press.

———. 2004. "Global Anxieties, Concept-Metaphors, and Pre-theoretical Commitments in Anthropology." *Anthropological Theory* 4, no. 1: 71–88.

———. 2007. *The Subject of Anthropology: Gender Symbolism and Psychoanalysis*. Cambridge: Polity Press.

———. 2011. *Still Life: Hopes, Desires, and Satisfactions*. Cambridge: Polity Press.

———. 2014. "If Intimacy Is the Answer, Then What Is the Question?" Opening address for the conference "Probing the Intimate: Cross-Cultural Queries of Proximity and Beyond," Cambridge, UK, May 12.

Morales-Diaz, Enrique. 2002. "Catching Glimpses: Appropriating the Female Gaze in Esmeralda Santiago's Autobiographical Writing." *Centro Journal* 14, no. 2: 131–47.

Morley, David. 2003. *Television, Audiences, and Cultural Studies.* New York: Routledge.

Al-Munajjid, Mohammad Salih. 2003. "Ruling on Wearing Shorts When Playing Sport and Exercising." At http://islamqa.info/en/22963.

Musharbash, Yasmine. 2007. "Boredom, Time, and Modernity: An Example from Aboriginal Australia." *American Anthropologist* 109, no. 2: 307–17.

Nagel, Joane. 1998. "Masculinity and Nationalism: Gender and Sexuality in the Making of Nations." *Ethnic and Racial Studies* 21, no. 2: 242–69.

Najmabadi, Afsaneh. 1993. "Veiled Discourse—Unveiled Bodies." *Feminist Studies* 19, no. 3: 487–518.

———. 1997. *The Erotic Vatan [Homeland] as Beloved and Mother: To Love, to Possess, and to Protect.* Cambridge: Cambridge Univ. Press.

Nash, Meredith. 2012a. "Weighty Matters: Negotiating 'Fatness' and 'In-Betweenness' in Early Pregnancy." *Feminism & Psychology* 22, no. 3: 307–23.

———. 2012b. "'Working Out' for Two: Performances of 'Fitness' and Femininity in Australian Prenatal Aerobics Classes." *Gender, Place, & Culture* 19, no. 4: 449–71.

Navaro, Yael. 2011. "Knowing the City: Migrants Negotiating Materialities in Istanbul." In *Cultures and Globalization: Heritage, Memory, and Identity*, edited by Helmut K. Anheier and Yudhishthir Raj Isar, 231–38. London: Sage.

Ng, Bo-sze. 2005. "Slimming Culture in Hong Kong: A Sociological Study." Master's thesis, Univ. of Hong Kong.

Nicolson, Paula, Rebekah Fox, and Kristin Heffernan. 2010. "Constructions of Pregnant and Postnatal Embodiment across Three Generations: Mothers', Daughters', and Others' Experiences of the Transition to Motherhood." *Journal of Health Psychology* 15, no. 4: 575–85.

Öncü, Ayşe. 1999. "Istanbulites and Others." In *Istanbul: Between the Global and the Local*, edited by Çağlar Keyder, 95–119. New York: Rowman and Littlefield.

Ong, Aihwa. 1990. "State versus Islam: Malay Families, Women's Bodies, and the Body Politic in Malaysia." *American Ethnologist* 17, no. 2: 258–76.

———. 2006. *Neoliberalism as Exception: Mutations in Citizenship and Sovereignty*. Durham, NC: Duke Univ. Press.

Organization for Economic Cooperation and Development (OECD). 2013. "Employment Rate of Women." In "Employment and Labour Markets: Key Tables from OECD," *OECD Employment Outlook 2013*, OECD Library, 5. At http://dx.doi.org/10.1787/empl_outlook-2013-en.

Örs, İlay Romain. 2018. *Diaspora of the City: Stories of Cosmopolitanism from Istanbul and Athens*. London: Palgrave Macmillan.

Ortner, Sherry B. 1981. "Gender and Sexuality in Hierarchical Societies: The Case of Polynesia and Some Comparative Implications." In *Sexual Meanings*, edited by Sherry B. Ortner and Harriet Whitehead, 359–409. Cambridge: Cambridge Univ. Press.

———. 2005. "Subjectivity and Cultural Critique." *Anthropological Theory* 5:31–46.

Osella, Caroline. 2012. "Desires under Reform: Contemporary Reconfigurations of Family, Marriage, Love, and Gendering in a Transnational South Indian Matrilineal Muslim Community." *Culture and Religion* 13, no. 2: 241–64.

Özbay, Cenk. 2010. "Nocturnal Queers: Rent Boys' Masculinity in Istanbul." *Sexualities* 13, no. 5: 645–63.

———. 2014. "Yirmi milyonluk turizm başkenti: İstanbul'da hareketliliklerin politik ekonomisi." In *Yeni Istanbul Çalışmaları: Sınırlar, Mücadeleler, Açılımlar*, edited by Cenk Özbay and Ayfer Bartu Candan, 166–97. Istanbul: Metis.

Ozgur, Iren. 2012. *Islamic Schools in Modern Turkey: Faith, Politics, and Education*. Cambridge: Cambridge Univ. Press.

Özyeğin, Gül. 2001. *Untidy Gender: Domestic Work in Turkey*. Philadelphia: Temple Univ. Press.

———. 2015. *New Desires, New Selves: Sex, Love, and Piety among Turkish Youth*. New York: New York Univ. Press.

Özyürek, Esra. 2006. *Nostalgia for the Modern: State Secularism and Everyday Politics in Turkey*. Durham, NC: Duke Univ. Press.

Pamuk, Orhan. 2005. *Istanbul: Memories of a City*. London: Faber and Faber.

Paradis, Elise. 2012. "Boxers, Briefs, or Bras? Bodies, Gender, and Change in the Boxing Gym." *Body & Society* 18, no. 2: 82–109.

Parla, Ayse. 2001. "The 'Honor' of the State: Virginity Examinations in Turkey." *Feminist Studies* 27, no. 1: 65–88.

Parla, Ayşe, and Ceren Özgül. 2016. "Property, Dispossession, and Citizenship in Turkey; or, the History of the Gezi Uprising Starts in the Surp Hagop Armenian Cemetery." *Public Culture* 28, no. 3: 617–53.

Pascoe, Cheri J. 2011. *Dude, You're a Fag: Masculinity and Sexuality in High School.* Berkeley: Univ. of California Press.

Patel, Priti, Joanna Lee, Rebecca Wheatcroft, Jacqueline Barnes, and Alan Stein. 2005. "Concerns about Body Shape and Weight in the Postpartum Period and Their Relation to Women's Self-Identification." *Journal of Reproductive and Infant Psychology* 23, no. 4: 347–64.

Paulson, Susan. 2005. "How Various 'Cultures of Fitness' Shape Subjective Experiences of Growing Older." *Ageing and Society* 25, no. 2: 229–44.

Pearson, Giles. 2012. *Aristotle on Desire.* Cambridge: Cambridge Univ. Press.

Peirce, Leslie P. 1993. *The Imperial Harem: Women and Sovereignty in the Ottoman Empire.* New York: Oxford Univ. Press.

Pekcan, Gülden, and N. Karaadaoglu. 2000. "State of Nutrition in Turkey." *Nutrition and Health* 14, no. 1: 41–52.

Pile, Steve. 1996. *The Body and the City: Psychoanalysis, Space, and Subjectivity.* London: Routledge.

———. 2008. "Where Is the Subject? Geographical Imaginations and Spatializing Subjectivity." *Subjectivity* 23, no. 1: 206–18.

Poole, Marilyn. 2001. "Fit for Life: Older Women's Commitment to Exercise." *Journal of Aging and Physical Activity* 9, no. 3: 300–312.

Al Qurtubi, Imam. 2003. *Tafsir Al Qurtubi: Classical Commentary of the Holy Qur'an.* London: Dar-al-Taqwa.

Raab, Alon K. 2012. "Sport, Politics, and Society in the Arab World" (review). *Middle East Journal* 66, no. 3: 558–59.

Ramazanoğlu, Yıldız. 2000. *Osmanlı'dan Cumhuriyet'e kadının tarihi dönüşümü.* Istanbul: Pınar Yayınları.

Rasmussen, Martin, and Karin Laumann. 2014. "The Role of Exercise during Adolescence on Adult Happiness and Mood." *Leisure Studies* 33, no. 4: 341–56.

Rendell, Jane. 2006. *Art and Architecture: A Place Between.* London: I. B. Tauris.

Rickman, Allyson, and John Nauright. 2007. "Globalization and the Fitness Industry: A Case Study of 24 Hour Fitness and Its Expansion into Asia." *International Journal of Fitness* 3, no. 2: 17–24.

Rofel, Lisa. 1999. *Other Modernities: Gendered Yearnings in China after Socialism*. Berkeley: Univ. of California Press.

———. 2007. *Desiring China: Experiments in Neoliberalism, Sexuality, and Public Culture*. Durham, NC: Duke Univ. Press.

Rozario, Santi. 2011. "Islamic Piety against the Family: From 'Traditional' to 'Pure' Islam." *Contemporary Islam* 5, no. 3: 285–308.

Rubin, Gayle. 1975. "The Traffic in Women: Notes on the 'Political Economy' of Sex." In *Toward an Anthropology of Women*, edited by Rayna Reiter, 157–210. New York: Monthly Review Press.

Ruddick, Sara. 1980. "Maternal Thinking." *Feminist Studies* 6, no. 2: 342–67.

Şahin, Öznur. 2018. "From Home to City: Gender Segregation, Homosociality, and Publicness in Istanbul." *Gender, Place, & Culture* 25, no. 5: 743–57.

Saktanber, Ayse. 2002. *Living Islam: Women, Religion, and the Politicization of Culture in Turkey*. London: I. B. Tauris.

Salamandra, Christa. 2012. "The Muhannad Effect: Media Panic, Melodrama, and the Arab Female Gaze." *Anthropological Quarterly* 85, no. 1: 45–77.

Şallı, Ebru. 2005. *Hamilelikte sağlıklı ve güzel kalmak*. Istanbul: Gendaş Yayınları.

Samie, Samaya F., and Sertaç Sehlikoglu. 2014. "Strange, Incompetent, and Out-of-Place: Media, Sportswomen, and the London 2012 Olympics." *Feminist Media Studies* 15, no. 3: 363–81.

Sandikci, Ozlem, and B. Iljan. 2004. "Dowry: A Cherished Possession or an Old-Fashioned Tradition in a Modernizing Society?" In *Contemporary Consumption Rituals: A Research Anthology*, edited by Cele C. Otnes and Tina M. Lowrey, 149–80. London: Routledge.

Savacool, Julia. 2009. *The World Has Curves: The Global Quest for the Perfect Body*. New York: Rodale.

Schauer, Terrie. 2005. "Women's Porno: The Heterosexual Female Gaze in Porn Sites 'for Women.'" *Sexuality and Culture* 9, no. 2: 42–64.

Schielke, Samuli. 2009. "Ambivalent Commitments: Troubles of Morality, Religiosity, and Aspiration among Young Egyptians." *Journal of Religion in Africa* 39, no. 2: 158–85.

————. 2015. "Living with Unresolved Differences: A Reply to Fadil and Fernando." *HAU: Journal of Ethnographic Theory* 5, no. 2: 89–92.

Schielke, Samuli, and Liza Debevec. 2012. *Ordinary Lives and Grand Schemes: An Anthropology of Everyday Religion*. New York: Berghahn Books.

Seber, Gülten. 2013. "Kadın çalışmalarında yapamadıklarımız." *Anadolu University Journal of Social Sciences* 13, special issue: 27–33.

Sehlikoglu, Sertaç. 2010. "'We Have Always Been Modern': Narratives from the Women-Only Gyms in Istanbul." Master's thesis, Univ. of Toronto.

————. 2013a. "Boundaries of a Veiled Female Body: Islamic Reflections on Women's Sporting Bodies in Relation to Sexuality, Modesty, and Privacy." *Anthropology News* 53, no. 6: 34–35.

———— (username: Random). 2013b. "ISMEK step-aerobics class." YouTube video, at https://youtu.be/6XcjIj5_Nqw.

———— (username: Random). 2013c. "Sinem Trainer." YouTube video, at http://youtu.be/DHvfvMB94JY.

————. 2014. "Imagining the Self as Sporting Body." At http://www.culanth.org/fieldsights/495-sports-deviation.

————. 2015a. "The Daring *Mahrem*: Changing Dynamics of Public Sexuality in Turkey." In *Gender and Sexuality in Muslim Cultures*, edited by Gul Ozyegin, 235–52. Surrey, UK: Ashgate.

————. 2015b. "Female Bodies and State Power: Women-Only Sport Centers in Istanbul." In *Women's Sport as Politics in Muslim Contexts*, edited by Homa Hoodfar, 102–35. London: Women Living under Muslim Laws.

————. 2015c. "Public Intimacies, Intimate Publics: Natural Limits, Creation, and the Culture of Mahremiyet in Turkey." *Cambridge Journal of Anthropology* 33, no. 2: 77–89.

————. 2016. "Exercising in Comfort: Islamicate Culture of Mahremiyet in Everyday Istanbul." *Journal of Middle East Women's Studies* 12, no. 2: 143–65.

————. 2017. "Sports and Gender in Turkey." In *Encyclopedia of Women & Islamic Cultures*, edited by Suad Joseph and Elora Shehabuddin. Leiden: Brill. At https://referenceworks.brillonline.com/entries/encyclopedia-of-women-and-islamic-cultures/sports-turkey-COM_002076.

————. 2018. "Revisited: Muslim Women's Agency and Feminist Anthropology of the Middle East." *Contemporary Islam* 12, no. 1: 73–92.

Sehlikoglu, Sertaç, and Aslı Zengin. 2015. "Introduction: Why Revisit Intimacy?" In "Intimacy Revisited," edited by Sertaç Sehlikoglu and Aslı

Zengin, special issue of *Cambridge Journal of Anthropology* 33, no. 2: 20–25.

Sfeir, Leila. 1985. "The Status of Muslim Women in Sport: Conflict between Cultural Tradition and Modernization." *International Review for the Sociology of Sport* 20, no. 4: 283–306.

Shafak, Elif. 2012. *The Gaze*. London: Penguin.

Shahrokni, Nazanin. 2014. "The Mothers' Paradise: Women-Only Parks and the Dynamics of State Power in Iran." *Journal of Middle East Women's Studies* 10, no. 3: 87–108.

Sibley, David. 2002. *Geographies of Exclusion: Society and Difference in the West*. London: Routledge.

Simon, William, and John H. Gagnon. 1986. "Sexual Scripts: Permanence and Change." *Archives of Sexual Behavior* 15, no. 2: 97–120.

Sirman, Nükhet. 2005. "The Making of Familial Citizenship in Turkey." In *Citizenship in a Global World: European Questions and Turkish Experiences*, edited by Fuat Keyman and Ahmet İçduygu, 147–72. London: Routledge.

Şişman, Nazife. 2005. *Küreselleşmenin pençesi İslam'ın peçesi*. Istanbul: Insan Yayınları.

———. 2006. *Emanetten mülke: Kadın, beden, siyaset*. Istanbul: İz.

Skalli, Loubna H. 2006. *Through a Local Prism: Gender, Globalization, and Identity in Moroccan Women's Magazines*. Lanham, MD: Lexington Books.

Skouteris, Helen, Roxane Carr, Eleanor H. Wertheim, Susan J. Paxton, and Dianne Duncombe. 2005. "A Prospective Study of Factors That Lead to Body Dissatisfaction during Pregnancy." *Body Image* 2, no. 4: 347–61.

Smith-Hefner, Nancy J. 2006. "Reproducing Respectability: Sex and Sexuality among Muslim Javanese Youth." *RIMA: Review of Indonesian and Malaysian Affairs* 40, no. 1: 143–72.

Soja, Edward W. 1989. *Postmodern Geographies: The Reassertion of Space in Critical Social Theory*. London: Verso.

Spielvogel, Laura. 2003. *Working Out in Japan: Shaping the Female Body in Tokyo Fitness Clubs*. Durham, NC: Duke Univ. Press.

Stewart, Kathleen. 2007. *Ordinary Affects*. Durham, NC: Duke Univ. Press.

———. 2008. "Weak Theory in an Unfinished World." *Journal of Folklore Research* 45, no. 1: 71–82.

Strathern, Marilyn. 1990. *The Gender of the Gift: Problems with Women and Problems with Society in Melanesia*. Berkeley: Univ. of California Press.

Svendsen, Lars. 2005. *A Philosophy of Boredom*. Translated by John Irons. London: Reaktion Books.

Tadiar, Neferti Xina M. 2004. *Fantasy Production: Sexual Economies and Other Philippine Consequences for the New World Order*. Hong Kong: Hong Kong Univ. Press.

Talimciler, Ahmet. 2006. "Ideolojik bir meşrulaştirma araci olarak spor ve spor bilimleri." *Spor Yönetimi ve Bilgi Teknolojileri* 1, no. 2: 35–40.

Tanpınar, Ahmet Hamdi. 2014. *Time Regulation Institute*. Translated by Maureen Freely and Alexander Dawe. Edited by Pankaj Mishra. London: Penguin.

Tanyeli, Uğur. 2013. *Toplumsal cinsiyet örüntülerini fiziksel çevre bağlamında okumak: 18. Yüzyıldan bu yana İstanbul'un kadınları, mekanları ve korkuları*. Istanbul: Osmanlıdan Günümüze Cinsiyet, Mahremiyet ve Mekan Çalıştay.

Tee, Caroline. 2016. *The Gülen Movement in Turkey: The Politics of Islam and Modernity*. London: I. B. Tauris.

Teychenne, Megan, Kylie Ball, and Jo Salmon. 2008. "Physical Activity and Likelihood of Depression in Adults: A Review." *Preventive Medicine* 46, no. 5: 397–411.

Tober, Diane M., and Debra Budiani. 2007. "Introduction: Why Islam, Health, and the Body?" *Body & Society* 13, no. 3: 1–13.

Trodd, Colin. 2003. "The Discipline of Pleasure; or, How Art History Looks at the Art Museum." *Museum and Society* 1, no. 1: 17–29.

Tugal, Cihan. 2009. "The Urban Dynamism of Islamic Hegemony: Absorbing Squatter Creativity in Istanbul." *Comparative Studies of South Asia, Africa, and the Middle East* 29, no. 3: 423–37.

Turam, Berna. 2007. *Between Islam and the State: The Politics of Engagement*. Stanford, CA: Stanford Univ. Press.

Türker, Orhan. 2000. *Galata'dan Karaköy'e: Bir liman hikayesi*. Istanbul: Sel Yayıncılık.

———. 2001. *Fanari'den Fener'e: Bir Haliç hikayesi*. Istanbul: Sel Yayıncılık.

———. 2003. *Halki'den Heybeli'ye*. Istanbul: Sel Yayıncılık.

———. 2004. *Prinkipo'dan Büyükada'ya: Bir Prens Adasının hikayesi*. Istanbul: Sel Yayıncılık.

———. 2006. *Therapia'dan Tarabya'ya: Boğaz'ın diplomatlar köyünün hikayesi.* Istanbul: Sel Yayıncılık.

———. 2008. *Halkidona'dan Kadiköy'e: Körler ülkesinin hikâyesi.* Istanbul: Sel Yayıncılık.

———. 2016. *Pera'dan Beyoğlu'na: İstanbul'un Levanten ve azınlık semtinin hikayesi.* Istanbul: Sel Yayıncılık.

Turner, Edith. 2012. *Communitas: The Anthropology of Collective Joy.* Edited by Laurel Kendall. New York: Palgrave Macmillan.

Tuzcuoğulları, Cemal, E. Barbaros Tuzcuoğulları, and Ö. Tarkan Tuzcuoğulları. 2001. *Atatürk ve spor.* Ankara: Takav Yayıncılık.

Tuzen, Mustafa, and Mustafa Soylak. 2007. "Evaluation of Trace Element Contents in Canned Foods Marketed from Turkey." *Food Chemistry* 102, no. 4: 1089–95.

Üçok, Bahriye. 1985. *Atatürk'ün izinde bir arpa boyu.* Ankara: Türk Tarih Kurumu Basımevi.

Ünal, R. Arzu. 2019. "Fashioning the Female Muslim Face: From 'Hiding One's Beauty' to 'Managing One's Beauty.'" In *Beauty and the Norm: Debating Standardization in Bodily Appearance,* edited by Claudia Liebelt, Sarah Böllinger, and Ulf Vierke, 177–99. London: Palgrave Macmillan.

Unusan, Nurhan. 2007. "Consumer Food Safety Knowledge and Practices in the Home in Turkey." *Food Control* 18, no. 1: 45–51.

Urry, John. 1990. *The Tourist Gaze: Leisure and Travel in Contemporary Societies.* London: Sage.

Vaka, Demetra. 1971. *The Unveiled Ladies of Stamboul.* Istanbul: Books for Libraries Press.

Vatansever, Z., A. Gargili, N. S. Aysul, G. Sengoz, and A. Estrada-Peña. 2008. "Ticks Biting Humans in the Urban Area of Istanbul." *Parasitology Research* 102, no. 3: 551–53.

Vom Bruck, Gabriele. 1997. "Elusive Bodies: The Politics of Aesthetics among Yemeni Elite Women. In Memory of Amatullah Al-Shami." *Signs* 23, no. 1: 175–214.

Wacquant, Loïc. 2004. *Body & Soul: Notebooks of an Apprentice Boxer.* Oxford: Oxford Univ. Press.

Wallace, Arlene M., Diane B. Boyer, Alice Dan, and Karyn Holm. 1986. "Aerobic Exercise, Maternal Self-Esteem, and Physical Discomforts during Pregnancy." *Journal of Nurse-Midwifery* 31, no. 6: 255–62.

Wang, Thomas W., and Barbara S. Apgar. 1998. "Exercise during Pregnancy." *American Family Physician* 57:1846–59.

Watve, Milind G., and Chittaranjan S. Yajnik. 2007. "Evolutionary Origins of Insulin Resistance: A Behavioral Switch Hypothesis." *BMC Evolutionary Biology* 7, no. 1: 61–74.

Weiss, Brad. 2009. *Street Dreams and Hip Hop Barbershops: Global Fantasy in Urban Tanzania*. Bloomington: Indiana Univ. Press.

Wells, Jonathan C. K. 2010. *The Evolutionary Biology of Human Body Fatness: Thrift and Control*. Cambridge: Cambridge Univ. Press.

Werbner, Pnina. 2007. "Veiled Interventions in Pure Space: Honour, Shame, and Embodied Struggles among Muslims in Britain and France." *Theory, Culture, & Society* 24, no. 2: 161–86.

White, Jenny B. 2002. *Islamist Mobilization in Turkey: A Study in Vernacular Politics*. Seattle: Univ. of Washington Press.

———. 2003. "State Feminism, Modernization, and the Turkish Republican Woman." *National Women's Studies Association Journal* 15, no. 3: 145–59.

White, Sarah C. 1997. "Men, Masculinities, and the Politics of Development." *Gender & Development* 5, no. 2: 14–22.

Yanagisako, Sylvia Junko, and Jane Fishburne Collier. 1987. "Toward a Unified Analysis of Gender and Kinship." In *Gender and Kinship: Essays toward a Unified Analysis*, edited by Jane Fishburne Collier and Sylvia Junko Yanagisako, 14–50. Stanford, CA: Stanford Univ. Press.

Yanardağoğlu, Eylem, and Imad N. Karam. 2013. "The Fever That Hit Arab Satellite Television: Audience Perceptions of Turkish TV Series." *Identities* 20, no. 5: 561–79.

Yarar, Betül. 2005. "'Civilized Women' and 'Light Sports': Modernisation, Women, and Sport in the Early Republican Period of Turkey ('Uygar Kadınlar' Ve 'Hafif Sporlar': Turkiye'de Cumhuriyetin İlk Yıllarında Modernleşme, Kadın Ve Spor)." *Kadin/Woman 2000* 6, no. 2: 1–35.

Yeğenoğlu, Meyda. 1998. *Colonial Fantasies: Towards a Feminist Reading of Orientalism*. Cambridge: Cambridge Univ. Press.

Yesil, Bilge. 2015. "Transnationalization of Turkish Dramas: Exploring the Convergence of Local and Global Market Imperatives." *Global Media and Communication* 11, no. 1: 43–60.

Yıldız, Doğan. 1979. *Türk spor tarihi*. Ankara: Eko Matbaası.

———. 2002. *Çağlarboyu Türkler'de spor*. Istanbul: Telebasım.

Yılmaz, Meral. 1997. "Aerobik 'herkes' için." *Aksiyon*, May 24.

Yonucu, Deniz. 2008. "A Story of a Squatter Neighborhood: From the Place of the 'Dangerous Classes' to the 'Place of Danger.'" *Berkeley Journal of Sociology* 52:50–72.

You, Haili. 1994. "Defining Rhythm: Aspects of an Anthropology of Rhythm." *Culture, Medicine, and Psychiatry* 18, no. 3: 361–84.

Young, Iris Marion. 1984. "Pregnant Embodiment: Subjectivity and Alienation." *Journal of Medicine and Philosophy* 9, no. 1: 45–62.

Young, Michael. 1988. *The Metronomic Society: Natural Rhythms and Human Timetables.* Cambridge, MA: Harvard Univ. Press.

Yumlu, Konca. 2014. "Toplumsal cinsiyet ve medya." *Ileti-ş-im*, no. 21: 151–55.

Yurdadön, Ergun. 2004. "Sport in Turkey: The Post-Islamic Republican Period." *Sport Journal* 7, no. 1: n.p.

Yuval-Davis, Nira, and Floya Anthias, eds. 1989. *Woman, Nation, State.* London: Macmillan.

Ze'evi, Dror. 2006. *Producing Desire: Changing Sexual Discourse in the Ottoman Middle East, 1500–1900.* Berkeley: Univ. of California Press.

Zengin, Aslı. 2011. *İktidarın mahremiyeti: İstanbul'da hayat kadınları, seks işçiliği ve şiddet.* Istanbul: Metis.

———. 2014. "Trans-Beyoğlu: Kentsel dönüşüm, şehir hakkı ve trans kadınlar." In *Yeni Istanbul çalışmaları: Sınırlar, mücadeleler, açılımlar,* edited by Cenk Özbay and Ayfer Bartu Candan, 360–75. Istanbul: Metis.

Zeybek, Sezai Ozan. 2014. "İstanbul'un yuttukları ve lustukları: Köpekler ve mesneler üzerinden İstanbul tahlili." In *Yeni Istanbul çalışmaları: Sınırlar, mücadeleler, açılımlar,* edited by Cenk Özbay and Ayfer Bartu Candan, 262–81. Istanbul: Metis.

Index

Abu-Lughod, Lila, 67, 79

açık (vs. *kapalı*), 154–55

Afsaruddin, Asma, 142, 168

agency, 68–70, 103–4, 209–10; and body, 218; creative, 70; feminist, 67–70; and gender, 61; and imagination, 137; and self, 11, 64–65; of space, 117. *See also* gaze

Ahıska, Meltem, 40

Akdağ, Recep, 92

Alemdaroğlu, Ayça, 2, 38, 86

Al-Ghazali, Abu Hamid, 64–66

altchronic practices, 206–9

Anderson, Laurie, 158–59

Appadurai, Arjun, 103

autonomy, 58, 67, 209–11; practice of, 58; relationality-autonomy dualism, 67

avret, 47–48

awareness, injecting, 95

awrah, 47–48

Babayan, Kathryn, and Afsaneh Najmabadi. *See* Islamicate

Bali, Rifat, 120

banality, 139, 248

başörtüsü, 97, 125; and *köylülük*, 122, 154–55. *See also* bonnet

Bayat, Asef, 209

Bayram, Fatma, 236–37

B-Fit, 14–15, 18, 132–35

bilinç aşılamak, 95

binaries, 13, 72–73; gender, 41, 147, 170, 178; global-local, 102; Hegelian, 66; insider-outsider, 144; Kemalist, 36–37; modesty and sexuality, 50; piety–everyday Islam, 72; relevance of, 71–74; religious-secular, 67; sacred-profane, 71–73; traditional-modern, 72–73. *See also* desire: Hegelian; subjectivity: complex

bioschedules, 231

Bizimkiler series, 1–2

body: postnatal, 218, 223–28; prenatal, 193, 217–19, 230

bonnet, 52–53, 180

borderscapes, 182–84

boredom, 57

Bosphorus Sea, 119

brands (high-end and fake), 129–30

Butler, Judith, 66–67

carcinogens, 242

Castoriadis, Cornelius, 209

çeyiz, 219

civilizing, 35, 86–87

comfort. *See rahat*

SERTAÇ SEHLIKOGLU is Abdullah Mubarak Al-Sabah Research Fellow in Middle Eastern and Islamic studies at Pembroke College, Cambridge, and an affiliated lecturer in social anthropology in the faculty of Asian and Middle Eastern studies at the University of Cambridge.

Select Titles in Gender, Culture, and Politics in the Middle East

---

For a full list of titles in this series, visit
https://press.syr.edu/supressbook-series/gender
-culture-and-politics-in-the-middle-east/.